MW01061645

Endorsements: *A Minute of Vision for Men*

Do you have one minute a day to invest in yourself? Pastor Roger Patterson looks at sports through a different lens and helps us learn about life, love, and how to be the man God created us to be. *A Minute of Vision for Men* is consistent with Psalm 32:8, instructing and teaching men in the way they should go. It is a must-read for every man longing to be better in the marketplace, at home, and in the fields of life.

JAMES BROWN
Network broadcaster at CBS Sports and News

Short . . . sweet . . . and to the point. *A Minute of Vision for Men* will help you be the man you were created to be!

CHRIS BROUSSARD
Senior writer at *ESPN The Magazine* and founder of The K.I.N.G. Movement

A Minute of Vision for Men is a great starter to growing as a man of God. It will flicker the inner passion God has given you to grow in wisdom and your daily devotion to the Lord.

CHARLIE WARD
1993 Heisman Trophy winner

A Minute of Vision for Men is a strong tool to lead any man into spiritual growth in just one minute a day. These daily nuggets of wisdom speak to the real life of men in a very practical way. This devotional presents a daily thought with Scripture that is not intimidating or overwhelming. It gets to the point and speaks right to the heart. A must-have!

DARRYL STRAWBERRY
Four-time World Series champion

My walk and relationship with God is at its best when I am experiencing tangible growth and change on a daily basis. This devotional allows me to do just that in a way that I haven't come across before.

It paints imagery into my head that allows my time with God to be practical and real; it generates conversation with him in a way that makes me feel like he is sitting in the same room with me. This devotional allows me to take my time with God and really apply it to my life, and it has allowed me to daily see and feel growth and change in my relationship with Christ.

DAN ORLOVSKY
Quarterback of the Detroit Lions; twelve-year NFL veteran

This is a must-read! The inspiration Pastor Patterson gives in these daily readings will start or end your day right and leave an epic impact on your life. This isn't just for those seeking spiritual inspiration but for all those who need that little extra to enhance their day and their life. I won't miss a day—nor should you. I pray this is the first of many more books of inspiration by Roger. Thank you for the inspiration!

SEAN SALISBURY
Former NFL quarterback; cohost of *Prime Cut*, SB Nation Radio's national drive-time radio show

A Minute of Vision for Men is a relevant daily devotional for all men. The compact daily readings are both motivating and inspiring, while at the same time they provide a challenging word. I would recommend this devotional to all men, regardless of their stage in life.

BUBBA CROSBY
Former New York Yankee

A Minute of Vision for Men is an exceptional tool for anyone who strives for daily excellence in their personal and professional life. It offers a short yet profound opportunity for reflection, guidance, and motivation, which are keys to success. Roger has done a tremendous job putting into his book an influence and charisma that until now only those of us who know him personally have reaped the benefits of.

TODD WHITTING
Head baseball coach at the University of Houston

Every man needs to be challenged from time to time. *A Minute of Vision for Men* will challenge you to be the man God created you to be and the man your family desperately needs you to be.

MAJ. JEFF STRUECKER (RET.)
US Army Ranger of the Year (1996); author of *The Road to Unafraid*, detailing his involvement in Black Hawk Down

A Minute of Vision for Men is a gift. The devotionals are simple and easy to read, yet packed with great punch and opportunities for reflection. Roger addresses seemingly all the major facets of a man's life: how he gets significance, what temptations he needs to avoid . . . essentially, how he can become the man, father, and husband he is called to be. I strongly encourage men to invest a mere minute a day and let their lives be transformed.

DAVID GOW
CEO of SB Nation Radio

Roger Patterson delivers daily biblical devotions that will teach you to live with a more expectant faith, allowing you to take even better aim at the path that God has prepared just for you. Roger is a gifted storyteller and a Bible scholar who will help get your day off to a God-honoring start with the daily wisdom in these devotions. I know you will be greatly encouraged by *A Minute of Vision for Men*.

DARRIN GRAY
Director of Partnerships at All Pro Dad, the national fatherhood program founded by Tony Dungy

I met Roger when I was playing second base and Roger was our catcher on the Little League ball field. That was a long time ago, but I remember being a bit jealous of Roger because his position required a suit of armor while I just had a hat and glove. Catchers need armor to effectively fulfill their position. The same is true for the man of God. We need the armor of God, and most of us just pick up a hat or glove a couple of Sundays a month. More is required to fulfill our position at home and work—we need daily armor. *A Minute of Vision for Men* will help you do just that.

The short-but-precise thought and Scripture will arm you daily for the battle and set you on a victorious path!

GREGG MATTE
Pastor of Houston's First Baptist Church and author of *Unstoppable Gospel*

As the pastor of the NFL Houston Texans, I'm constantly searching for resources that edify the spiritual warriors inside these modern-day gladiators I work with each day. Roger Patterson has met that need! He has developed a treasure chest full of insightful nuggets of truth that will enrich the minds of men who will dig into it.

GREG TYLER
Team pastor of the Houston Texans

I know Roger Patterson as a pastor and a friend. Roger has influenced so many over the years with his intriguing storytelling and impactful life lessons. If men will simply take a minute a day to read this book, that minute could ignite a flame toward becoming the men and leaders God desires us to be. Can you spare a minute a day?

DOUG PAGE
Senior pastor of First Baptist Church, Grapevine, Texas

You have time for this! Dr. Patterson combines God's Word, wisdom from inspired leaders, highlights—and lowlights—from the world of sports, and life experience in a compelling and practical daily devotional. Concise and convicting, each day's devotion brings a no-excuses challenge to drive us to be our intended and better selves.

BRAD CHILDERS
President and CEO of Archrock, Inc.

Roger Patterson has done it! He has provided men with a short and simple way to start the day with a spiritual vision. His voice is authentic, and his message relevant. I urge every guy to read this book, one minute at a time, and give a copy to a friend.

BILL PERKINS
Author of *When Good Men Are Tempted*, *Six Battles Every Man Must Win*, and *Six Rules Every Man Must Break*

Roger Patterson is a man's man upon whom God has placed extra measures of wisdom and discernment. Roger learns from every encounter and every experience. In *A Minute of Vision for Men*, he communicates the insights he has gained in a way that appeals to men of all ages and interests. This is not your ordinary daily devotional, but rather a fun and interesting book that provokes thought and can't help but improve you every day. Dads, read this with your sons—sports and hunting are involved, not to mention common sense. Oh, and your son will love the time with you.

MICHAEL SHELLEY
Retired state president of U.S. Bank Arkansas; father of three; grandfather of thirteen; proud to be a friend of Roger Patterson for two decades

Finally, a devotional that's not just for the contemplative types! Roger Patterson's new book, *A Minute of Vision for Men*, shows that any man, at any stage in life, can build a successful devotional life. With 365 minutes designed to give you greater traction in your spiritual life, this book helps men to think about, and see, the spiritual side of life. Pick it up, open it up, and invest one minute a day. You'll be glad you did.

DR. DAVID EDWARDS
Author of *Life Verse*

365 MOTIVATIONAL MOMENTS

A MINUTE OF
VISION
FOR
MEN

TO KICK-START YOUR DAY

TYNDALE
MOMENTUM™

The nonfiction imprint of
Tyndale House Publishers, Inc.

Visit Tyndale online at www.tyndale.com.

Visit Tyndale Momentum online at www.tyndalemomentum.com.

TYNDALE, Tyndale Momentum, and Tyndale's quill logo are registered trademarks of Tyndale House Publishers, Inc. The Tyndale Momentum logo is a trademark of Tyndale House Publishers, Inc. Tyndale Momentum is the nonfiction imprint of Tyndale House Publishers, Inc., Carol Stream, Illinois.

A Minute of Vision for Men: 365 Motivational Moments to Kick-Start Your Day

Designed by Mark Anthony Lane II

Published in association with the literary agency of Mark Sweeney & Associates, Naples, FL.

For information about special discounts for bulk purchases, please contact Tyndale House Publishers at csresponse@tyndale.com or call 800-323-9400.

ISBN 978-1-4964-1777-0

Printed in the United States of America

23	22	21	20	19	18	17
8	7	6	5	4	3	2

To Brady, Cooper, and Carson . . .
You are my motivation for this project.
I pray that I will live up to the words on these pages.
I love you with all my heart!
Dad

Introduction

Welcome to *A Minute of Vision for Men*. My hope is that this book will share timely wisdom in such a time-constrained world. These daily minutes are drawn from sports headlines, from moments with my wife or kids, and from Scripture. For the last few years, I've had the privilege of sharing these one-minute daily thoughts on the radio. We have seen this grow from one station, Houston's KGOW, to over three hundred stations throughout North America, Africa, Europe, and Australia.

One of the passions driving this project is my desire to engage men where they're at while also helping them succeed spiritually. During my years as a pastor, I have learned that there are a number of men who want to grow spiritually but aren't sure how to do it. Though successful in nearly every other area of their lives, they are intimidated by spiritual things, including the Bible and devotional books that take fifteen to twenty minutes a day to read. *A Minute of Vision for Men* is written to engage you in a daily thought from Scripture that should take just about a minute. In short, this book is a starting point to help you grow spiritually or a supplement to what you are already doing.

With 365 different readings in this book, I am well aware that you are going to connect with some of these daily moments more than others. If you are a husband and father, I hope to give you some nuggets of wisdom to deploy in your home. If you aren't yet married or a parent, I trust that these readings will begin to prepare you for that season or encourage you in your current relationships with women and young people. If your kids are already grown, then let the readings that speak about parenting add value to you so that you can pass it on to others. I know that you are part of a diverse audience reading this book, and I believe that the discipline of engaging with Scripture on a daily basis will pay big dividends over time.

No matter where I have traveled in the world, one of the common problems I see is that men don't know how or aren't willing to engage in the battle of living up to their God-given potential. Instead, they settle for less than what is best for them, their families, and their careers. *A Minute of Vision for Men* is a daily investment of vision for your life. May we see the tide of men rising up to become what God designed us to be!

Dr. Roger Patterson
Bellaire, Texas
March 1, 2016

JANUARY

The Man You Were Meant to Be

Priorities matter. When our list of priorities puts us at the top of the food chain, things get out of line. But when God is our highest priority, the significance of our families and the proper order of the other things in our lives become clear.

In his book *The Making of a Man*, Heisman Trophy winner Tim Brown writes about his shifting priorities: "My life was about more than me and football. My faith had matured and deepened. I'd always believed in God, but now I was fully committed to Him. As a husband and father, I became more devoted to my family than ever. I was becoming the man I was meant to be."[1]

Notice what the Bible says about the impact and fruit of a man whose priorities are in order. Psalm 1:1-3 states, "Oh, the joys of those who do not follow the advice of the wicked, or stand around with sinners, or join in with mockers. But they delight in the law of the LORD, meditating on it day and night. They are like trees planted along the riverbank, bearing fruit each season. Their leaves never wither, and they prosper in all they do."

Becoming the man you are meant to be begins with reordering your priorities: God first, family second, career third. Enjoy the blessings that flow when you become the man you were meant to be. Remember, from proper priorities, proper choices flow. What are your priorities as you start off this year?

Oh, the joys of those who do not follow the advice of the wicked, or stand around with sinners, or join in with mockers. But they delight in the law of the LORD, meditating on it day and night. They are like trees planted along the riverbank, bearing fruit each season. Their leaves never wither, and they prosper in all they do.
PSALM 1:1-3

---

[1] Tim Brown and James Lund, *The Making of a Man* (Nashville, TN: Thomas Nelson, 2014), 4.

A Personal Training Plan

In his book *The One Year Uncommon Life Daily Challenge*, Tony Dungy talks about the importance of having self-control, being disciplined, getting into shape, and committing to a plan. As a player at training camp, Dungy was amazed by how some of the other players would show up out of shape and unprepared.[2] In the same way athletes train their bodies to be able to run faster and lift more weight, as leaders of our families, we need to train ourselves to be better men.

First Corinthians 9:27 says, "I discipline my body like an athlete, training it to do what it should. Otherwise, I fear that after preaching to others I myself might be disqualified."

How are you training to be the better husband, father, friend, or employee that you long to be? Making time for reading Scripture, praying, and exercising is a good starting point. Many guys I know also meet together in a weekly small group setting to fellowship and sharpen one another.

Being the man you were meant to be takes the intentional discipline of an athlete training for competition.[3] Don't let up, and do your best not to go it alone. Develop a plan, and stick to the plan so that you will be ready for the challenges of each day.

I discipline my body like an athlete, training it to do what it should. Otherwise, I fear that after preaching to others I myself might be disqualified.
1 CORINTHIANS 9:27

---

[2] Tony Dungy and Nathan Whitaker, *The One Year Uncommon Life Daily Challenge* (Carol Stream, IL: Tyndale, 2011), January 1.

[3] Check out www.allprodad.com, which offers a variety of resources to help you grow.

Everybody Needs a Coach

Everybody needs a coach. I realized that fact the other day when I was lying flat on my back, doing reverse crunches. You see, without my coach, I wouldn't do reverse crunches.

Tom Landry, the Dallas Cowboys head coach for nearly thirty years, said, "The job of a football coach is to make men do what they don't want to do in order to achieve what they've always wanted to be." Inherent in this quote is the admission that men don't always want to pay the price necessary to become who they are destined to be. Additionally, we don't always know what to change or even how to make the changes that are necessary to grow. Coaches can see these deficiencies and challenge us.

Proverbs 13:20 states, "Walk with the wise and become wise; associate with fools and get in trouble." Who we associate with informs what we become. If you want to be wise and excel, find someone who has been where you want to go. Look for godly qualities in his life. When you find a coach, listen to him, and begin to implement his counsel. As you walk through life, consider the company you keep, and make the adjustments in those relationships so that nothing holds you back from becoming the man that God is calling you to be.

Walk with the wise and become wise; associate with fools and get in trouble.
PROVERBS 13:20

Success Is an Action

Personal-development expert Darren Hardy says, "Action is the great separator." I've had a million good ideas, but they are just that—ideas. Until you put it on paper, map it out, and commit to a plan of action, you just have an idea. Once you get it on paper, you then have to execute it. Until you take action, you are no different from the next person who is excited about some idea.

People who are successful are willing to take action. But they don't just take any action—they take the right action.

While getting my doctorate, I learned the importance of taking the right action. Before I could write my doctoral thesis, I had to write a prospectus. This thirty-five-page paper was a road map of the action I was going to take to fulfill my "idea" that would contribute to the academic community. Fortunately, I had good advisers who assisted me and helped me know what needed to be included and what needed to be left out. After I got through this phase, I was allowed to continue writing my thesis. I'll never forget finishing my oral defense of my thesis before three professors and hearing them say, "Congratulations, Dr. Patterson."

Few characters in Scripture are as bold as Peter. Look at his boldness when he takes action to walk on water. Matthew 14:28-29 states, "Peter called to him, 'Lord, if it's really you, tell me to come to you, walking on the water.' 'Yes, come,' Jesus said. So Peter went over the side of the boat and walked on the water toward Jesus."

With the Lord's permission, Peter experienced something no one else has. As John Ortberg says, "If you want to walk on water, you have to get out of the boat." Action truly is the great separator.

Peter called to him, "Lord, if it's really you, tell me to come to you, walking on the water." "Yes, come," Jesus said. So Peter went over the side of the boat and walked on the water toward Jesus.   MATTHEW 14:28-29

Success Is an Attitude

Winston Churchill once said, "Attitude is the little thing that makes a big difference." In essence, Churchill was saying that our attitude controls the trajectory of each and every day of our lives. Our attitude, if not intentionally molded, will call us to a path of least resistance and minimal effort.

When I became the senior pastor of West University Baptist and Crosspoint Church, the first asset that I brought as the new leader of the congregation was an "expectant" attitude. Nearly six years later, I still sign every official correspondence with some form of the phrase "Expecting Greater Things." Sometimes I sign with the words "Still Expectant" or "Staying Expectant."

After being on staff for thirteen years and then becoming the senior leader of the church, I knew that if I didn't insert an attitude that conveyed a bright future, I wouldn't lead us very far. Before I took the reins, Dr. Barry Landrum had led us very effectively for thirteen years. We could have gotten comfortable and complacent, but I believed that God wanted to do more than we could ask, think, or imagine.

There are two key passages that inspire my expectant attitude. The first is John 14:12, which states, "I tell you the truth, anyone who believes in me will do the same works I have done, and even greater works, because I am going to be with the Father." These great works, which the New International Version calls "greater things," aren't works in greater quantity but quality.

The second passage that comes to mind is Ephesians 3:20-21: "All glory to God, who is able, through his mighty power at work within us, to accomplish infinitely more than we might ask or think. Glory to him in the church and in Christ Jesus through all generations forever and ever! Amen." These verses set the attitude of success in my heart and in our congregation.

All glory to God, who is able, through his mighty power at work within us, to accomplish infinitely more than we might ask or think. Glory to him in the church and in Christ Jesus through all generations forever and ever! Amen.
EPHESIANS 3:20-21

Success Is an Atmosphere

Today is my wife's birthday. What a gift Julee is to me! I am thankful that I get to wake up with her every day. I am thankful that wherever I go in our home, I see her influence. She has created an amazing atmosphere for our family so that each member of our family can be successful.

Not only is success an action and attitude, but success is also an atmosphere. The successful people I know have this in common: they surround themselves with other successful people. They have a coach or mentor who has gone where they have yet to go. They learn from other successful people via podcasts or books. They are continually absorbing things that will help them grow. Somewhere along the way, these people figured out that to move beyond the crowd, they had to make some changes that would propel them forward. A major change that they have made is choosing the right companions for the journey.

One of the big ideas that I want my children to understand is the importance of surrounding themselves with the right friends. So I say to them, "If you surround yourself with lazy people, you'll be lazy. If you surround yourself with deceptive people, you will be deceptive. If those in your continual company are foolish, guess what? You, too, will be foolish."

You see, success is an atmosphere as much as it is an action or attitude. Surround yourself with the people who will not only push you, challenge you, and push you out of your comfort zone, but who also love the Lord and want to serve and please him. Remember again the words of Proverbs 27:17, which states, "As iron sharpens iron, so a friend sharpens a friend."

As iron sharpens iron, so a friend sharpens a friend.   PROVERBS 27:17

The Importance of Thinking Ahead

Wayne Gretzky once said, "A good hockey player plays where the puck is. A great hockey player plays where the puck is going to be."

Customary advice says, "Live in the present. The past is behind you, and the future is so uncertain." But living in the present can be quite difficult given all the distractions around us. While writing today's devo, I have been interrupted by three text messages and one urgent e-mail. It's easy to get distracted by that request we just received in an e-mail while working on our current task.

Although we don't want to be distracted by the future, living in the present is best informed when we have a vision for our future. I settled the vision for my life on December 1, 2009. Julee and I were on a Royal Caribbean cruise, thirteen nautical miles off the coast of Cuba. I was enjoying the moment, for sure. But in that moment, I was also dreaming about how to live out my days and how to articulate that desire. It was on that ship that I decided how I was going to try to live what I call "the exponential life." I want to live in such a way that how I lead, speak, and act can affect not only those in my own life but those in the age to come. When I invest in others who invest in others, the ripple effect is immeasurable in my life and in the generations that will follow.

Matthew 25:23 states, "The master said, 'Well done, my good and faithful servant. You have been faithful in handling this small amount, so now I will give you many more responsibilities. Let's celebrate together!'" I pray I hear these words, or something like them, from our Lord. Because of this vision, I can look back on days gone by and evaluate, look ahead in order to dream and plan, and make sure that I am using each moment I have been given for what matters most.

The master said, "Well done, my good and faithful servant. You have been faithful in handling this small amount, so now I will give you many more responsibilities. Let's celebrate together!" MATTHEW 25:23

Guard Your Heart

I wrote a book just for my son Brady when he turned thirteen, because I wanted to make sure he knew my heart, hopes, and expectations for him. I want to share the opening page of *Thirteen Going on Eighteen: Becoming a Man of Influence* with you, as I think it sets the tone for what it really takes to live a life that seeks to continually move forward:

Lou Holtz, legendary college football coach, once said, "I can't believe that God put us on this earth to be ordinary." I agree wholeheartedly with Coach Holtz. You were put on this earth not to be ordinary but to be extraordinary.

Proverbs 4:23 states, "Guard your heart above all else, for it determines the course of your life." Remember, you were put on this earth to be extraordinary, so I want to challenge you to guard your heart. Your heart is the totality of your mind, will, emotions, and expectations. In the Scriptures, your heart represents the depth of your gut or inner bowels. Sounds gross, doesn't it?

In life, there will be moments when you are so disappointed that your gut actually aches. These moments of deep pain happen when you realize the depth of your mistakes or when someone hurts you to your core.

These moments happen with disappointment and when you come up short on a goal you have been pursuing. It is critical that you don't allow these moments to define you and keep you down. In other words, when these gut-wrenching moments take place, do everything you can to not become embittered by them. Remember, your heart is the wellspring of your life. If it gets polluted, then your life will get bogged down. If you get bogged down, then you will fear moving forward. If you fear moving forward, you will never become the man you were created to be. So, if you want to be more than ordinary, begin and continue by guarding your heart, for it is the wellspring of life.

Guard your heart above all else, for it determines the course of your life.
PROVERBS 4:23

Knowing the Land

Ten thousand acres is hard to get your mind around. Ten thousand acres is the size of a ranch I visited when a friend took us deer hunting there. Twenty deer blinds are spread across the property for hunters to use as they harvest deer. The house on the ranch is built for large groups who come in and hunt together. The fire pit is one of the biggest I have ever seen!

On the first morning of our hunt, about an hour before the sun came up, we got into the Polaris and journeyed to the back of the property. It took us about thirty minutes to arrive at our destination. What impressed me most was that our host, who enjoys taking his family, his friends, and his clients hunting at this ranch, knew every turn to get there. He knew the land so well that he didn't need the sunlight to show him which way to go.

As a leader, do you know the landscapes of your home, business, and community in this way? Do you know how to navigate difficult times because of the amount of time you have spent in the land and the way you have loved those around you?

Proverbs 27:23 states, "Know the state of your flocks, and put your heart into caring for your herds." Knowing the land, knowing the condition of your flocks, and knowing how to lead them well takes time and energy, but the effort is worth it.

Know the state of your flocks, and put your heart into caring for your herds.
PROVERBS 27:23

The Peace of Christ at the Sock Hop

Free agency is a phenomenal tool for players in professional sports. In years past, once you were drafted, the team that picked you controlled your rights. That is why so many teams could establish long-standing dynasties, keeping their players all under one roof for multiple years. When free agency entered the game, enabling the players to get out onto the open market, the days of the dynasty were seemingly disrupted. This opened the door for players to seek the best fit for where they were in their careers.

A friend I saw at a daddy-daughter sock hop was weighing three different career opportunities. He was under pressure to pick between the three jobs, and I could see the angst on his face. When we spoke briefly, he told me that his decision was one hour overdue. I looked at him, called him by name, and said, "Let the peace of Christ rule your heart." The next time I saw him at church, he said, "On paper, I took the third-ranked opportunity. With the others, I felt sick to my stomach, and so I did what you said. This is the one where I had peace."

Remember, opportunity can create growth if we search things out. When it is decision time, consider Colossians 3:15, which states, "Let the peace that comes from Christ rule in your hearts. For as members of one body you are called to live in peace."

Let the peace that comes from Christ rule in your hearts. For as members of one body you are called to live in peace.　　　　　COLOSSIANS 3:15

Running Five Miles

There are some guys who look like they were built to run. I am not one of them, but Mike Bonem is. He is tall, lean, and very fast. He ran cross-country at Rice University and is still a runner to this day. Mike and I had the privilege of serving on a church staff together for a number of years, and we even wrote a book together. He is a dear friend, and I am glad we got to run part of life's race together.

Not built to run like Mike, I go out for jogs and have even worked my way up to running four or five miles at a time. To run that far, I have to frequently take on shorter distances and build up to a longer run. As I've jogged, I've learned that I get stronger when I am consistent. When I develop endurance little by little, I'm not as fatigued at the 3.5- and 4-mile marks of my longer runs.

Don't you wish that you could develop endurance in just a short time? But it takes time to build endurance of any sort—physically, relationally, spiritually, or financially. Further still, the truth is that we won't make it far in this life if we don't develop endurance in these areas.

Romans 5:3-4 states, "We can rejoice, too, when we run into problems and trials, for we know that they help us develop endurance. And endurance develops strength of character, and character strengthens our confident hope of salvation."

When we choose to see each day as an opportunity to build endurance, we make deposits into our future. When the longer run comes, we will need to draw on that strength and use it to see us through. Build endurance today by challenging yourself—physically, relationally, spiritually, and financially.

We can rejoice, too, when we run into problems and trials, for we know that they help us develop endurance. And endurance develops strength of character, and character strengthens our confident hope of salvation.
ROMANS 5:3-4

Stay Coachable

When I would get a whipping as a kid, my dad always took the opportunity to teach me afterward. Looking back, I remember how he would try to reinforce his love for me after the discipline. What makes me laugh today is that when I was a teenager, there were times when my dad would look at me and say, "You're not too big for a spanking."

Now as an adult, I may be too big for the form of discipline my father gave me, but I'm aware that I'm not too big to have a coach. To me, a coach is someone who has successfully played the position that I am playing. It is my desire to learn from my coach's successes and failures and to try to implement the lessons I learn in my local context.

Dan Hall, president of On Course Solutions, has been my professional coach for nearly five years. Dan has pastored for many years in a variety of church settings. His wisdom, expertise, and insight have been a true blessing to me.

Coaches are blessings, but only if we stay coachable. If we aren't coachable, we will hear them say, "I tried to tell you that a few months back," and we will shake our heads, realizing that they were right. This has happened with me a few times since Dan began walking with me.

Listen to the affirmation the Bible gives to having a wise coach in your life. Proverbs 25:12 in the English Standard Version states, "Like a gold ring or an ornament of gold is a wise reprover to a listening ear."

Remember, you aren't too big for discipline! Put your ear near a coach, and enjoy the growth that comes from his lessons.

Like a gold ring or an ornament of gold is a wise reprover to a listening ear.
PROVERBS 25:12, ESV

Keep the Momentum Going

With a 15–1 record, the Carolina Panthers secured the first seed of the NFC and clinched home-field advantage through the play-offs for the 2015–16 NFL season. After a bye week, the Seattle Seahawks came to Charlotte. Many touted this as the best play-off game of the weekend.

Though the Panthers had enjoyed a week off, they kept the mojo going. They jumped on the Seahawks, and before the Seahawks could get things figured out, the Panthers were up 31–0. It was reminiscent of the Giants versus Panthers game just a few weeks earlier in the regular season. As in the Giants game, the Seahawks were able to stifle the offense of the Panthers in the second half and make a game of it. The Seahawks had a great second half, although the game ended with a score of Panthers 31, Seahawks 24.

Keeping momentum in life requires a concentrated effort. It is natural for us, like the Panthers, to turn our focus and efforts in another direction when things are going well. We also have a tendency to coast. Paul, after encouraging Timothy as a gifted young pastor, challenged him to not let up on the progress he was making: "Keep a close watch on how you live and on your teaching. Stay true to what is right for the sake of your own salvation and the salvation of those who hear you" (1 Timothy 4:16). Momentum, when you lose it, is difficult to recapture. So, when you get it going, keep it going.

Keep a close watch on how you live and on your teaching. Stay true to what is right for the sake of your own salvation and the salvation of those who hear you. **1 TIMOTHY 4:16**

To Kneel or to Spike

In the heat of the moment, situational awareness sometimes gets lost. As the Washington Redskins were seeking to clinch the NFC East title in 2015, with six seconds remaining in the first half, Redskins quarterback Kirk Cousins mistakenly took a knee when he was supposed to spike the ball to stop the clock.

His mistake cost his team a guaranteed three points, because instead of stopping the clock, his actions ensured that the clock would run out. Cousins didn't let his mistake ruin the rest of the game. He finished the day completing thirty-one of his forty-six pass attempts, throwing four touchdowns and passing for 365 yards. Fortunately, his mistake did not cost the team the game, as they defeated the Philadelphia Eagles 38–24. After the game, Cousins admitted that there was confusion on the play call and, in the moment, he made the wrong decision. He owned his mistake and focused on making things right in the second half.

How often do you make poor decisions when there is confusion and pressure? I am sure we can all relate to Cousins's error because we have made our own. We have said things we wish we could take back. We have acted foolishly, hurting those we care about because of our selfishness and pride. If we make too many of these types of errors, it will certainly hurt the relationship, sometimes beyond repair. If you have made a poor decision recently and hurt someone you care about, humble yourself and seek his or her forgiveness.

Proverbs 6:2-3 tells us, "If you have trapped yourself by your agreement and are caught by what you said—follow my advice and save yourself, for you have placed yourself at your friend's mercy. Now swallow your pride; go and beg to have your name erased."

Admit you are wrong, seek forgiveness, and play a great second half with humility so that you can win the day.

If you have trapped yourself by your agreement and are caught by what you said—follow my advice and save yourself, for you have placed yourself at your friend's mercy. Now swallow your pride; go and beg to have your name erased.
PROVERBS 6:2-3

Lessons from the Bengals

When the Pittsburgh Steelers were matched up with the Cincinnati Bengals in the 2015–16 AFC wild card game, the teams had a history of unsportsmanlike conduct on the field. But in spite of the bad blood between them, it was kept under the boiling point most of the game.

With the Steelers down by one point and two minutes to go, inexperienced Landry Jones stepped onto the field to run the two-minute offense for the Steelers. To Jones's dismay, the nemesis of the Steelers offense, Bengals middle linebacker Vontaze Burfict, stepped in front of his pass and intercepted it, seemingly securing the win. Burfict and his buddies ran all the way to the opposite end of the field, through the end zone, and up into the tunnel as they celebrated what appeared to be a certain Bengals victory. But the game wasn't over yet.

The Steelers regained possession, and after an effective drive and a couple of penalties handed to the Bengals for fouls, the Steelers were able to score, moving on in the play-offs and sending their rival into the off-season.

I believe the focus and self-control that Bengals' coach Marvin Lewis instilled in his players going into this game left his team when Burfict and his cronies were running up the tunnel with well over a minute and a half left to play.

Self-control is a must in athletics and in life. It is a shame that the uncontrolled actions of a few players cost so many other teammates, coaches, Bengal employees, and Cincinnati fans a magical season. The same could be said about the husband and father who gets caught up in adultery. All the years of investment into his wife, his kids, and his career can be gone with one moment that lacks self-control. Focused self-control is vital to be successful in a world full of temptation. Remember, it is always available to you. Second Timothy 1:7 states, "God has not given us a spirit of fear and timidity, but of power, love, and self-discipline."

God has not given us a spirit of fear and timidity, but of power, love, and self-discipline.   2 TIMOTHY 1:7

Revived by Failure

Michael Jordan once said, "I've missed more than nine thousand shots in my career. I've lost almost three hundred games. Twenty-six times, I've been trusted to take the game-winning shot and missed. I've failed over and over. . . . And that is why I succeed." To Jordan, failure was fuel.

When Jesus' disciple Peter failed, it was a big-time failure. After declaring that he would never betray Jesus, Peter caved to the pressure of the moment and denied Jesus three times after Jesus' arrest.

What I want you to consider today is how Jesus met Peter in his failure. He didn't tell Peter, "Pull yourself up by your bootstraps." In this crisis, Jesus gave love and forgiveness to Peter and then expanded his vision.

John 21, which takes place after Jesus' resurrection, shows Peter and the disciples out on the boat, throwing out their nets all night without any luck. When Jesus appears, he tells the disciples to cast the nets on the other side.

This is the second time we see Jesus telling the disciples to cast their nets on the other side of the boat. The first time happened at Peter's calling. In the first story, the catch was so plentiful that the boats began to sink and the nets began to break. The second story records that 153 fish were caught because this time, the nets held.

After the disciples returned to shore, John 21 tells us that Jesus repeatedly asked Peter if he loved him. Verse 17 tells us, "A third time [Jesus] asked him, 'Simon son of John, do you love me?' Peter was hurt that Jesus asked the question a third time. He said, 'Lord, you know everything. You know that I love you.' Jesus said, 'Then feed my sheep.'"

In Peter's failure, Jesus met him at the place of his original calling to remind him that there was a bigger plan for his life. Don't get stuck in your mistakes. Go back to that place where he called you, and meet with him again. You, too, will be humbled and amazed!

A third time [Jesus] asked him, "Simon son of John, do you love me?" Peter was hurt that Jesus asked the question a third time. He said, "Lord, you know everything. You know that I love you." Jesus said, "Then feed my sheep."
JOHN 21:17

You Can't Teach Tall

He's six foot five at fourteen years of age. He is a great kid, a smart kid, and a talented athlete. He swims for a regional club here in Houston and plays for the parks-and-recreation basketball team I coach.

The problem, though, is that Daniel doesn't yet realize his size. We have him in the middle because he is tall and can dominate the boards, but that only happens when he wants it to. His instincts tell him to take his game outside, but at this point, because of his size, he will have the most success if he stays in the post and learns to bang it out down low. Part of his problem is that he doesn't yet know how tall he really is and how his height can help him dominate the middle. I tell him at every practice, "Daniel, realize your size. Understand how God made you, and maximize that."

That's good counsel for our everyday lives, isn't it? When we realize how we have been created by God, and the way he has gifted us, we can play to our potential.

First Peter 4:10 states, "God has given each of you a gift from his great variety of spiritual gifts. Use them well to serve one another." We still need to work on our weaknesses, but we also need to maximize our strengths. What gifts has God given you so that you can serve others? What is it that only you can bring to the team you are on? Stand up in that, because you can't teach tall!

God has given each of you a gift from his great variety of spiritual gifts. Use them well to serve one another.   1 PETER 4:10

To Have Success, Give Your Life Away

The great Walter Payton, Super Bowl–winning running back for the Chicago Bears, once said, "I want to be remembered as the guy who gave his all whenever he was on the field." Payton had made the decision to give his time on the football field all that he had and was publicly declaring this pursuit. Ironically, Payton gave a tremendous amount outside football as well. His off-the-field contributions were so well known that the NFL Man of the Year award, given to a player who exhibits a humanitarian spirit off the field, was named for Payton after his death. Players who now receive this recognition receive the Walter Payton NFL Man of the Year award.

Giving is a decision. Most people in life are takers, not givers. Takers get all they can, can all they get, and sit on the can. Takers are selfish people interested only in themselves. On some level we are all takers, aren't we? It's easy to take but difficult to give. Giving is an attitude that sees a greater purpose to life, and it begins with a decision point.

Proverbs 11:30 says, "The seeds of good deeds become a tree of life." Make a decision to cast seeds of giving to, sharing with, and blessing those in need. Partner with organizations like the Salvation Army, Goodwill, and local missions. Look for children who don't have a father, and see if there might be a way to mentor them. Find a widow in your community, and check on her. These are just a few ways to cast seeds of good deeds. Over time, they will become a tree of life so that others can find the comfort of the shade.

The seeds of good deeds become a tree of life.　　　　　　　　PROVERBS 11:30

More Knee Bend

When Tom Brady won his fourth Super Bowl, a note that he wrote to himself was found in his locker. It read, "Bend knees more on drop." He knew that he needed to throw from a power position, so he repeated to himself over and over again the need for more bend in his knees.

When pundits comment on a quarterback's throwing ability, they often talk about his arm strength. But arm strength is a myth. Arm strength will take a quarterback only so far. His real power comes from his legs and his core. The power to throw the ball with greater velocity or distance comes from the power generated in the knees through the upper torso. Brady's note only affirms that.

Isn't it fascinating that to achieve the greatest success in his profession, Tom Brady is going back to the basics that he learned in seventh or eighth grade? Back in seventh or eighth grade, we were learning all sorts of fundamentals about life. Let's not forsake that teaching, because it was given to us so that we might be successful.

Proverbs 4:3-4 says, "I, too, was once my father's son, tenderly loved as my mother's only child. My father taught me, 'Take my words to heart. Follow my commands, and you will live.'"

Fundamental things we learned as kids will carry us through our lives. Go back to the basics of being gracious, chivalrous, servant hearted, and hospitable. Don't forsake the fundamentals.

"I, too, was once my father's son, tenderly loved as my mother's only child. My father taught me, 'Take my words to heart. Follow my commands, and you will live.'" **PROVERBS 4:3-4**

I'm Glad I Didn't Stay in Bed

At eleven years of age, being patient and waiting for a deer to come by is difficult. Even at my age, waiting for a trophy buck can seem very trying. This particular morning was cold. The temperature was in the low thirties, and it was the second day of the hunt. We hadn't gotten much sleep the night before, and getting out in the cold while being sleepy seemed miserable.

When I went to wake my boys up, Cooper, my youngest son, said, "I'm not going. I'm too tired." I told him, "Coop, we didn't come all this way to sleep in. I'm coming back in five minutes." He said, "Okay," and then got up with his brother a few minutes later.

We layered up, got to the stands, and began to wait. I was with my older son, Brady, in one stand, and my friend John, our guide and host, was with Coop. It wasn't long after sunup when Brady and I heard the shot ring out through the crisp morning air. Moments later, we got a picture on my phone of Cooper with his first buck.

Proverbs 6:9 says, "Lazybones, how long will you sleep? When will you wake up?" It's easy to stay in bed, but the reward waits for those who get up and get at it. After we circled up with Cooper and John around his eight-point, Coop said to me, "Dad, I'm glad I didn't stay in bed."

Lazybones, how long will you sleep? When will you wake up?

PROVERBS 6:9

This One's for Pat

When he was awarded the Vince Lombardi Trophy after Super Bowl 50, Denver Broncos general manager John Elway declared, "This one's for Pat." Pat Bowlen, the owner of the Broncos since 1984, has had the highest winning percentage in the NFL with more regular-season wins than any other franchise from 1984 to 2015.

Bowlen, known for his concept of "team," makes others in his organization feel valued and appreciated. On the day after the Broncos won the 2015 season's AFC Championship, ESPN's Adam Schefter was reflecting on his time as a "cub reporter" covering the Broncos when he was twenty-three years old. Shefter pointed out that twenty years later, the same people who wandered the halls at the Broncos offices back then are the people wandering the halls today. This loyalty is a tribute to Bowlen's leadership and the way he values his people.

When Denver defeated the Packers 31–24 in Super Bowl XXXII, Bowlen declared, "This one's for John." Elway had a chance to return that favor eighteen years later. Bowlen, not present because of his ongoing fight with Alzheimer's disease, received back the blessing he had given years before in front of his beloved city and a global audience watching the game.

I am reminded of Proverbs 11:11, which states, "Upright citizens are good for a city and make it prosper," and Proverbs 11:25, which states, "The generous will prosper; those who refresh others will themselves be refreshed." Who do you need to bless today?

The generous will prosper; those who refresh others will themselves be refreshed.

PROVERBS 11:25

Layers of Frustration

Super Bowl 50 proved to be a very frustrating game for Carolina Panthers quarterback Cam Newton. Newton was sacked seven times and only completed eighteen of forty-one passes. The Broncos pass rush was so dominant that Newton, the league's MVP, never got settled. His frustration spilled over after the game as he inappropriately walked out of his media interview.

Frustration is like an onion. The longer it has to grow, the more layers it will develop. Since I learned this lesson the hard way, I have always tried to allow frustration to be a catalyst for progress in my life. But even this is a skill to be developed. If we steward frustration well, as I hope Cam Newton will, it can be a powerful force for solid change and real improvement. But as a parent watching my son struggle with a situation at school, I have really been challenged to know what to do with my frustration.

Here is what I have learned: the longer I allow frustration with others to grow, the quicker bitterness will take root, settle in, and impact other areas and relationships in my life.

Ephesians 4:31-32 gives us a great solution: "Get rid of all bitterness, rage, anger, harsh words, and slander, as well as all types of evil behavior. Instead, be kind to each other, tenderhearted, forgiving one another, just as God through Christ has forgiven you." If you sense bitterness developing, cut it off and cut it out at the root as soon as you can. Replace it with the intentional choice to forgive, be kind, and be a servant to those who have frustrated you.

Get rid of all bitterness, rage, anger, harsh words, and slander, as well as all types of evil behavior. Instead, be kind to each other, tenderhearted, forgiving one another, just as God through Christ has forgiven you.   EPHESIANS 4:31-32

Taking It All In

After the 20–18 defeat of the Patriots in the 2015 season's AFC Championship game, Sal Paolantonio interviewed Peyton Manning. The Denver Broncos quarterback became the oldest quarterback ever to go to a Super Bowl, surpassing his boss, John Elway, the Broncos general manager.

Manning took his time on the field that Sunday evening, seemingly soaking in the confetti, looking up to his family, and enjoying the satisfaction of the moment. The victory was even sweeter than his past successes because of the adversity Manning had faced before the game. With every pundit betting against him and siding with one of the NFL's greatest quarterbacks of all time, Tom Brady, Manning did what he had been doing for eighteen seasons. He led his team to the conference championship.

Paolantonio asked him how satisfying a victory it was, and Manning replied, "I'm just taking it all in." My friend, Mike Van Hoozer, in his book, *Moments: Making Your Life Count for What Matters Most*, calls this moment a moment of reflection, where you take time to embrace, enjoy, and engage completely in the moment.

There are many moments in the Old Testament when the people of Israel were called to celebrate and remember significant victories. Leviticus 23:41 shows us one such call to a celebration, the Feast of Tabernacles: "You must observe this festival to the LORD for seven days every year. This is a permanent law for you, and it must be observed in the appointed month from generation to generation."

Taking it all in involves celebrating. The Lord made sure that Israel knew that in their celebrations, he was to be honored. Before you move on to the next battle, savor the victory by taking the moment in. Reflect and then remember to thank the Lord.

You must observe this festival to the LORD for seven days every year. This is a permanent law for you, and it must be observed in the appointed month from generation to generation.　　　　　　　　　　　　　　　LEVITICUS 23:41

A Crime in Sport

As the 2016 Australian Open began, the BBC and BuzzFeed reported that sixteen of the top fifty tennis players in the world had been approached about throwing their matches in the previous ten years. Ironically, one of the major sponsors of the Australian Open is an online gambling company.

Novak Djokovic, the number-one-ranked player in the world, when asked about the scandal, said that in years past his people had been approached about throwing a match, reportedly offering Djokovic up to $200,000. Djokovic said, "Somebody may call it an opportunity. For me, that's an act of unsportsmanship, a crime in sport, honestly. I don't support it. I think there is no room for it in any sport, especially in tennis."[4]

When you are willing to bend the rules, there is a high probability that you are willing to break the rules also. But when you leave room in your life to play outside the rules, you are sure to be found out. Numbers 32:23 says, "If you fail to keep your word, then you will have sinned against the LORD, and you may be sure that your sin will find you out."

If a report were leaked about playing outside the lines at your job, or with women, might your name appear on it? Remember, there is great comfort in integrity. "Whoever walks in integrity walks securely, but he who makes his ways crooked will be found out" (Proverbs 10:9, ESV).

Whoever walks in integrity walks securely, but he who makes his ways crooked will be found out.   **PROVERBS 10:9, ESV**

---

4 Jim Caple, "Novak Djokovic's People Offered $200K for Star to Lose Match," *ESPN*, January 26, 2016, http://espn.go.com/tennis/story/_/id/14594431/novak-djokovic-says-was-offered -200000-lose-match-2007.

Anyone Can Start . . . Few Finish

The South African Kalahari Augrabies Extreme Marathon is, as you can tell by the name, more than just a marathon. According to the race's website, "The event goes way beyond merely covering 250 kilometers in extreme conditions; it is a challenge to get past what normal people would regard as crazy, and achieve one's personal goals."

I have not run a marathon, nor do I have any plans to do so. But I have learned that anyone can start something, but few finish it. You see, there is a cost involved in crossing the finish lines of life. This cost is sweat, tears, hard work, and perseverance. This cost isn't paid once, but over and over again as one builds up the stamina to go the distance of the race. It is the case in finances, in marriage, in education, and in business.

I have to confess that I have started many times. I have started a diet, I have started a program, and I have started toward a goal. I also have to confess that finishing is hard, and I don't always realize the cost involved when I start out, because I don't add up what it takes to get there.

Our Christian walk is the most important race we need to complete. Jesus' words in Luke's Gospel ring true when it comes to finishing as his disciple. He said, "Don't begin until you count the cost. For who would begin construction of a building without first calculating the cost to see if there is enough money to finish it? Otherwise, you might complete only the foundation before running out of money, and then everyone would laugh at you. They would say, 'There's the person who started that building and couldn't afford to finish it!'" (Luke 14:28-30).

Is your faith growing today in such a way that you know you will finish and receive the victor's crown? As the apostle Paul instructs us in 1 Corinthians 9:24, "Don't you realize that in a race everyone runs, but only one person gets the prize? So run to win!"

Don't you realize that in a race everyone runs, but only one person gets the prize? So run to win!   1 CORINTHIANS 9:24

Thanks for Being My Coach

One of my favorite roles as a father is that of coach. Coaching has provided sacred time with my children and a way for me as a pastor to be involved in the lives of people in our community. Some of my most satisfactory moments of ministry have come from coaching my kids on their sports teams.

At eleven years of age, my son Cooper's use of the English language is often limited to one or two words at a time. So when he said to me, "Hey, Dad, thanks for being my coach," my ears perked up. What a blessing to hear!

Before our football draft one season, I did two funerals within a three-day period. The men who died were in their seventies. When their children were young, one of these men had been a softball coach and the other a Scout leader. As their grown children came to visit me in my office, to a person they reflected on how their fathers had been present in their lives. I asked them for an example or two, and their answers spoke of the leadership their dads exhibited on the ball fields and at the pack meetings.

First John 2:14 speaks about the impact dads can have on their children. Notice the strength and victory wrought in the young men because of the mature lives and faith of their fathers: "I write to you, fathers, because you know him who is from the beginning. I write to you, young men, because you are strong, and the word of God abides in you, and you have overcome the evil one" (1 John 2:14, ESV).

Dad, there are no greater gifts to give your kids than your time and your presence. That leadership will be felt for years to come. Right before the football draft that year, I sent a note to the other coaches and said, "Guys, win or lose, what we will do for the next ten weeks really does matter."

I write to you, fathers, because you know him who is from the beginning. I write to you, young men, because you are strong, and the word of God abides in you, and you have overcome the evil one. 1 JOHN 2:14, ESV

A Spark off the Bench

During the last week of the 2015 regular season, some thought Broncos coach Gary Kubiak, with a play-off berth already clinched, would play Peyton Manning so he could see what Manning had left in the tank before going into the play-offs. Manning, in the throes of his eighteenth NFL campaign, had missed the previous six weeks with an injury to his foot, and the Broncos had handed the reins to Brock Osweiler. Although Manning was ready to play, Kubiak chose to stick with Osweiler and named Manning the backup, a role he played for the very first time in his Hall of Fame career.

Since New England lost earlier in the day, the number one seed was up for grabs. The Broncos struggled against a mediocre Chargers team, and despite turning the ball over five times, they were only down 13–7 when Manning entered the game in the third quarter.

The crowd rose to their feet when number eighteen took the field. There seemed to be a new energy to the offense. A few plays later, the Broncos had tied the game and went on to win 27–20 over the Chargers, finishing the season 12–4 and clinching the number one seed going into the play-offs.

Good leaders spark their teams in ways that others can't. When Joshua took command of Israel after Moses' death, the Israelites promised, "We will obey you just as we obeyed Moses. And may the LORD your God be with you as he was with Moses" (Joshua 1:17). To be the leader that sparks his team, you must pay the price, pour into others, and when the opportunity presents itself, go execute.

We will obey you just as we obeyed Moses. And may the LORD your God be with you as he was with Moses.   JOSHUA 1:17

From Blunder to Blessing

Without Trevone Boykin, the Texas Christian University Horned Frogs struggled to find their way in the 2016 Valero Alamo Bowl. Boykin, who had led his team for multiple seasons, was sent home due to an assault charge stemming from a bar fight. Now backup quarterback Bram Kohlhausen had a chance to redeem Boykin's blunder and turn out a victory.

Kohlhausen, who lost his dad in November 2015, led his team back from a thirty-one-point deficit to tie the game and push it into overtime. Getting the ball first, the Horned Frogs scored a touchdown. The Oregon Ducks fought back, but after three overtimes, the Horned Frogs were the Alamo Bowl champions. In a classy, gracious move, Kohlhausen dedicated the victory to Trevone Boykin, who missed his last college start because of his bad choices.

The gospel of Christ redeems us, too. Ephesians 1:13-14 tells us, "You Gentiles have also heard the truth, the Good News that God saves you. And when you believed in Christ, he identified you as his own by giving you the Holy Spirit, whom he promised long ago. The Spirit is God's guarantee that he will give us the inheritance he promised and that he has purchased us to be his own people. He did this so we would praise and glorify him." Our Lord takes our blunders and forgives them through his death on the cross. Once we receive his forgiveness, he grants us a life we don't deserve, dedicating himself to us by giving us the Holy Spirit, guaranteeing our victory for all eternity.

You Gentiles have also heard the truth, the Good News that God saves you. And when you believed in Christ, he identified you as his own by giving you the Holy Spirit, whom he promised long ago. The Spirit is God's guarantee that he will give us the inheritance he promised and that he has purchased us to be his own people. He did this so we would praise and glorify him.

EPHESIANS 1:13-14

Tripping the Referee

Coaching "Rec League" basketball is a blast. There isn't any pressure beyond the time you devote to the game that day. As my kids have gotten older and their skills have improved, I have enjoyed the faster pace and quality of play.

Yet there are days when I feel that the pace of the referees could pick up a bit. They call game after game, age group upon age group, enjoying the game they love as a second job on the weekends. But I get frustrated that they miss so much because their pace seems to still be on the third- and fourth-grade level from a few hours before.

In those moments of frustration, I need to remember that even a fool is considered wise when he keeps his mouth shut. Although they're working a second job on the weekends, these men are the authority in charge, and my team and my sons will think of them in proportion to how they see me treat them.

Authority figures are becoming increasing targets of disdain and violence in our time. From the two young high school football players who assaulted a referee by blindsiding him during a play, to videos that emerge on the Internet of parents attacking referees at peewee football games, to Jarmal Reid of the Oregon State Beavers tripping the ref in the backcourt because Reid didn't get the call he thought he deserved, athletes, coaches, and many parents have lost regard for authority.

But Scripture calls us to honor authority. Romans 13:1 states, "Everyone must submit to governing authorities. For all authority comes from God, and those in positions of authority have been placed there by God." Will you submit to those in authority who have been placed in their positions by God?

Everyone must submit to governing authorities. For all authority comes from God, and those in positions of authority have been placed there by God.

ROMANS 13:1

Where I Can Come and Be a Kid

The Walter Payton NFL Man of the Year Award is given to the player who is selected by a panel of judges for having the biggest impact on his community. When 2015 nominee Connor Barwin joined the Philadelphia Eagles, he committed to giving back to the city by investing in the city parks through his foundation.

The son of a city manager, Barwin bikes nearly everywhere he goes in Philly. He sees the city from a unique vantage point because of what his father taught him and because of the speed with which he can travel the streets. The NFL Network, covering all the Walter Payton NFL Man of the Year finalists, ran a story about Barwin's investment in the city parks. One little girl said, "I love coming here because it's where I can come and be a kid." Creating spaces where children can feel safe and free in the inner city is beautiful. Barwin is committed to renovating city parks so that people young and old can gather, play, and be refreshed.

When I saw this story, I was reminded of Proverbs 11:24-25: "Give freely and become more wealthy; be stingy and lose everything. The generous will prosper; those who refresh others will themselves be refreshed."

As I read this proverb, I see that there is a blessing that is activated when I bless others. Somehow, in God's economy of things, he brings blessings into the life of the one who is openhanded and is putting others' interests ahead of his own. Consider this an invitation to go refresh someone's life today, and enjoy the blessings that come to that person's life and yours.

Give freely and become more wealthy; be stingy and lose everything. The generous will prosper; those who refresh others will themselves be refreshed.
PROVERBS 11:24-25

Tenacious Leadership

After three ACL tears, rehabs, and returns to play, there doesn't seem to be anything that Thomas Davis, Carolina Panthers linebacker, can't overcome. Davis, who broke his arm in the 2015 NFC Championship game against the Arizona Cardinals, declared that he would play in the Super Bowl that year. He was quoted as saying, "Come on, you know me, right? I ain't missing the Super Bowl, you better believe that."[5]

Tenacity to see the job through marks great athletes, great doctors, great leaders, and great men. To be a great husband and father, you must keep your destination in mind. The words you say and the actions you choose should flow out of a tenacious desire to love your wife and children in such a way as to make it through any adversity that may come.

Having a vision of golfing, fishing, or hunting with your sons when they are forty and you are seventy should help you deal with the crises of today. Being there to walk your daughter down the aisle and give her to her new husband should compel you to live well today. Seeing the family gathered around you and your wife at your fiftieth wedding anniversary should be a motivating vision for how you can make investments toward that future moment. Your attitude ought to be, "Come on, you know me, right? I ain't missing those moments."

Look at the tenacious vision and love of our God as stated in Jude 1:24: "Now all glory to God, who is able to keep you from falling away and will bring you with great joy into his glorious presence without a single fault."

Do you see the vision that God has for us? May we also have a clear vision for our future and a tenacious love that helps us navigate our choices today!

All glory to God, who is able to keep you from falling away and will bring you with great joy into his glorious presence without a single fault. JUDE 1:24

---

[5] Jeanna Thomas and Luke Zimmermann, "Can Thomas Davis Play in the Super Bowl with a Broken Arm?" *SB Nation*, January 25, 2016, http://www.sbnation.com/nfl/2016/1/25/10826270/thomas-davis-broken-arm-play-super-bowl-50-panthers-broncos.

FEBRUARY

A Commitment to Excellence

NBA executive Pat Reilly once said, "Excellence is the gradual result of always striving to do better." Sometimes we think that striving for excellence means being perfect, but excellence is about doing the best we can with what we have been given. The great coach Vince Lombardi said, "The quality of a person's life is in direct proportion to their commitment to excellence, regardless of their chosen field of endeavor."

The apostle Peter proclaims in 2 Peter 1:3 that "God has given us everything we need for living a godly life." He declares that God's glory and excellence call us to himself. Since God demonstrates excellence, we, too, are to demonstrate this. Peter continues this thought and challenges us to make application to our lives:

> In view of all this, make every effort to respond to God's promises. Supplement your faith with a generous provision of moral excellence, and moral excellence with knowledge, and knowledge with self-control, and self-control with patient endurance, and patient endurance with godliness, and godliness with brotherly affection, and brotherly affection with love for everyone. (verses 5-7)

Take a moment to look at your life. Does it reflect a commitment to excellence and godliness? As men, we should set the tone in striving toward godliness. Respond to the promises of God, and ask for the Holy Spirit to fill you and enable you to grow a little bit more each and every day. Someone who is committed to excellence doesn't settle for the status quo. He pays attention to the details, puts in the required time, and performs with consistency. Sticking with the status quo might feel comfortable, but God's call runs much deeper.

God has given us everything we need for living a godly life.   **2 PETER 1:3**

Easy Learning

When athletes make the jump from middle school to high school, the game speeds up. When they jump from high school to college, it gets even faster. When an athlete gets to the pros, the game gets even faster—that is, until it slows down. You see, there comes a time when after significant study and experience, the game gets easier instead of harder—slower instead of faster.

But that knowledge of the game can come only when athletes seek to learn. Proverbs 14:6 says, "A mocker seeks wisdom and never finds it, but knowledge comes easily to those with understanding."

Unfortunately, mockers don't take time to learn from their experience. Coaches can speak into their lives, but then mockers simply ignore the words of wisdom. On the other hand, those who are teachable are eager to learn. They have a "Put me in, coach" mentality. They can't get enough drills, and they are eager to do the extra film study to master their game.

I have the privilege of being Dr. Jim Tour's pastor. He is an example of a man of great understanding. Dr. Tour is the T. T. and W. F. Chao Professor of Chemistry, as well as a professor of computer science, materials science, and nano-engineering at Rice University. Professionally, he is an elite scientist. As a man of prayer, he is very persistent in his requests. When I asked him if he was having any breakthroughs in his research, Jim told me, "We have breakthroughs every single week." You see, Jim prays for the Lord to give him knowledge as he does the most cutting-edge research in nanotechnology.

Consider this Scripture the next time you need knowledge:

"The eyes of the LORD keep watch over knowledge"
(Proverbs 22:12, NIV).

Learn from your experience, master your craft, and ask the Lord for breakthroughs. The learning will come easier than you think if you stick with it.

A mocker seeks wisdom and never finds it, but knowledge comes easily to those with understanding.　　　　　　　　**PROVERBS 14:6**

Better Than the Big Game

In 2014, before the Seattle Seahawks beat the Denver Broncos in Super Bowl XLVIII, several members of the team sat down with a Seattle pastor who asked them about their faith in Jesus Christ. Rocky Seto, one of the coaching staff, replied, "If we ever were to win the Super Bowl, we'd be able to tell everyone that Jesus is still better. Because as much as we worship this thing called a ring and a championship, Jesus is way better still."

As you know, the Seahawks won in 2014, but in 2015 they tasted that bitter, final-moment defeat. Loss is painful, no matter what. But I am confident that those players and coaches who have their trust in Christ were able to wake up the next morning and say, "Jesus is better still."

The Bible testifies to the greatness of Jesus Christ and shows us that nothing can compare to him. Hebrews 1:3-4 says, "The Son radiates God's own glory and expresses the very character of God, and he sustains everything by the mighty power of his command. When he had cleansed us from our sins, he sat down in the place of honor at the right hand of the majestic God in heaven. This shows that the Son is far greater than the angels, just as the name God gave him is greater than their names."

Do you declare the greatness of Jesus Christ in both victory and loss? Do you have a foundation that helps you keep perspective when you win in the workplace? When something you have worked for falls through, do you still cling to the greatness of Jesus Christ? No matter what you experience, I hope that you can say with confidence, "Jesus is better still."

The Son radiates God's own glory and expresses the very character of God, and he sustains everything by the mighty power of his command. When he had cleansed us from our sins, he sat down in the place of honor at the right hand of the majestic God in heaven. This shows that the Son is far greater than the angels, just as the name God gave him is greater than their names.
HEBREWS 1:3-4

Getting an Adjustment

I have a great chiropractor. Dr. Eric Tondera attends my church, and our families have been friends for years. When I met Eric nineteen years ago, we were playing in a young-marrieds softball league. I had just aggravated my back, and during our at bat, he told me to lie on the ground so that he could stretch my hamstrings. Since that time nearly two decades ago, I have had to see Eric for a few more adjustments to my lower back.

While writing the final draft of this book, I found my back hurting from sitting too long. It got so bad that when I got up in the middle of the night, my lower back locked up on both sides, and the pain drove me to my knees. After taking some ibuprofen and icing my back for a few hours, I went to see Dr. Tondera for an adjustment and got even more relief. The following day there was a little stiffness, but all the pain was resolved.

When a chiropractor adjusts you, he manipulates your joints with great strength and power. The adjustment isn't pleasant, but it brings great relief. When the chiropractor pops your neck, it can really set you free from pain. But you have to trust him to properly adjust your neck.

Not only is my chiropractor my doctor, but he is also my friend. He is honest with me about my weight and the causes of my pain, as a good doctor and friend should be. Proverbs 27:6 states, "Wounds from a sincere friend are better than many kisses from an enemy." The New International Version says that the wounds of a friend can be "trusted." If your friend speaks truth to you, it is for a needed adjustment that is for your good. Embrace the painful words, and get your life back in alignment, because your friend is only trying to spare you from painful days ahead.

Wounds from a sincere friend are better than many kisses from an enemy.
PROVERBS 27:6

Act Like You've Been There

Tony Dungy, Super Bowl–winning head coach of the Indianapolis Colts, said about their Super Bowl victory, "Our goal was to win a Super Bowl, but also to win in the right way, to be role models to our community, to represent Indianapolis, . . . and the National Football League." Inherent in this quote is vision: Coach Dungy envisioned not only winning the Super Bowl but also winning it with class and character.

Proverbs 29:18 says, "When people do not accept divine guidance, they run wild." That divine guidance is vision, and successful people know that they need it.

Once successful people receive vision for their lives, they begin to picture the day when they have arrived at that place. When they do get there, they aren't surprised that they're successful. They may be overwhelmed by how much success they have, but they are never surprised that they have it. You see, people enjoy success because they have envisioned the victory. Their vision moves them toward success. Andy Stanley says, "Vision is seeing something that could be while being fueled by the conviction that it should be."

After you receive the vision for your life, lay out a process to get there—mile markers, stepping-stones, and goals. What will it take to reach your destination? How many resources will it take? How do you get there with class, as Coach Dungy did? Start with these two questions: What in my life could be? Better yet, what *should* be? Get the divine guidance you need by asking the Lord to make his vision for you clear.

When people do not accept divine guidance, they run wild.   PROVERBS 29:18

The Pain of Pruning

I have four bougainvillea plants on my back deck. I first saw the bougainvillea when I went to San Jose, California, to speak at a leadership conference. I stayed at a hotel that had trained their bougainvillea beautifully, and they were in full bloom. I thought, *I wonder if I could grow that at home.*

I don't have a green thumb. I am good with a lawn mower, but tending to a growing plant isn't my strength. I'm excited that my bougainvillea are still growing and blooming, but they are nowhere near what I saw in San Jose. I know that I need to prune them, but a part of me doesn't want to cut off what is growing, because I am not confident in the result. At least I have some blooms now, and I don't want to go through the pain of losing them if I do the pruning and training wrong.

I can draw some parallels in my own life and leadership journey when I sense there is a season of pruning that needs to take place. On a personal level, there are times when I've got to get some things under control at home that I may have neglected. On a professional level, sometimes it's just time to move on from an employee who is preventing progress.

Change can be difficult if you think about it for too long. Sometimes, though painful, the best course for all involved is to cut off a branch so that the resources will be redirected to what is most fruitful. In John 15:1-2, Jesus says, "I am the true grapevine, and my Father is the gardener. He cuts off every branch of mine that doesn't produce fruit, and he prunes the branches that do bear fruit so they will produce even more." Remember, pruning is painful, but its intended purpose is to help what is bearing fruit to be even more fruitful.

I am the true grapevine, and my Father is the gardener. He cuts off every branch of mine that doesn't produce fruit, and he prunes the branches that do bear fruit so they will produce even more.
JOHN 15:1-2

FEBRUARY 7
It's Not Over 'til It's Over

If you watched Super Bowl XLIX, you saw a hard-fought game by both the New England Patriots and the Seattle Seahawks. It was a constant give-and-take with big plays and high emotions. With just over two minutes left in the fourth quarter, the Patriots scored to get ahead by four points.

The Seahawks had plenty of time and, it appeared, the right plan to march down the field and win the game. After a miraculous catch and a short run, the Seahawks were at the goal line. With only twenty seconds left in the game, it looked like a Seahawks repeat victory was inevitable.

But an undrafted rookie for the Patriots, Malcolm Butler, kept his focus on the game, remembered this signal the Seahawks gave from film study, and intercepted the ball, securing another Super Bowl victory for the Patriots. It was an improbable finish to an amazing game.

In Scripture, there are a large number of improbable finishes. When Israel was pressed on all sides, God told Gideon to gather troops to fight the Midianites. What God called him to do next was astounding. He was told to scale back his fighting force from thirty thousand to three hundred men. Through Gideon's obedience, God taught him that anything was possible with the Lord's help. Judges 7:9 states, "That night the LORD said, 'Get up! Go down into the Midianite camp, for I have given you victory over them!'"

Do you have areas in your life where it looks like defeat is inevitable? Remember, with the Lord on your side, victory is always available. Keep your head in the game, and stay focused, because there is still time on the clock. Remember, "It's not over 'til it's over."

That night the LORD said, "Get up! Go down into the Midianite camp, for I have given you victory over them!" JUDGES 7:9

Jealousy: The Most Dangerous Emotion

In his book *The One Year Uncommon Life Daily Challenge*, Tony Dungy warns against the jealousy he sees in professional sports. Dungy says, "It's a challenge at times. Each year thirty-one teams watch the Super Bowl champion—the goal they also shared but fell short of."[6]

So many of us struggle with this dangerous emotion. We tend to see what other people have and lose sight of all the good things in our own lives. We see our neighbor buying a new car, or someone else getting promoted instead of us, and we wonder why we didn't get what he or she did. This is the way life goes.

We went to a friend's house to watch the Super Bowl one year. My friend and his wife had just finished turning their backyard into a wonderful outdoor living space. It had a pool, hot tub, pergola, wood-burning fireplace, dining table, seating group, and Ping-Pong table. Another friend who was there looked at me quickly and said, "Roger, I need a sermon on coveting, right now."

You see, she was saying, "I'm jealous, and I want what they have." We laughed, because she said what I was thinking. But remember, if you harbor jealousy in your heart, it will begin to affect your attitude toward those who have what you want. It will lead you to discontentment, leaving you ungrateful for what you have been given. It will cause you to live for the wrong things, and you will miss so many of the simple joys of life.

Proverbs 27:4 says, "Anger is cruel, and wrath is like a flood, but jealousy is even more dangerous." Listen to Coach Dungy's counsel as we conclude our time together today: "Never let jealousy take hold. It always leaves a bad taste in your mouth."[7]

Anger is cruel, and wrath is like a flood, but jealousy is even more dangerous.

PROVERBS 27:4

---

[6] Tony Dungy and Nathan Whitaker, *The One Year Uncommon Life Daily Challenge* (Carol Stream, IL: Tyndale, 2011), August 8.
[7] Ibid.

Jesus, the Guilt Offering

My friend Mike Person is the executive producer at SB Nation Radio. Mike has been in radio production for years. He loves the Lord and has a great talent for lining up guests for his shows. When we started *Vision for Life Radio: Where Faith and Sports Collide*, Mike landed Coach Bobby Bowden and Heisman Trophy winner Charlie Ward for my very first show.

For Super Bowl 50, Mike and his team at SB Nation Radio went to Radio Row in San Francisco. As he was booking guests for the SB Nation Radio network, he sent me a picture of Baltimore Ravens running back Justin Forsette. Forsette's hat was on backwards, and it read, "JESUS." I love that Forsette was making it known that he is a Christ follower.

It seems that as things progress toward Christ's return, opinions about faith are beginning to polarize. You are either for Jesus or you aren't, and there isn't a lot of middle ground. Those who are against Christ are mocking him more and more. Just watch HBO's Bill Maher to witness this mocking. I believe this disrespect of Christ is in direct correlation to the foolishness of our country.

Proverbs 14:9 says, "Fools mock at the guilt offering, but the upright enjoy acceptance" (ESV). When there is an increase in folly and a disregard for God, the guilt offering that brings men peace with God is mocked more and more.

Our nation has progressively moved away from a fear of the Lord. He is not revered in the courtroom. He is not revered in the White House. He is not revered in the public square. There is a great disrespect and disregard for God, and this leads to an increase of fools and folly all around.

Don't be a fool and disregard your maker. Fear the Lord and enjoy the guilt offering, the Lord Jesus, who paid the price for your sin.

Fools mock at the guilt offering, but the upright enjoy acceptance.
PROVERBS 14:9, ESV

Not Lost but Home

Hall of Fame coach Vince Lombardi once said, "Football is like life. It requires perseverance, self-denial, hard work, sacrifice, dedication, and respect for authority."

There is a lot of wisdom in his words. Playing any sport at a high level is hard. But life is even harder. The sufferings and hardships of this life don't distinguish between rich or poor, famous or common, white or black. NBA coach Monty Williams lost his wife, Ingrid, suddenly and prematurely when she was killed in a head-on collision. Former NFL quarterback Randall Cunningham lost his son Christian in a drowning. Coach Bobby Bowden has had to bury two grandsons and a son-in-law. Green Bay Packers quarterback and, later, coach Bart Starr also lost a son.

When Coach Williams eulogized his wife, he said, "This is hard for my family." Then Coach Williams spoke with hope. He finished his thought and said, "But it will work out."

We often say we have lost a person when he or she dies. But Coach Williams would probably challenge the use of the word *lost*. When he gave that amazing eulogy, he boldly said, "My wife is in heaven. . . . My wife is where we all need to be, and I am envious of that. . . . We didn't lose her. When you lose something, you can't find it. I know exactly where my wife is." To that I say amen. The truth of the matter is that Ingrid Williams is more alive today than she has ever been. The Scripture declares the hope of our salvation: "Yes, we are fully confident, and we would rather be away from these earthly bodies, for then we will be at home with the Lord" (2 Corinthians 5:8).

You see, when someone who knows Christ dies, he or she isn't lost. That person has gone home. We can be confident that if we are saved by Christ, to be absent from the body is to be present with the Lord.

Yes, we are fully confident, and we would rather be away from these earthly bodies, for then we will be at home with the Lord. 2 CORINTHIANS 5:8

Date Night

Hall of Fame coach Tom Landry once said, "Today, you have 100 percent of your life left." Whether you realize it or not, you have 100 percent of your marriage left as well. Some would argue with me on that point because they don't believe their marriage will last another month.

But what if you lived as if you had 100 percent of your marriage left beginning today? What would you change about your part of the relationship? You see, every relationship is a two-way street, but you can control only how you carry yourself in the marriage. I want to challenge you to consider how you can play great special teams through special moments like date night. Date night is life giving to a marriage. It demonstrates to your spouse that she is a priority. It gives both of you a break from work, kids, and schedules that can easily get out of control. Date night is an opportunity to pursue your spouse again, inviting her to come away with you.

The Old Testament book Song of Songs is one of the most erotic love stories in literature. It is the story of lovers pursuing each other and inviting each other into an embrace. Many a man will stop pursuing his wife, and as a result, the intimacy of the marriage will be extinguished. Notice how the king pursues his wife in Song of Songs 2:10-12:

> My lover said to me, "Rise up, my darling!
> Come away with me, my fair one!
> Look, the winter is past, and the rains are over and gone.
> The flowers are springing up, the season of singing birds has come,
> and the cooing of turtledoves fills the air.

There is wisdom in the invitation to "come away." Set a date, and go enjoy the blessing of being together. Make it special, and ask God to renew you as a husband. Keep pursuing your wife, and remember that today, you have 100 percent of your marriage left.

My lover said to me, "Rise up, my darling! Come away with me, my fair one!"
SONG OF SONGS 2:10

Dating Your Daughter

As Valentine's Day approaches, I want to turn your focus to your daughter. There is no doubt in my mind that you are going to show your significant other how special she is on Valentine's Day. But I want to invite you to see Valentine's Day as an opportunity to do something special for your daughter as well. It is a chance for you to begin to "date" your daughter and show her that you are holding her heart.

Unless we show our daughters how a real man carries himself, they will settle for far less than what we or the Lord would have for them. In light of all you do, let me tell you that dating your daughter takes intentionality and consistency. Further, if we don't do this, we can expect that our little princesses will learn about dating from teenage boys. The last place that I want my little girl learning about a relationship with a man is with a teenage boy.

Let's show our little girls, our teenage girls, our college girls, what it is to be loved, cherished, protected, respected, and affirmed. Don't just do it once and think you can check it off the list, but do it over and over again, so that she gets it.

Our daughters allow us to hold their hearts for only a short time. I know that you will never let go, but at some point she will give that heart to another man. It is your job to show her what type of man to consider.

Ecclesiastes 3:1 tells us, "For everything there is a season, a time for every activity under heaven." Guys, don't let this time with your daughter go by without showing her what it is to really be cherished. Make the most of this season so that when she enters the next, she will be as prepared as possible for what lies ahead.

For everything there is a season, a time for every activity under heaven.
ECCLESIASTES 3:1

The Best Thing a Dad Can Do

Hall of Fame basketball coach John Wooden once said, "The most important thing a father can do for his kids is to love their mother." I think he is absolutely right.

The problem that I often encounter as a husband is that I love myself more than I love my wife. Julee and I have been married for twenty-one years, and we have described our marriage as quite blissful. But I still fall into the same pit all too often—the pit of selfishness and self-love—and the biggest problem is that I often fail to see it.

The cure for my selfishness is humble service, known as the sacrificial love of Jesus. Philippians 2:3-5 states, "Don't be selfish; don't try to impress others. Be humble, thinking of others as better than yourselves. Don't look out only for your own interests, but take an interest in others, too. You must have the same attitude that Christ Jesus had."

When I actively serve my wife's interests ahead of my own, I am declaring my love for her. The longer we are married, the more I realize that this needs to be an intentional decision every day, because this kind of love is not driven by emotion. It is easy to slip into selfishness and not even realize it. I want to challenge you to take on the same attitude of Christ and put your wife's needs ahead of your own. You will love her well, and your children will see it firsthand.

Don't be selfish; don't try to impress others. Be humble, thinking of others as better than yourselves. Don't look out only for your own interests, but take an interest in others, too. You must have the same attitude that Christ Jesus had.
PHILIPPIANS 2:3-5

Cherish the Gift of Your Wife

Bud Grant, former head coach of the Minnesota Vikings, said, "A good football coach needs a patient wife, a loyal dog, and a great quarterback—but not necessarily in that order." There is no position on the field that can replace the quarterback. To win football games, you must have a good one. But to win at home, guys, we must value our wives.

Over our twenty-one years of marriage, my wife, Julee, and I have had our differences and our challenging moments, like every other couple. But the vast majority of our married life has been great. I am proud to write that and am thankful for my wife. I am blessed beyond measure to be married to Julee Lyn Patterson.

Proverbs 18:22 says, "The man who finds a wife finds a treasure, and he receives favor from the LORD." Men, we must believe this passage of Scripture with all of our hearts. When the Bible says a wife is a treasure, rest assured it means that God gave us our wives. God's gift to Adam was Eve, and though they didn't have the perfect relationship, the Bible calls her his perfect complement. I would suspect that you don't have the perfect relationship either, but your wife is a great complement to you.

I want to remind you today that God sees your wife as a treasure and that in giving her to you, he has shown you favor. I want to challenge you to find a way to cherish your wife as the treasure she is! Honor her this week with a surprise that declares your love and her worth to you. May the Lord bless your marriage this year beyond measure!

The man who finds a wife finds a treasure, and he receives favor from the LORD.
                                                          PROVERBS 18:22

Go

I'm having fun coaching my son Brady's basketball team. We have eight athletes on our team in the Bellaire Parks and Recreation league. It is fun coaching fourteen- and fifteen-year-olds because they are becoming better athletes. Now that the players are older, their basketball IQ has developed, and they are learning to work as a team, looking for ways to break down their opponents.

With the group of athletes I have, I find myself hollering, "Go!" when we get a turnover. The two-three zone defense we play, and the swarming intensity of our defense, has created a lot of turnover opportunities for us. We can outrun anybody, and our depth allows us to stay fresh.

You know, life is fun when you are on a team and you have each other's backs. It is refreshing to win as a team. The Bible speaks about the power of working together and playing as a team in Ecclesiastes 4:9-12:

> "Two people are better off than one, for they can help each other succeed. If one person falls, the other can reach out and help. But someone who falls alone is in real trouble. Likewise, two people lying close together can keep each other warm. But how can one be warm alone? A person standing alone can be attacked and defeated, but two can stand back-to-back and conquer. Three are even better, for a triple-braided cord is not easily broken."

Value the team you are on, and work at working well together. When you do, you can really go!

Two people are better off than one, for they can help each other succeed.
ECCLESIASTES 4:9

When Fog Settles In

Have you ever been stuck in the fog? I once took my family on a cruise, where we had a tremendous time making memories, laughing, and eating too much. When it came time to disembark and get back to our real lives, we couldn't go anywhere. The fog in the harbor was so thick that the port authority closed all traffic going in and out. The delay lasted nearly ten hours, and all we could do was wait it out on the ship.

There are some situations and seasons in our lives that bring a thick fog with them. When it settles in and is so thick that you can't really progress and aren't sure which way to go, what do you do? You can take a tip from our time being stuck on the cruise ship and "EAT" all you can. This is an acronym I picked up from a coach I deeply respect:

Effort: Give your best effort on what you can control.
Attitude: Have the best attitude you can in spite of the challenging circumstances.
Technique: Master your technique by putting your head down and making the most of the situation you are in.

Listen to the counsel of the psalmist who found himself in a season of waiting: "Trust in the Lord and do good; dwell in the land and cultivate faithfulness. Delight yourself in the Lord; and He will give you the desires of your heart" (Psalm 37:3-4, NASB).

When you are stuck waiting, make the most of the situation by cultivating faithfulness. Then you will be prepared when the sun shines through again.

Trust in the Lord and do good; dwell in the land and cultivate faithfulness. Delight yourself in the Lord; and He will give you the desires of your heart.
PSALM 37:3-4, NASB

Pornography Is an Intimacy Killer

In February 2016, former NFL player and *Brooklyn Nine-Nine* actor Terry Crews took to his Facebook page to discuss his long-standing addiction to pornography. Crews was quoted as saying, "For years, years, years, my dirty little secret was that I was addicted to pornography. . . . It really, really messed up my life in a lot of ways."[8] At forty-seven, Crews revealed the addiction he'd had since he was twelve years old.

I find it refreshing that a man in his position would openly admit the impact that pornography had on his life. It caused significant pain in his marriage, and reportedly, he and his wife both attended therapy for the challenges the addiction brought them. In an article about his addiction, Crews said, "Every man out there desires intimacy. . . . But the problem is, pornography is an intimacy killer."[9]

Some studies indicate that the chemical reactions that take place in a man's brain while viewing pornographic images are as addictive as cocaine. The only way that I have found that men can get free of this particular addiction is to bring it into the light and seek help. They must then employ safeguards for the rest of their lives.

John 3:21 says, "Those who do what is right come to the light so others can see that they are doing what God wants." Bringing our lives into the light will enable us to get the help we need to overcome that which has entangled us. Are you addicted to pornography? Share your problem with a pastor, and ask him to help you get the help you need. Get involved with a men's group that will challenge you and hold you accountable. Put filters on your computer and phone. Live in the light. May you, too, have the courage to stand up against the stronghold of pornography!

Those who do what is right come to the light so others can see that they are doing what God wants.
JOHN 3:21

---

8 Desiree Murphy, "Terry Crews Gets Candid about His Porn Addiction: 'It Really Messed Up My Life,'" ET Online, February 24, 2016, http://www.etonline.com/news/183023_terry_crews_gets_candid_about_porn_addiction_it_really_messed_up_my_life/.
9 Ibid.

Man Up

One of the things we love about sports is what the extremely talented athletes who play them can do under pressure. For some players, those in-the-moment actions establish their legacies. We cheer for young athletes with potential to seize the opportunities and endure the pressure so that they can cement their legacies. Let's be honest: performance under pressure is what separates the men from the boys, the great from the good.

In Super Bowl 50, Carolina Panthers quarterback Cam Newton faced the pressure of the number-one-ranked defense in the NFL. The Denver Broncos front seven harassed Newton the entire game, sacking him seven times. As the clock wound down, it seemed that Newton wouldn't emerge the victor by overcoming that pressure. To Newton's credit, rarely did the offensive package call for an extra tight end or halfback to stay in and block for him. Instead, the offensive coordinator left it to his offensive line and Newton's ability to scramble to keep the MVP quarterback on his feet and out of trouble. I would suspect that Newton will take his game to another level during the off-season and come back even better.

Pressure can make us stronger. In the book of James, we are told to consider it pure joy when we encounter trials that test us, because perseverance is being developed (see James 1:2-4).

If you are in the cauldron of pressure, I want to encourage you to embrace it and to man up. Proverbs 24:10 says, "If you fail under pressure, your strength is too small." And we don't want to have small strength.

Man up by being courageous, being strengthened, and choosing to persevere!

If you fail under pressure, your strength is too small. PROVERBS 24:10

Knowing What Matters Most

One of the things I have had trouble learning to say is the word *no*. By nature, I am an extrovert, a people pleaser, and a problem solver. But my coach Dan Hall, president of On Course Solutions, has continually challenged me to see why I say yes or no.

Dan once asked me to declare what I have already said yes to. These are my most important tasks and responsibilities. He has taught me that if I don't know what my top priorities are, I won't ever have the freedom to say no. The longer we have walked together, the more I have learned that he is right.

Jesus was a master of saying no because of what he had already said yes to. In Mark 1:37-38 we see Jesus in prayer: "When they found him, they said, 'Everyone is looking for you.' But Jesus replied, 'We must go on to other towns as well, and I will preach to them, too. That is why I came.'"

The crowd is assembled, his followers are urging him there as well, but Jesus says, "No, I'm headed this way." Jesus could say no because he had already said yes to the plan of the Father.

What have you already said yes to? If you are married and have kids, there are two of your answers. Remember, knowing what you will and won't do is crucial to your success and fulfillment.

When they found him, they said, "Everyone is looking for you." But Jesus replied, "We must go on to other towns as well, and I will preach to them, too. That is why I came."   MARK 1:37-38

Closing the Loop

During the 2013 Discover BCS National Championship game, Eddie Lacy of the Alabama Crimson Tide made his way to the highlight reel by sending a defender on the Notre Dame defense to the ground. It was a spin move finished off with a stiff-arm that amazed all looking on. Alabama went on to win that game 42–14 in a rout of the number-one-ranked Fighting Irish.

Have you ever been stiff-armed? The stiff-arm is an amazing tool for running backs because it seems to give them an unfair advantage over the defense. As they break into the open field, many running backs shift the ball to the outside arm and extend the inside arm straight out into the face mask of a defensive player and shed him off.

We often communicate via the stiff-arm. We do it by not responding to a difficult person. What we need to understand is that in relationships, lack of communication is still a type of communication. It is a stiff-arm, often given when we don't know how to deal with an annoying, difficult person. We stiff-arm others when we fail to reply to an e-mail, ignore a phone call, or avoid returning a text message.

Let's remember the Golden Rule of Luke 6:31, which says, "Do to others as you would like them to do to you." Certainly, no one is perfect in this, and there are times when we forget to close the loop. But when it is more of a pattern than a misstep, you might want to see if it is eroding your trustworthiness.

Do to others as you would like them to do to you.   LUKE 6:31

You Are Going to Make It

Just before he went on a few road trips to check out colleges, Jake, a high school senior, went with his friends to play Frisbee golf at Rice University. While there, he decided to jump on the trampoline for just a few minutes. Unfortunately, Jake never got to go on those road trips, because he fractured bones on both sides of his ankle while jumping on the trampoline.

After surgery to insert nine screws, and a few weeks of doing nothing at home, Jake got his doctor's permission to return to school. However, when Jake and his grandmother got to the nurse's office, the nurse told him that he wouldn't be allowed to return to school. He was still wearing a soft cast, and she was concerned there were just too many students who could injure him further. While Jake was waiting for the nurse's final ruling, a small boy who had to use a walker approached Jake. This boy's legs were deformed, and every step was a struggle for him. He neared Jake, standing eye-to-eye as Jake sat in his wheelchair, and said, "When you go to rehab, do whatever the therapists tell you. Work as hard as you can and try really hard. You are going to make it."

Jake responded with a quick high five and a "Thanks, man!" His grandmother was taken aback by this courageous young man who had just encouraged her grandson to give it his best.

First Peter 5:12 says, "My purpose in writing is to encourage you and assure you that what you are experiencing is truly part of God's grace for you. Stand firm in this grace." What if, like Peter and this young man with a walker, we saw it as our purpose to encourage others so that they would experience God's grace? An encouraging word is refreshing to those going through difficult times. Let them know, "You are going to make it!"

My purpose in writing is to encourage you and assure you that what you are experiencing is truly part of God's grace for you. Stand firm in this grace.

1 PETER 5:12

In Season and out of Season

I've had a few opportunities to join the guys of *Prime Cut*, SB Nation Radio's nationally syndicated afternoon drive time show, to share about matters of faith and how they intersect with the sports world. These moments have been quite fun for me, because I had planned to go into sports broadcasting when I was in high school. Many of the guys at SB Nation Radio have become my friends, and when I have done segments with them, they have allowed me to openly share my opinion and faith perspective.

I have been asked questions about Russell Wilson's contract size and whether or not God really spoke to him when he threw that interception on the two-yard line in Super Bowl XLIX. I have been asked how I thought Monty Williams's faith was going to sustain him through the sudden loss of his wife, Ingrid, after she was killed in a head-on collision. As I have gone back and listened to the segments afterward, I have tried to learn from my time on air. I want to make sure I am representing the Lord well.

When we are asked a question about our faith, how should we respond? Second Timothy 4:2 tells us to "preach the word; be ready in season and out of season" (ESV).

I count it a privilege to be able to answer questions about faith and how it impacts and intersects with those in the sports world on a program that is being broadcast in over sixty markets. But you don't have to be on a radio program or be interviewed by media to effectively speak of your faith.

I have learned that when we are put in a positon to answer questions about our faith, we need not panic, be nervous, or wonder if we gave the right answer. Instead, in the moment, we can simply pray, *Lord, use me to honor you*, and answer the questions graciously and honestly so that we can bear witness to Christ and bring glory to the Father.

Preach the word; be ready in season and out of season.　　　2 TIMOTHY 4:2, ESV

Yesterday Ended Last Night

The 2015–16 Houston Rockets had a disappointing first half of the season. After going to the Western Conference Finals at the end of the previous season, the Rockets, just a few games into the 2015–16 campaign, fired head coach Kevin McHale. In my estimation, McHale was the one who got them to play defense in 2015 when they really didn't want to put in the effort. So, after a bizarre move by the owner, Les Alexander, the Rockets struggled to play defense well without McHale's leadership.

I am well aware that this is only my opinion of what happened to the Rockets. It could be that McHale was the one not serving the organization well. Whatever the case, we live in a "What have you done for me lately?" world. Governing how you will adapt to change and work through those shifts will require you to have the right mind-set.

Proverbs 6:6-8 challenges us to not sit on our laurels, regretting our past mistakes or admiring our trophies in the trophy case: "Take a lesson from the ants, you lazybones. Learn from their ways and become wise! Though they have no prince or governor or ruler to make them work, they labor hard all summer, gathering food for the winter."

John Maxwell, author and worldwide leadership trainer, used to keep a sign on his desk that read, "Yesterday Ended Last Night." It was a constant reminder to him that the successes or failures of the previous day or season would have little impact on his success going forward.

Did you have a good day yesterday? Be thankful, but keep at it. Do you have regrets from yesterday? Learn from your mistakes, but find grace. Whatever the case, remember, "Yesterday ended last night."

Take a lesson from the ants, you lazybones. Learn from their ways and become wise! Though they have no prince or governor or ruler to make them work, they labor hard all summer, gathering food for the winter.

PROVERBS 6:6-8

As for Me and My House

In February 2016, Ingrid Williams, wife of NBA assistant coach of the Oklahoma City Thunder Monty Williams, was killed in a head-on collision with a woman traveling ninety-two miles per hour in a forty-mile-per-hour zone. Because Monty Williams had been in the NBA as a player or coach since the early nineties, the league took her loss hard.

Many people watched the video where Williams eulogized his wife. By the time I watched the video, it already had 6,267,419 views. I first heard the eulogy on SB Nation Radio's *Prime Cut* drive time show with former ESPN hosts Steve Bunin and Sean Salisbury. Bunin was extremely honest when he said, "I don't know that I could be so quick to forgive," after hearing Williams publicly declare, "We hold no ill will toward the Donaldson family." I had similar thoughts to Bunin's as well.

Williams encouraged the audience to pray for the Donaldsons, because they, too, lost a loved one. He declared, "In my house we have a sign that says, 'As for me and my house, we will serve the Lord.' We cannot serve the Lord if we do not have a heart of forgiveness. That family didn't wake up wanting to hurt my wife."

Now you know why there were over 6.2 million views. This response is so counterintuitive it can come only from a heart that has been radically transformed by the gospel. Williams boldly declared, "All of this will work out . . . as hard as it is . . . it will work out. I know this because I have seen this in my life." He quoted the verse that I want to leave you with today, then encouraged those gathered for the funeral that this would work out. Romans 8:28 declares, "We know that God causes everything to work together for the good of those who love God and are called according to his purpose for them." God is good, and no matter what you are facing, he is working for your good.

We know that God causes everything to work together for the good of those who love God and are called according to his purpose for them. ROMANS 8:28

Acts of Chivalry

I love the work of the team at All Pro Dad. They help guys become the men we were created to be through articles on their website.[10] While reading one of their articles, "10 Acts a Chivalrous Husband Does for His Wife," I was reminded how important these little things can be. Here are a few:

1. When walking on the street, walk on the street side of the sidewalk.
2. When it's raining, don't hesitate to get soaked getting her an umbrella.
3. In the mornings, take delight in the chance to make your wife's coffee or tea.[11]

This third one is my favorite. It is a joy to me to start my wife's day off with the gift of a cup of coffee. She can easily make her own coffee, but if I ever have the chance, I take the opportunity to serve her.

Guys, these intentional acts of service create an atmosphere of blessing in your relationship. I call it the "principle of intentionality," which declares, "Today, I have the opportunity to serve and bless my spouse." You will be amazed at the way your wife reciprocates when you build this principle into your daily life. If you model this for your sons, they, too, will pick up on it when they begin to get involved in relationships. This will also set a great example for your daughters, so they know what qualities to look for in a future husband. Ephesians 5:25-26 states, "Husbands, this means love your wives, just as Christ loved the church. He gave up his life for her to make her holy and clean, washed by the cleansing of God's word."

What are some other ways you can be the gentleman your wife needs?

Husbands, this means love your wives, just as Christ loved the church. He gave up his life for her to make her holy and clean, washed by the cleansing of God's word.
EPHESIANS 5:25-26

---

[10] Check them out at www.AllProDad.com. You can also subscribe to their daily e-mail, which will give you practical tools and tips for being a great father.

[11] "10 Acts a Chivalrous Husband Does for His Wife," *All Pro Dad*, http://www.allprodad.com /10-acts-a-chivalrous-husband-does-for-his-wife/.

The Eyes Have It

It is pretty humbling to pay a visit to a man on his deathbed. Wayne had fought a long battle with cancer, and his time on this earth was drawing to an end. As Wayne lay in the care of hospice, Pastor Chuck and I went to convey God's love for him and open the door to any needed spiritual conversations.

As we stood over Wayne and greeted him, there was a warmth and glow in his eyes that I rarely see at that level of suffering. Wayne's mind was still sharp, and he reached out with his hands to greet us. He had struggled for quite some time to speak well, because half of his tongue was removed with the cancer. But on this day, we had no trouble understanding him.

I asked him when he accepted Christ as his Savior, and he indicated that he did it when he was a little boy. When I asked him if there was anything that he needed to talk about, he quickly and confidently said no, while shaking his head as if to say, "I am content." His favorite Scripture was the lengthy poem about time in Ecclesiastes 3. I read it, Chuck then prayed, and Wayne gave a resounding, "Amen!"

Ecclesiastes 3:1-2 says, "For everything there is a season, a time for every activity under heaven. A time to be born and a time to die." As Wayne's time to die approached, his eyes said so much that day. I'll never forget it. Wayne hardly spoke ten words, but he communicated volumes. He couldn't fool us, as a man's eyes don't lie when he is on his deathbed. Had Wayne been bitter, we would have seen it in his eyes. Had he not believed, we would have known it from his eyes. Instead his eyes conveyed that he was ready. How about you? What will your eyes convey when it is your time to die?

For everything there is a season, a time for every activity under heaven. A time to be born and a time to die. ECCLESIASTES 3:1-2

Don't Coach Mad

Rick Pitino, the head basketball coach of the Louisville Cardinals, once said, "Don't coach mad." I think we could expand this in a myriad of ways:

Don't lead mad.
Don't work mad.
Don't parent mad.
Don't play mad.
Don't be a mad spouse.

Proverbs 29:22 states, "An angry person starts fights; a hot-tempered person commits all kinds of sin." This Scripture shows us that an angry person has a wake of conflict in his life, and it counsels us to not get caught up in it. Unfortunately, there are angry people all around us, and it is hard not to be impacted by the choices that they make.

It is easy to talk about others being angry. But the more important reflection to consider is a personal one. Are you angry? Those who are angry are usually those who have been wounded. When their hurts aren't healed, those hurts will express themselves in a myriad of ways. One common way is that pain gets turned into anger, and if I have seen it once, I have seen it many times—hurt people tend to hurt other people.

If this is your story, I want to encourage you to seek counseling. Ultimately, it is going to involve forgiveness—being forgiven by Christ and allowing Christ to help you forgive those who hurt you. A certified professional Christian counselor can walk you through this process. It may get worse before it gets better, but if you see it through to the end, you will be so glad that you did.

An angry person starts fights; a hot-tempered person commits all kinds of sin.
PROVERBS 29:22

Teamwork Is a Beautiful Thing

Legendary Duke Blue Devil head basketball coach Mike Krzyzewski once said of working as a team, "To me, teamwork is the beauty of our sport, where you have five acting as one. You become selfless."

As I gathered my first- and second-grade Kangaroos together at half-time, I told the girls how proud I was of them. This was the first half of our next-to-last game of the season. It was also the first time that they had embraced passing the ball to one another. Now, I didn't break out quoting Coach K, but I did tell them that they were acting selflessly when they would pass up a shot and pass the ball off to their teammate. I contrasted that to playing selfishly, where all a player cares about is getting her own shots. For the Kangaroos that day, the results going into halftime were profound. We had scored at least eighteen points in the first half, with all the girls getting a shot at the basket.

The concept of teamwork is extremely important to the success of any team. All coaches talk about working as one unit. Teamwork and selflessness create the backbone of a great team, and without them a team cannot realistically compete. You can have a group of superstars, but if they do not work well as one unit, chances are they are not going to be as successful as you would think.

I love how Philippians 2:3-4 puts it: "Don't be selfish; don't try to impress others. Be humble, thinking of others as better than yourselves. Don't look out only for your own interests, but take an interest in others, too."

You see, humility is the key to playing as a team. We naturally look at our own interests, but elevating others is an intentional choice. Do this at home, at work, and at play, and watch the victories begin to pile up.

Don't be selfish; don't try to impress others. Be humble, thinking of others as better than yourselves. Don't look out only for your own interests, but take an interest in others, too.
PHILIPPIANS 2:3-4

MARCH

A Good, Good Father

There she was, sitting at the gate to the school yard, just a few feet away from her teacher, with tears dripping down her first-grader cheeks. Her eyes were red, and her nose had a sniffle. She was at an after-school pickup location that was different for her, because the instructions had changed. Her eyes looked through the crowd to see who would come, wondering if they would come, or if she had been forgotten. It was a tough way for this precious little girl to end her day.

Then her daddy came. As soon as he saw her, he asked the person he was talking to on his phone, "Can I call you back? My daughter is crying." He got down on his knee as she stood up, and she ran to his arms. He immediately began to comfort her, to let her know he was just a minute behind and that he would never forget her and leave her alone. The words to Chris Tomlin's song "Good Good Father" rang out in my mind when I saw this father get to his knee to comfort his little girl.

Whatever your earthly dad was like, the Bible reveals an incredible heavenly Father, who is perfect in all of his ways. Like this young daughter whose father reassured her, you are loved, not forgotten, not forsaken, and not alone.

First John 3:1 says, "See how very much our Father loves us, for he calls us his children, and that is what we are!" I just want to remind you today that our heavenly Father is a good, good Father.

See how very much our Father loves us, for he calls us his children, and that is what we are!

1 JOHN 3:1

Confusion Is the Answer

There have been two distinct times in my life when a moment of confusion directed me to the answer for a significant decision. One was when our daughter, Carson, broke her elbow launching herself off the swing set. At one of her checkups, the doctor didn't like how the X-ray looked. He thought she would need surgery to heal properly, and he wanted to send her for a CAT scan to double-check everything. When we arrived for the scan, we were told our insurance didn't cover it and we would have to pay $1,200.

After getting up from the floor, giving the attendant my credit card, and waiting quite a while, I was asked, "Has she ever had X-rays?" Impatiently I said, "Yeah, across the street thirty minutes ago." He replied, "Well, if you don't have them we will have to get some more." At that moment my phone rang, the attendant came out to get my daughter for more X-rays and the CAT scan, and I wasn't sure what to do. I felt pressure from the attendant, impatience from the lab assistant, and concern in my own heart from bearing the costs that my insurance should have carried. It was a chaotic moment for sure. Before the attendant could take my daughter in for the scan, my wife said, "Just cancel, and let's regroup." What wisdom! First Corinthians 14:33 states, "God is not a God of disorder but of peace." Although I believed that the confusion was part of the answer, the confusion of the moment was actually redirecting us to say no.

God did not confuse us at that lab, but he did use the confusion to redirect us, lead us to peace, and protect our resources. A few days later, we saw a specialist, and not only did Carson not need surgery, but her entire course of treatment was redirected. When you don't have a peace, look for the Lord to lead you to his peace another way.

God is not a God of disorder but of peace.　　　　1 CORINTHIANS 14:33

Hard Conversations

What is it like to negotiate a new contract as a professional athlete? How do you argue your value and worth, especially when you are getting older? Hard conversations are difficult for some. They come easier for others, and for even a few, they seem to just naturally fit their personality. Thank the Lord for agents!

I have progressed in my life to the point where I realize the benefit of hard conversations. They used to be difficult for me. But after a few laps around the track, I have realized that some of the most difficult conversations I have had have borne the most fruit in my life.

What is the aim of hard conversations? Is their purpose just to convey information, to get a person to submit, or is it something much greater? My purpose in having hard conversations is threefold.

Most important, I want to discover or reaffirm that the other person and I have the same heart. You see, I believe that if we have the same heart—a heart that desires the greater good and a similar outcome—we will make tremendous progress to get things cleared up. With the same heart, anything is possible.

Second, I am trying to discern what offense I may have committed. If I have offended my brother or sister, I need to humble myself and apologize for it. If I have been wrong, intentionally or unintentionally, I need to know it so that I can take responsibility and ask for forgiveness.

Third, I am trying to ascertain the path forward so I know what a win looks like. If I am to lead or follow, if I am to wait, or even if I am to just leave things at a place of peace, I need to know where the relationship is headed and what is expected.

What I know to be true is the call to unity that Scripture gives us. Psalm 133:1 says, "Behold, how good and how pleasant it is for brothers to dwell together in unity!" (NASB). May all of our conversations bring us to unity. If they have to be hard, may they bear fruit.

Behold, how good and how pleasant it is for brothers to dwell together in unity!
PSALM 133:1, NASB

From Common to Exceptional

What makes a player with common talent become exceptional? What makes an athlete who has had a mediocre few seasons turn the corner and become great? In the steroid era of baseball, a number of players went from having common talent to having exceptional talent through the use of performance-enhancing drugs. These enhancers were kept hidden, but when they came out, the impact dishonored the game that America has loved for more than a century.

Other athletes have transitioned from common to exceptional because of their discipline and work ethic. Houston Texan Whitney Mercilus finished the 2015 season having what many called a "breakout" year. He finished with twelve sacks in the regular season and three sacks in their play-off loss to the Chiefs. Mercilus took the more disciplined approach to performance enhancement by hiring a personal chef to change his eating habits, limiting red meat in his diet, and upping his workout regimen in the off-season. When I saw him before the New England Patriots game and complimented him for his season, he said, "Finally, I am healthy."

Health comes into our lives when we get rid of the common things and set ourselves apart for something exceptional. The apostle Paul challenged Timothy to this exceptional life by saying to him in 2 Timothy 2:20-21, "In a wealthy home some utensils are made of gold and silver, and some are made of wood and clay. The expensive utensils are used for special occasions, and the cheap ones are for everyday use. If you keep yourself pure, you will be a special utensil for honorable use. Your life will be clean, and you will be ready for the Master to use you for every good work."

Setting yourself apart takes discipline, but it's worth it. Set yourself apart, and enjoy the fruit that is borne through disciplined holy living.

In a wealthy home some utensils are made of gold and silver, and some are made of wood and clay. The expensive utensils are used for special occasions, and the cheap ones are for everyday use. If you keep yourself pure, you will be a special utensil for honorable use. Your life will be clean, and you will be ready for the Master to use you for every good work. 2 TIMOTHY 2:20-21

Who Is Your Source?

One of the biggest mistakes that married people make is viewing their spouse as their source for joy, peace, and hope. When this happens, there is a relational breakdown. This breakdown is inevitable because one's spouse can never fill the holes in one's soul. A lack of awareness of this fact, though, leads to many frustrating and disappointing moments as well as deep relational pain.

Did you know that God never intended for you to view your spouse as your source for joy, peace, and hope? God intended to give man to woman and woman to man to complement each other and provide community and companionship. But he didn't try to give the woman to the man or the man to the woman to make one the source of joy, peace, and hope for the other. Only God can do this, because only he is the source of these things.

My favorite verse in the New Testament is Romans 15:13: "I pray that God, the source of hope, will fill you completely with joy and peace because you trust in him. Then you will overflow with confident hope through the power of the Holy Spirit." God longs to pour into our lives the very things we need.

Ask the Lord to give you the joy and peace that you need so that you can have an overflowing hope. Then, see your spouse as God intended—as a blessing and gift from God to be a complement to you.

I pray that God, the source of hope, will fill you completely with joy and peace because you trust in him. Then you will overflow with confident hope through the power of the Holy Spirit. ROMANS 15:13

Respect through Humility

We often gain respect in our society by how well we perform. If we are straight-A students, we make the honor roll and get awards. If we surpass our quarterly sales goals, we get bonuses and pats on the back. If we see an athlete make an amazing play on the field, we honor him or her with accolades, tweets, and retweets. We naturally reward great performance with recognition that declares, "We respect that about you."

But have you ever considered how your humility can lead to more respect from those in your circle of influence? Coach Mike Krzyzewski says, "When a leader takes responsibility for his own actions and mistakes, he not only sets a good example, he shows a healthy respect for people on his team."

Pride causes us to make excuses or blame others for our mistakes. It is a peculiar thing in us that causes us to not admit when we are wrong. But making excuses or even bluffing your way through your mistakes only leads to an awareness by those on your team that you cannot be trusted. If you can't be trusted, you will be minimized, and your influence will dry up.

Proverbs 18:12 states, "Haughtiness goes before destruction; humility precedes honor." Being unwilling to own your mistakes is deadly in relationships. Gain respect by showing ownership of your mistakes. Your team will appreciate the respect you show them by doing this, and they will repay you with a mutual respect that strengthens your bond.

Haughtiness goes before destruction; humility precedes honor.   PROVERBS 18:12

A Strong Cup of Joe

Here's an honest admission: I love my morning coffee. I like it in the midmorning and even late afternoon. Periodically, I'll have decaf in the evening. I didn't start drinking coffee until I was nearly thirty years old. But now, I don't know how I could live without it. When I don't have my morning cup of joe, I get headaches, and I am sure I am not the happiest guy to be around. But when that happens, all I know to do is push through.

There is another Joe I know who has learned how to push through. He is a third-year medical student who has struggled and overcome a tremendous amount already. He overcame a serious stuttering problem, not just once, but twice. He had to change course in college a few times. He was rejected by multiple medical schools in the United States and had to leave his family and his country to study at St. George's in Grenada.

While visiting with his parents, I told them that Joe is going to go a long way in life because he has already learned how to overcome. He knows how to deal with adversity. He knows what it takes to persevere. He knows what it means to go to battle and be strengthened in it. He's going to be a "strong cup of Joe."

Hebrews 11:34 says, "Their weakness was turned to strength. They became strong in battle and put whole armies to flight." It is in the battle, during those adverse times, when our weakness gets turned into strength. As we learn the determination to fight, the willingness to stand, the grit to persevere, the Lord makes us strong.

Their weakness was turned to strength. They became strong in battle and put whole armies to flight. **HEBREWS 11:34**

Searching It Out

One of the greatest lessons I have learned is how being presented with opportunities can create growth in my life. When a door opens and an opportunity presents itself, I need to know where to set my foot. My relationship with God has grown the most through seeking his guidance about these opportunities.

Proverbs 25:2 has helped me tremendously in knowing how to navigate opportunity. The verse says, "It is God's privilege to conceal things and the king's privilege to discover them."

There is an old poker phrase that describes a player's desire not to reveal his cards. This person is described as "playing it close to the vest." Sometimes I feel that God plays it close to his vest. So often in our lives when an opportunity presents itself, we are so eager to get from point A to point B that we fail to ask God for direction and seek his will. In doing that, we miss the moments between these destinations and the opportunity to grow closer to him.

The English Standard Version translates the word *privilege* in this verse as "glory." It is the idea that it is good, glorious, and beneficial for God to conceal matters. Additionally it is good, glorious, and beneficial for kings to have to search them out. You and I are the kings of this passage. We govern the affairs of our households, and sometimes our workplaces, and it is our responsibility to search God's concealed will out.

Since this is the case, I have concluded that our Lord is just as interested in the process and the journey between these destinations as where we will end up. You see, it is the process and the journey between destinations that cultivates the growth in our lives. So God will play it close to the vest and get glory by concealing a matter, and because we have to search it out, we will benefit by having a closer relationship with him.

It is God's privilege to conceal things and the king's privilege to discover them.
PROVERBS 25:2

Calling Players Up

Good point guards, forwards, and quarterbacks know how to raise up the teammates around them. They don't hesitate to lead their teams on the court or the field. Challenging a young athlete in one of these positions to play this way can be difficult. When young, they are usually the most talented kids on the team. As a result, they have a lot of experience scoring.

As they get older, not only are these players expected to score but they are also expected to lead their teams. There is a pressure to know each individual's responsibility on every play, and to challenge their teammates to step up when the moment is upon them. Though there is pressure to perform, these players don't always recognize their added responsibilities. A good coach will call it out of them, and his or her relationship with the players will determine how well that player responds and steps into the role.

In Israel, Elisha served Elijah the prophet for many years. He was the *sharath* (pronounced *shaw-roth*), a Hebrew term that indicates that Elisha was the special assistant to a very important person. Elijah, the prophet, cultivated a strong relationship to Elisha, his young aide, and it made the young man want to step into Elijah's role when the prophet's ministry for Israel was over.

As Elijah's final moments on earth approached, he asked Elisha to stay put as he walked on. This happened three times, and all three times, here is how Elisha replied: "As the LORD lives, and as you yourself live, I will not leave you" (2 Kings 2:4, ESV).

Elisha loved Elijah. He served Elijah well, and when it was his time, he went on to have a very effective ministry because he had the influence of Elijah in his life. Remember, strong relationships yield strong impact. If you call someone up, be there to invest in them so that they see the way to go.

As the LORD lives, and as you yourself live, I will not leave you.

2 KINGS 2:4, ESV

Seeing and Knowing

Donner Atwood, a retired pastor in the Reformed Church in America, tells a story in the *Christian Globe*. Atwood helps us see the loving hand of our God over our lives. He writes,

> One night a house caught fire and a young boy was forced to flee to the roof. The father stood on the ground below with outstretched arms calling to his son, "Jump! I'll catch you." He knew the boy had to jump to save his life. All the boy could see, however, was flames, smoke, and blackness. As can be imagined, he was afraid to leave the roof. His father kept yelling, "Jump! I'll catch you." But the boy protested, "Daddy, I can't see you." The father replied, "I can see you, and that's all that matters."[12]

Isn't it comforting to know that we have a good heavenly Father who cares for us? He sees what we cannot see. Most importantly, he sees us, and he has given us the Holy Spirit, who will always be with us.

John 14:16-17 declares, "I will ask the Father, and he will give you another Advocate, who will never leave you. He is the Holy Spirit, who leads into all truth. The world cannot receive him, because it isn't looking for him and doesn't recognize him. But you know him, because he lives with you now and later will be in you."

No matter what fires you are facing today, you have an Advocate, the Holy Spirit, who is working in and through your life for good.

I will ask the Father, and he will give you another Advocate, who will never leave you. He is the Holy Spirit, who leads into all truth. The world cannot receive him, because it isn't looking for him and doesn't recognize him. But you know him, because he lives with you now and later will be in you.

JOHN 14:16-17

---

12 "Sermon Illustrations: Faith," *Christian Globe*, http://www.christianglobe.com/Illustrations /a-z/f/faith.htm.

March Madness

Yes, it's that time of year when college basketball seems to take over our lives. Intense efforts are poured into selecting the perfect bracket as we search the Internet for stats of upsets and for teams that have injuries. Top sports analysts and even the president himself make their picks. Friends gather to cheer and discuss the wins and losses that will occur in the next few weeks.

March Madness is full of enthusiasm and excitement. But this year, let me challenge you to pause and ask yourself: Do I pour the same energy into my relationship with Christ that I do when filling out my bracket?

Does this question make sense, or is it madness? If it doesn't make sense to you, let me challenge you with this Scripture: "The message of the cross is foolish to those who are headed for destruction! But we who are being saved know it is the very power of God" (1 Corinthians 1:18).

If the message of the Lord's cross doesn't fully make sense to you, then maybe you are not yet a Christian and a beneficiary of his cross. If you are a Christian but your priorities aren't what they should be, what needs to change? Consider the words of Romans 3:22-25:

> We are made right with God by placing our faith in Jesus Christ. And this is true for everyone who believes, no matter who we are. For everyone has sinned; we all fall short of God's glorious standard. Yet God, in his grace, freely makes us right in his sight. He did this through Christ Jesus when he freed us from the penalty for our sins. For God presented Jesus as the sacrifice for sin. People are made right with God when they believe that Jesus sacrificed his life, shedding his blood.

Let this year's March Madness be about more than just basketball. Let it be about life change by coming to the cross and being made right with God.

The message of the cross is foolish to those who are headed for destruction! But we who are being saved know it is the very power of God.

1 CORINTHIANS 1:18

Stick-to-itiveness

The great Tom Landry once said, "Setting a goal is not the main thing. It is deciding how you will go about achieving it and staying with that plan." One of the things that I admire the most about my wife is her ability to set a goal, make a plan, and stay on track. She is tenacious and unrelenting.

I believe God knew that I would need a mate with stick-to-itiveness because I am easily distracted, diverted, and taken off course. Her discipline far exceeds mine, and it challenges me to grow in my discipline.

The book of Proverbs is full of advice about being disciplined in every area of our lives—in friendship, in business, in marriage, and in our finances. The book opens with these words:

> These are the proverbs of Solomon, David's son, king of Israel.
> Their purpose is to teach people wisdom and discipline, to
> help them understand the insights of the wise. Their purpose is
> to teach people to live disciplined and successful lives, to help
> them do what is right, just, and fair. (Proverbs 1:1-3)

You still need discipline, whether you are like my wife or easily distracted like me. Consider turning to the pithy wisdom of Proverbs. Since college, I have been investing my time striving to read a chapter of Proverbs each and every day. Given my need for discipline, I am far from perfect on this quest. But I will testify to the fact that investing in a chapter a day has helped me tremendously to acquire a more disciplined and prudent life.

Notice also the purpose of Proverbs: "To teach people to live disciplined and successful lives." Who doesn't want a successful life? Get into Proverbs, and heed its instruction. You will be glad you did.

These are the proverbs of Solomon, David's son, king of Israel. Their purpose is to teach people wisdom and discipline, to help them understand the insights of the wise. Their purpose is to teach people to live disciplined and successful lives, to help them do what is right, just, and fair. **PROVERBS 1:1-3**

Remember the Fundamentals

Duke Blue Devils coach Mike Krzyzweski once said, "There are five fundamental qualities that make every team great: communication, trust, collective responsibility, caring, and pride. I like to think of each as a separate finger on the fist. Any one individually is important. But all of them together are unbeatable."

I love the fact that to accomplish something great, coaches know that you can't forsake the fundamentals of human relationships. Just as there are fundamentals to playing roles in life and positions on a court, there are fundamentals that lead to relational and team success.

One of the most important fundamentals we should remember is love, as defined by 1 Corinthians 13. Former head coach of the Atlanta Hawks Lenny Wilkens would say, "If you want it, you've got to give it." So let's grade ourselves when it comes to living out the fundamental of love:

Is your communication gracious and kind, or is it selfish and rude?
Are you cultivating trust by being a person of integrity?
Are you doing your part in carrying your responsibilities?
Are you caring for the mission and proud to be on the team?

What kind of grade did you get today? Remember, today is an opportunity to get better. Ask the Lord to give you the love you need to be a great teammate.

Love is patient and kind. Love is not jealous or boastful or proud or rude. It does not demand its own way. It is not irritable, and it keeps no record of being wronged. It does not rejoice about injustice but rejoices whenever the truth wins out. Love never gives up, never loses faith, is always hopeful, and endures through every circumstance. Prophecy and speaking in unknown languages and special knowledge will become useless. But love will last forever!
1 CORINTHIANS 13:4-8

Stop and Tell Lester Thanks

Every community has a Lester—that person with too much life left to live to be as encumbered as he is because of illness or an accident. I met Lester on a jog. I was halfway through my three-mile run when I finally decided today was the day that I would stop. As I approached, I took out my earbuds, lifted my sunglasses, and met this man who is out with his walker every single day.

I had wanted to stop before, but I wasn't sure what I would say. But today I took the time to thank Lester. I slowed my gait and said, "Sir, what is your name?" With a half smile on his face and a twinkle in his blue eyes, he said with slurred speech, "Lester." I then said, "Well, Lester, it is nice to meet you. I want you to know that you are an inspiration. I see you out here working to get better, and it makes *me* want to get better. Thank you." I think he was dumbfounded, but he looked me in the eye and said, "Thank you."

Proverbs 27:17 states, "As iron sharpens iron, so a friend sharpens a friend." Be thankful for those like Lester who inspire you to continue on no matter the challenge before you. Also, know that you don't have to be disabled like Lester to inspire others and sharpen them with your life.

As iron sharpens iron, so a friend sharpens a friend.　　　　PROVERBS 27:17

The Power of a Note

In the age of 140 characters, Facebook shout-outs, and e-mail communication, the handwritten note seems to be a thing of the past. Yet studies show that many young people are longing for a handwritten note because it would mean someone had taken the time to actually write his or her thoughts out and put them on paper.

As I write this, I look to the right and left of my computer station and see handwritten notes and cards that people graciously penned and sent to me. Some of the handwriting is from my little girl, Carson, whom I know won't be little for long. Her handwriting is in crayon, along with cute pictures and the words, "I love you, Daddy."

Then there is the card from a congregant who thanked me for the Easter message. To the right of that is a thank-you note from a father who had lost his twenty-year-old son. That card reminds me how fragile life is and how important pastoral ministry really is in people's lives. Another note is from an elderly lady in our congregation, Marilyn. Marilyn has been struggling with her health, so receiving a note of encouragement from her when she was the one who needed encouraging has really meant a lot to me.

Taking the time to handwrite a note gives weight to the message you want to convey. Proverbs 16:24 says, "Kind words are like honey—sweet to the soul and healthy for the body." Go ahead and post, tweet, and hit send, but for those special things, consider taking a few extra minutes to put it in writing.

Kind words are like honey—sweet to the soul and healthy for the body.
PROVERBS 16:24

Who's He?

Houston Rockets guard Jason Terry caught the eye of media members and a national television audience when the Rockets played the Cleveland Cavaliers in January 2016. The Rockets lost that game to the Cavs, with a final score of 91–77. A humorous moment happened when the deep bench of Cleveland checked in for garbage time. With 2:09 left to play, Jason Terry and Sasha Kaun were matched up for the inbound pass.

Terry, unconcerned with what would happen to the ball, just couldn't figure out who he was guarding. Instead of trying to defend the inbound pass, Terry kept trying to get a look at the name on the back of that big Cavalier's jersey. On ESPN's *His & Hers*, hosts Michael Smith and Jemele Hill played the clip multiple times to note just how funny it was that Terry didn't know Kaun's name.

Aren't you glad that isn't the case with our heavenly Father? The agnostic believes that if there is a god, he is not interested in the lives of humanity. The deist says that God created the world, then stepped back and just let things take their natural course. But our heavenly Father, revealed through the Holy Bible, knows us intimately.

Psalm 139:13-14 says, "You made all the delicate, inner parts of my body and knit me together in my mother's womb. Thank you for making me so wonderfully complex! Your workmanship is marvelous—how well I know it." No matter what you may be facing today, God knows exactly who you are, where you are, and what you are going through. He loves you and longs for you to know his love.

You made all the delicate, inner parts of my body and knit me together in my mother's womb. Thank you for making me so wonderfully complex! Your workmanship is marvelous—how well I know it. **PSALM 139:13-14**

Dirty Delly

In January 2016, Matthew Dellavedova, the Australian-born Cleveland Cavalier, was voted by twenty-four of his peers as the dirtiest player in the NBA. Some of this reputation came from the way his style of play was perceived in the 2015 NBA finals. Delly, as many in the league call him, plays a hard-laced, scrappy brand of basketball. He is a far cry from the likes of Rodman and Laimbeer and the bad boys in Detroit. Dellavedova received nearly two times the votes as the next player. The survey, conducted by *Los Angeles Times* writer Broderick Turner, allowed players to remain anonymous when they submitted their list of dirtiest players.

Have you ever received harsh words about your work from an anonymous source? They are hard to hear, because you have no ability to defend yourself. When it has happened to me, it has caused a bevy of emotions, including sadness, anger, and frustration. After the initial shock, I have tried to step back and see if what was being said had any truth to it. Here are a few Scriptures that can assist you if you find yourself in this place.

The first is Proverbs 26:2, which states, "Like a fluttering sparrow or a darting swallow, an undeserved curse will not land on its intended victim." Take courage in this message, and let the words of the anonymous coward fall from your ears.

The second Scripture is Proverbs 12:1, which says, "To learn, you must love discipline; it is stupid to hate correction." If there is something to be learned, then step back and look for it, regardless of how the message came to you. If you position yourself to be a lifelong learner, then there is something to be gained by this that will be to your benefit.

Like a fluttering sparrow or a darting swallow, an undeserved curse will not land on its intended victim.
PROVERBS 26:2

The Same Amount of Time

Basketball legend Jim Valvano learned something very valuable that we need to learn as well. He once said, "There are 86,400 seconds in a day. It's up to you to decide what to do with them."

We are probably aware of the number of hours in a day, but we need to remember that we truly do get to decide how to use that time. So how are you spending your 86,400 seconds each day? If you are anything like me, you find yourself working on your computer or your tablet while spending time with your kids. It's easy to take the time we've been given for granted, so we trade time *with* our kids for time *near* our kids. The older my children get, though, the more I understand how precious time really is.

When this book is released, I will have a little over two and a half years left with my oldest at home. He will be off to college before I know it, and between now and then, he is going to be stretching his wings to fly a bit.

Dr. David Klingler, former Heisman Trophy candidate, NFL quarterback, and now professor at Dallas Theological Seminary, has a clear sense of his time. I invited him to take a spring break trip with me to Cuba to lecture in the seminary there. He declined, saying, "Roger, I only have two more spring breaks with my oldest at home. I am on the clock, and I am going to make the most of it." I'll never forget the time awareness he had, and I admire him for it.

Ephesians 5:15-17 states, "Look carefully then how you walk, not as unwise but as wise, making the best use of the time, because the days are evil. Therefore do not be foolish, but understand what the will of the Lord is" (ESV). The Bible declares time to be precious. What are you doing with your time today?

Look carefully then how you walk, not as unwise but as wise, making the best use of the time, because the days are evil. Therefore do not be foolish, but understand what the will of the Lord is. **EPHESIANS 5:15-17, ESV**

Daddy, What's Infinity?

Carson, my first-grade daughter, has been asking me about the number infinity lately. Her class has been studying numbers, and somewhere along the way, the concept of infinity came up. It is hard for me in my midforties to get my mind around, much less a six year old.

On January 24, 2016, *Capital OTC* reported that the world's largest prime number had been discovered by mathematician Curtis Cooper and his fellow researchers while they worked on the GIMPS project (Great Internet Mersenne Prime Search). These researchers use supercomputers to generate new prime numbers, and Cooper's team generated one with 22,338,618 digits.[13]

I guess I will have to share all this with Carson the next time she asks me about infinity.

Unless you are a researcher in the sciences, you probably don't live your life dealing with the infinitude of prime numbers. You are more concerned about day-to-day living. Well, what I love about the book of Proverbs is that it gives such practical instruction for our everyday lives. But even in this practical book of wisdom that informs my daily life, I also see eternity. Take a look at Proverbs 12:28 (NIV): "In the way of righteousness there is life; along that path is immortality." Getting on his path by trusting in Jesus' sacrifice on the cross for your righteousness will yield everlasting life.

It is hard to live in our day to day well if we haven't handled what we know and believe about eternity. Do you have this everlasting life?

In the way of righteousness there is life; along that path is immortality.

PROVERBS 12:28, NIV

---

[13] Justin Chase, "Scientists Discovered the Largest Prime Number," *Capital OTC*, January 24, 2016, http://www.capitalotc.com/scientists-discovered-the-largest-prime-number/214356/.

Hurt People Hurt People

The words of hurt people often hurt others. I want to encourage you to be ever mindful that your mouth is a loaded weapon. Use caution when you speak.

In my son Cooper's last season of machine-pitch baseball, I knew immediately that I had my hands full with one of the other coaches. We were in the draft room, and I was trying to help him out in a situation. Out of nowhere, he told me to mind my own business and that he would get it taken care of.

Throughout the season, that coach caused many problems for many people. He got into it with one of my buddies, who was coaching another team in the league. He even shot the bird at me and another coach and then lied and said he didn't do it. Why did this man act the way he did? Somewhere along the way, he had learned that to get his way, he had to hurt others—this is what bullies do. Perhaps he had been bullied in the past. Often mean people will bully others because they were bullied. They hurt others because they were hurt. Remember, hurt people hurt other people.

When my buddy had been mistreated, he called me and asked what he should do. He was hot about the way this man had treated him. I told him, "Coach, don't rebuke a fool, or you will be just like him." Challenging this man proved to be a fruitless endeavor. Instead, forgiveness was the way to go.

Colossians 3:13 states, "Bear with each other and forgive one another if any of you has a grievance against someone. Forgive as the Lord forgave you" (NIV). What do you do when someone hurts you? If you become angry and bitter, you will have a tendency to become just like him or her. That is why going to the Lord to help you forgive others is so important. If you aren't careful, you will become the person you despise.

Bear with each other and forgive one another if any of you has a grievance against someone. Forgive as the Lord forgave you.   COLOSSIANS 3:13, NIV

Mutual Commitment

Duke basketball coach Mike Krzyzewski once said, "Mutual commitment helps overcome the fear of failure—especially when people are part of a team sharing and achieving goals. It also sets the stage for open dialogue and honest conversation."

Marriage takes a mutual commitment. In his book *Love and Respect*, Dr. Emerson Eggerichs unpacks the simple yet profound truth that God created men to be respected and women to be loved.

Mutual commitment requires that both parties in a relationship go all in to provide what the other person needs so that the relationship can thrive. When you honor your wife with an unconditional love, you make her feel secure and established. When your wife returns your love with respect, your resolve to love her more and more will only compound.

But who goes first? A lot of times each person in the relationship is waiting for the other to go first. Pride gets in the way and says, "I'm not going to show her unconditional love until she shows me unconditional respect." If I have seen it once, I have seen it a hundred times!

But you are the spiritual leader of your home. That means you get to go first. You see, talking about being the spiritual leader is fun until you have to lead. But let me tell you, today is an opportunity to establish your wife and make her secure through unconditional love. When we create this type of climate, as Coach K advises, it will open up dialogue and honest conversation.

Ephesians 5:33 states, "Again I say, each man must love his wife as he loves himself, and the wife must respect her husband." Do it over and over, because this is what you have been called to do. Your wife will catch on, and you will enjoy the wins that come with your mutual commitment.

Again I say, each man must love his wife as he loves himself, and the wife must respect her husband.
EPHESIANS 5:33

The Power of the Gospel

All children need a father to coach them in life. Dads instill wisdom, discipline, accountability, and unconditional love in their children. This is the fundamental job of a father. At least it should be. But there has been a shift taking place in the American family since the emergence of "no-fault divorce." The great ideal that the family unit is the bedrock of the nation seems to have gone the way of wired telephones. As our culture evolves, we have fewer children than ever going to bed under the roof of two parents, and fewer dads who are intentionally coaching their children well.

In some pockets of our nation, we now have an entire generation of young men growing up without a father. The problem is that many of these young men end up in gangs because that is where they find the community, acceptance, and leadership they long for.

This is the story of Rick Vasquez, who serves on my church staff. Rick's father wasn't around much as he was growing up, so Rick didn't really know how to be a man. He entered a life of crime and was eventually sentenced to prison. Rick has great leadership gifts, and the gang leaders in prison recognized that. So they brought him in as a gang leader.

It wasn't until Rick was in solitary confinement that he came to know Jesus Christ.[14] Today he is sharing the gospel with whomever will listen to him. Rick now returns to the prisons to share his story with men who are incarcerated. He lives out Romans 1:16: "I am not ashamed of this Good News about Christ. It is the power of God at work, saving everyone who believes—the Jew first and also the Gentile." You see, the gospel does what dads can't. Let's get the gospel to this fatherless generation!

I am not ashamed of this Good News about Christ. It is the power of God at work, saving everyone who believes—the Jew first and also the Gentile.

ROMANS 1:16

---

[14] To hear a firsthand account of Rick's story, go to https://www.youtube.com/watch?v=V1yjsulxdKc.

The Way to Life

On the *Ellen DeGeneres Show*, Ronda Rousey, the famous women's MMA fighter and champion, admitted to Ellen that after her loss to Holly Holm in November 2015, she had considered taking her life. When I heard the interview, I wondered how she could have gotten to that place. Then Rousey spoke of how she had questioned herself, asking, "Who am I if I am not that anymore?" Fortunately, she was able to come out of that dark place and to be honest and vulnerable about her struggle.

I wonder if somehow Ronda Rousey believed a lie that would lead her to the conclusion that she was nothing without success. Maybe we all believe the lie that to never be beaten, to always win, is the way to the life we have always wanted.

Many of us are tempted to believe that climbing the ladder of success so that we can have a fortune and be recognized by our peers is the quest every man should take, because in that destination there is life. If something challenges that success, our foundation erodes.

Scripture tells us a few things to keep in mind as we walk life's road. First, Proverbs 29:25 says, "Fearing people is a dangerous trap." In other words, living for the approval of others is a most certain way to become captured by lies.

Second, whatever we do, we are to do it for the Lord. As you seek to excel, do it as unto the Lord. First Corinthians 10:31 states, "Whether you eat or drink, or whatever you do, do it all for the glory of God."

Third, the real way to life is found by being willing to receive correction when we are wrong, because it will set us on the right path, if we will listen. Proverbs 6:23 says, "Their command is a lamp and their instruction a light; their corrective discipline is the way to life."

Fear God, live for him, and listen for his leading. Let this be your foundation so you can keep fighting.

Their command is a lamp and their instruction a light; their corrective discipline is the way to life.
                                                          PROVERBS 6:23

Intentional Expectations

A dad's impact is profound and truly hard to measure. Coach John Wooden, in his book *Wooden*, states, "Being a role model is the most powerful form of educating. . . . Too often fathers neglect it because they get so caught up in making a living they forget to make a life."[15] I hope this can't be said of me or of you.

Steve Young's dad understood the importance of being a good role model. The Hall of Fame quarterback says of his father, "My dad, like any coach, has always stressed the fundamentals. He taught me responsibility, accountability, and the importance of hard work. As a teenager, when I wanted to start borrowing the car, my dad agreed under the condition I get a job so I could afford to put gas in it. It is lessons like these that have stuck with me over time."[16]

Proverbs 3:1-2 states, "My child, never forget the things I have taught you. Store my commands in your heart. If you do this, you will live many years, and your life will be satisfying." Mentoring, modeling, and intentional training are the responsibilities of a father. To do them, we must be present in our children's lives.

What are you intentionally pouring into your children? What principles, values, and words do you come back to that make it clear what high expectations you have? Young continues, "Though my father was tough, he was always in my corner, teaching me the value of hard work."[17]

Remember, what we emphasize gets realized. Be intentional about the time you spend with your children, and encourage them to rise to their potential.

My child, never forget the things I have taught you. Store my commands in your heart. If you do this, you will live many years, and your life will be satisfying.   PROVERBS 3:1-2

---

15 John Wooden and Steve Jamison, *Wooden* (New York: McGraw-Hill, 1997), 5.
16 Tom Limbert, *Dad's Playbook: Wisdom for Fathers from the Greatest Coaches of All Time* (San Francisco: Chronicle Books, 2012), 6.
17 Ibid.

Footprints

One of the most memorable African American quarterbacks of the 1990s was Randall Cunningham. Cunningham was an amazing athlete. After retiring in 1995, he came out of retirement to lead the Minnesota Vikings from 1997 to 1999. The 1998 season was his finest, as he led the Vikings to a 15–1 record, losing to the Falcons in the NFC Championship game.

I had the privilege of interviewing Cunningham for my radio show. His book *Lay It Down: How Letting Go Brings Out Your Best* was a large part of our conversation. This book details the process of moving forward after the Cunningham family lost their little boy Christian when he drowned in 2010.

In my interview with Cunningham, I asked him this question: "Your book is a very intimate view into the most horrific day of your life and that of your family, when your son Christian drowned. Tell us, if you would, how your faith enabled you to stand up in the midst of that pain."

This is what he had to say: "There are a lot of people that know the poem about footprints. Everything was going good and then [God] abandoned me at the difficult point of my life and they're basically saying I only saw my two footprints walking. And the poem goes on to say, 'No, that was me carrying you.' I experienced that."

Are you grieving? I want to remind you of Jesus' words. Matthew 5:4 states, "God blesses those who mourn, for they will be comforted." This was Cunningham's testimony, and it was one of the most profound conversations of my life. Are you stuck in your pain? Pick up Randall Cunningham's book, and allow the Lord to lead you through it. May you be comforted!

God blesses those who mourn, for they will be comforted.　　MATTHEW 5:4

Water Break

My wife has gotten me into the Insanity Max:30 workout routine, and I can testify that, as its name declares, it is insane. There are certain moves I can do that I don't mind at all. There are others that I can't even do yet, but maybe someday. Then there are those I would love to avoid because they are hard and they hurt, but I know that if I keep showing up, the benefit will be worth the price I pay.

Then there is my favorite part of the workout: the thirty-seconds of "Water Break." I love that part! For those precious seconds, I can stop, get a swig of water, and kind of catch my breath. In that moment, I am in my own semiretreat from the demands of the insane workout.

Jesus would often take a "water break" to leave the demands of the moment and get away to pray. Often, he would send his disciples to the other side of the lake so he could be alone with his heavenly Father. At other times, he would get up early in the morning, before the sun had come up, to spend time with his Father and pray.

How often do you take a break in your day to pray? In the heat of the battle, in the throes of your day, you don't have to go until you max out. No, you can stop and ask for wisdom, give thanks, or cast your anxiety on the Lord. Remember the words of the apostle Peter, who said in 1 Peter 5:6-7, "Humble yourselves under the mighty power of God, and at the right time he will lift you up in honor. Give all your worries and cares to God, for he cares about you."

Humble yourselves under the mighty power of God, and at the right time he will lift you up in honor. Give all your worries and cares to God, for he cares about you.   1 PETER 5:6-7

It Should Hurt

When Peyton Manning was released by the Indianapolis Colts in 2012 after he had sat out all season because of a neck injury, Colts owner Jim Irsay announced that the team would move in another direction instead of paying Manning the $28 million bonus that he was due. Manning's return to playing football was suspect, and Irsay did what he thought was best for his franchise.

Manning was clearly shaken up when the moment to say good-bye arrived. While fighting back tears, Manning said, "Nobody loves their job more than I do. Nobody loves playing quarterback more than I do. I still want to play. But there is no other team I wanted to play for. . . . We all know that nothing lasts forever. Times change, circumstances change, and that's the reality of playing in the NFL."

One of the things that we should keep in mind is that saying good-bye should hurt if we have lived our lives well. If we have given our all to our family, to our work, to our church community, good-byes should be painful.

When David and Jonathan parted ways, it was a painful good-bye for these best friends. First Samuel 20:41 states, "As soon as the boy was gone, David came out from where he had been hiding near the stone pile. Then David bowed three times to Jonathan with his face to the ground. Both of them were in tears as they embraced each other and said good-bye, especially David."

Until it is time to go to that next place, live every day where you are as though it will be the hardest thing for you to leave. If it hurts a lot when you leave, you have lived in that place and that season well.

As soon as the boy was gone, David came out from where he had been hiding near the stone pile. Then David bowed three times to Jonathan with his face to the ground. Both of them were in tears as they embraced each other and said good-bye, especially David.   1 SAMUEL 20:41

They Call Him Eeyore

In the Winnie-the-Pooh series, one character is known for his complaining. Eeyore the donkey is always blue. Do you know someone like this? No matter what encouragement you give the person, he or she will always find something to complain about and a reason to get sour. Maybe you frequently have your own Eeyore moments.

What causes this? Dr. Kevin Elko states, "Two culprits in our personality cause complaining: comparison and judgment."

Comparison creates discontentment because you want what someone else possesses. You believe that you are entitled to something more, so when you see someone with more, it makes you jealous. Judging others is the other form of complaining. People who judge others walk in an "I'm better than you" attitude. So even when they are not asked, they insert themselves into the situation to offer you advice, stir things up, and create problems. These people are complainers not from what they lack but from the status they believe they have achieved by comparing themselves to others.

First Timothy 6:5-8 warns of those with such attitudes:

These people always cause trouble. Their minds are corrupt, and they have turned their backs on the truth. To them, a show of godliness is just a way to become wealthy.

Yet true godliness with contentment is itself great wealth. After all, we brought nothing with us when we came into the world, and we can't take anything with us when we leave it. So if we have enough food and clothing, let us be content.

Be careful of the complainers in your midst. Choose contentment, and steer clear of those who stir up trouble.

True godliness with contentment is itself great wealth. After all, we brought nothing with us when we came into the world, and we can't take anything with us when we leave it. So if we have enough food and clothing, let us be content.

1 TIMOTHY 6:6-8

Two Feet Down

I have always wondered how hard it is for receivers to get their second foot down before going out of bounds. When they transition from the college to the pro game, I am assuming that they spend a significant amount of time mastering this. It is a shame when a wideout makes a spectacular downfield catch over his shoulder and barely misses. Sometimes the ball is thrown in a way that leads him just a bit too far outside, and he is unable to secure it while staying in bounds.

Tending to our souls also takes work. As a wideout is disciplined in his route running and as he practices the repetitions of getting two feet in bounds, we, too, need to be disciplined not to be led out of bounds by others. I look back over my time as a young man and wonder how much God may have spared me from in spite of some of my foolish relationships and actions.

One of the keys to tending our souls is to take inventory of the people that we spend time with. Proverbs 1:10 provides us a stern warning, from a father to his son: "My child, if sinners entice you, turn your back on them!" Scripture also declares in 1 Corinthians 15:33, "Don't be fooled by those who say such things, for 'bad company corrupts good character.'" If we aren't being disciplined in the relationships we choose, those we run with may just lead us out of bounds.

Don't be fooled by those who say such things, "for bad company corrupts good character."
                                                                    1 CORINTHIANS 15:33

Winning Ranked Forty-Eighth

After our first game in my daughter's coach-pitch softball league, I asked our league director if it was right for the coaches of the other team to have their girls round the bag at first base on their way to second when the ball is hit in the infield with a throw coming to first.

Initially, she said it was fine, as this was a strategy for tournament play. Feeling that it was both tacky and unsafe, I argued that the most important thing at this point in the season was teaching the proper fundamentals, and running through the bag was the proper play. After a few more e-mails and a phone call, she finally concurred. It took me reminding her that there is an orange safety bag at first base for a reason for her to see that this had to be addressed. But she said, "I will address it as a safety issue only."

Author Mark Hyman, professor of sports management at George Washington University, said, "We no longer value participation. We value excellence." This is another way of saying, "We value winning."[18] Don't get me wrong, winning and being excellent are good, and there is a time and place and age for it. But many push their teams at the young ages to win at all costs. They cut corners, or round the bag, in a way that dishonors the game, teaching their children that this is the way to compete. The Bible tells us what God thinks of this dishonesty. Proverbs 11:1 states, "The LORD detests the use of dishonest scales, but he delights in accurate weights."

Let's keep this in mind as we pursue the next championship trophy. Amanda Visek, also a professor at George Washington University, surveyed 150 children about what makes sports fun for them. The kids listed eighty-one different factors that made them happy playing sports. Winning ranked forty-eighth.

The LORD detests the use of dishonest scales, but he delights in accurate weights.

PROVERBS 11:1

---

[18] Michael S. Rosenwald, "Are Parents Ruining Youth Sports? Fewer Kids Play Amid Pressure," *Washington Post*, October 4, 2015, https://www.washingtonpost.com/local/are-parents-ruining-youth-sports-fewer-kids-play-amid-pressure/2015/10/04/eb1460dc-686e-11e5-9ef3-fde182507eac_story.html.

You Need to Floss Every Day

Going to the dentist is not one of my favorite things to do. As a matter of fact, I am writing this devotional from the dentist's reception area. After having fractured my teeth while playing a pickup game of basketball in high school, I have tried to stay out of the dentist's office as much as I can. Steel instruments scraping my teeth while I smell latex gloves just isn't something I enjoy.

But visiting the dentist's office a couple of times a year is mission critical for my overall health and well-being. The checkup reinforces what I am doing well, and the lecture from the hygienist motivates me to floss more.

The discipline of flossing removes the particles that can get in all the wrong places and cause decay. Like flossing, the spiritual discipline of confession removes the remnants of our mistakes because we take our sins to the Lord and ask him to cleanse us. I am afraid that, like flossing, we don't practice confession enough, because we don't take inventory of our ways enough. But a healthy heart and soul are worth the daily discipline of searching out our ways.

Psalm 139:23-24 states, "Search me, O God, and know my heart; test me and know my anxious thoughts. Point out anything in me that offends you, and lead me along the path of everlasting life." After the Lord points out your offensive ways, confess to him, acknowledging your errors. First John 1:9 declares this good news to us: "If we confess our sins to him, he is faithful and just to forgive us our sins and to cleanse us from all wickedness." Be cleansed of your ways that offend the Lord. Remember, just as flossing is good for the gums, confession is good for the soul.

Search me, O God, and know my heart; test me and know my anxious thoughts. Point out anything in me that offends you, and lead me along the path of everlasting life. **PSALM 139:23-24**

APRIL

Accomplishing the Unthinkable

Have you ever heard the expression "Who would've thought?" It is the question asked when the unthinkable or extremely improbable happens. I am sure this was the expression uttered over and over again by the opponents of the Sewanee University football team from 1899.

This team went 12–0 and outscored their opponents 322 to 10. The only team that scored on them was Auburn, coached by John Heisman himself. The Sewanee football players were called the "Iron Men," not just for their football abilities, but because they won five games in a six-day schedule that had them traveling 2,500 miles. Who would've thought?

Orin Lewis, one of the deacons in my church and the president of our not-for-profit clinic, experienced his own iron man moment when he was suddenly admitted to the hospital. Having run the Chevron Houston Marathon a few weeks prior, Orin knew that there was something wrong. When he got to the hospital, he could barely breathe, and he began to throw up blood. The doctors diagnosed Orin with a massive pulmonary embolism that was putting pressure on his heart, causing part of it to shut down. Orin was only hours away from death.

Orin's wife told me that he would be in the ICU for up to two weeks, if he survived. We prayed at church that day. We prayed as a staff. We prayed on Wednesday night at our healing service. We prayed and prayed and prayed. On Thursday, Orin went home, walked himself up the stairs, and even took his dogs out for a walk. It was miraculous.

I don't know if you ever feel like you are on a 2,500-mile road trip facing battle after battle. But I want you to know that there are challenges and improbabilities in your life that are easily handled by God. Remember Jesus' words of Matthew 19:26: "Humanly speaking, it is impossible. But with God everything is possible." Turn over your impossibilities to the Lord, because nothing is impossible with God.

Humanly speaking, it is impossible. But with God everything is possible.
MATTHEW 19:26

Bearing Fruit

One of the things I love most about the NFL draft is the moment when a team decides to move up the draft board to take a risk on a player. A team negotiates with another team to swap places, hoping that the player they really want will be available when they choose in their new draft position. The Minnesota Vikings did this in the 2014 draft. They traded two of their later-round draft picks to the Seattle Seahawks in order to secure the chance to pick Louisville Cardinals quarterback Teddy Bridgewater as the last pick of the first round. Many in Houston, where I live, thought Bridgewater would go to the Texans, who had the first pick of the second round. If so, it seems the Texans were willing to wait their turn for Bridgewater, whereas the Vikings were willing to pay a price and risk losing two other players to get their franchise quarterback.

You know, there is a fundamental principle in God's law that declares, "You reap what you sow." The risks you take and the decisions you make lead to a harvest of some sort. There is fruit, or lack thereof, from the decisions you make. So let me ask you, what does your harvest look like? What are you reaping at work, at home, and with your friendships? Are you increasingly becoming isolated and lonely? Are you doing things today that a year ago you would never have done?

Proverbs 14:14 states, "Backsliders get what they deserve; good people receive their reward." This Scripture is a simple reminder that when we sow good, we will be rewarded, and when we go astray, there will be consequences.

Remember, our lives, like a crop, bear fruit. The fruit is what is seen. But what determines the harvest is what is sown from one's heart.

Backsliders get what they deserve; good people receive their reward.
PROVERBS 14:14

Calling Balls and Strikes

Rogers Hornsby, who averaged hitting .400 over five years, was facing a rookie pitcher who threw three pitches that the umpire called balls, although the pitcher was sure they were strikes. When the rookie shouted a complaint, the umpire replied, "Young man, when you throw a strike, Mr. Hornsby will let you know."[19]

Some of the best umpires have unique and creative ways to call balls and strikes. What about you? As a parent, it is important that you let the rookies in your home know when they have thrown a strike or a ball.

When your kids do something special or accomplish a task that has previously been hard for them to do, let them know that they just threw a strike and cheer them on. When they misstep and don't do the basics, or fail to live up to the standard established, graciously correct them and let them know that they aren't living up to their potential. In essence, call a ball!

As you rear your children, create a way to communicate with them so that they will receive your instruction and take it to heart. Remember, you are correcting them because you love them. Here is a word to encourage your efforts, from Solomon, the wise king of Israel: "Direct your children onto the right path, and when they are older, they will not leave it" (Proverbs 22:6).

Direct your children onto the right path, and when they are older, they will not leave it.

PROVERBS 22:6

---

[19] "10 Ways to Get Your Wife to Respect Your Judgment," *All Pro Dad*, http://www.allprodad.com/10-ways-to-get-your-wife-to-respect-your-judgment/.

From Cloudiness to Clarity

One of the biggest challenges a man faces is knowing whether to stay or to go—to launch out on his own or to stay with the corporate gig. In those still, quiet moments, many a man wonders, *What if . . . ?* How do you know when it is time to stay or time to go? Scripture gives us many principles for movement.

Proverbs 14:8 says, "The prudent understand where they are going, but fools deceive themselves." You may be in the midst of cloudiness regarding your decision. I describe cloudiness as knowing that you need to go but not yet knowing where. If this is where you are, don't launch out yet, but begin to seek clarity. Clarity is understanding clearly and then launching out from there with a good plan.

Proverbs 19:2 tells us, "Enthusiasm without knowledge is no good; haste makes mistakes." Patiently journeying with God while seeking his leadership will direct you to a clear path—not only for your job but for your marriage, your money, your parenting, and your mission.

Your journey with God will produce wisdom for making decisions as you walk with him day by day. Bible teacher Beth Moore said, "Wisdom is knowledge applied. Head knowledge is useless on the battlefield. Knowledge stamped on the heart makes one wise." Wisdom calls for a diligent pursuit of carefully assessing where you have been, where you are, and where you are going. As you seek God's wisdom for your life, take your time, and journey from cloudiness to clarity.

Enthusiasm without knowledge is no good; haste makes mistakes.
PROVERBS 19:2

Hey, Look at Me

In the age of the selfie, we live in a world that says, "Hey, look at me!" Marketers are so savvy that they have developed the "selfie stick" in order for selfie picture takers to get an even better angle of themselves. I am afraid that if I used a selfie stick, all you would see is my increasingly balding head.

What we lack, though, in our culture are men and women who will say to their sons and daughters, their neighbors' children, the kids on the team that they coach, "Hey, look at me!" when it comes to being a good example. Proverbs 23:26 states, "O my son, give me your heart. May your eyes take delight in following my ways."

Solomon told his son to look at him, to follow after him, to go where he went and do what he did. Nearly half of the children being raised in this generation in the United States have no father in the home. As a result, the daily example that they are called to look toward isn't there. Might you be a surrogate father for a child on your street? Might you help fill the increasing gap in our homes so that this coming generation might know which way to go?

Rise up and live in such a way that you have no problem telling your sons, daughters, and other youth in your community to follow after you, because whether you realize it or not, they are already looking at you, wondering if you are one they can follow.

O my son, give me your heart. May your eyes take delight in following my ways.
PROVERBS 23:26

Managing like Tommy

The great Tommy Lasorda once said, "Managing is like holding a dove in your hand. Squeeze too hard and you kill it, not hard enough and it flies away." When coaches have retired and then come out of retirement to coach the game that they love, they often sense that things have changed. Their "old-school" tactics aren't having the results that they once did. When they realize that they are now in a different environment, they often question their ability to effectively lead when players don't respond to their natural leadership instincts. If they squeeze too hard, they might just bind up the team with fear. If they don't instill enough discipline, the team begins to break down from a lack of boundaries.

Parenting is a lot like that too, isn't it? If parents are too strict, it squashes the spirit of a child. If parents aren't willing to discipline, the child has no sense of boundaries and, like the dove, might fly away. This begs the question, How do you manage your kids like Lasorda managed his Dodgers?

The answer is to speak the truth in love. If all we do is speak truth, then we risk being legalistic, unmerciful, and abusive. If all we do is love, and never confront with truth, then anything goes. Ephesians 6:4 states, "Fathers, do not provoke your children to anger by the way you treat them. Rather, bring them up with the discipline and instruction that comes from the Lord."

In parenting, one of the most delicate skills is finding the right way to speak the truth in love. And trust me, as the father of two boys and a girl, I know you can't use the same approach with girls as you do with boys.

Fathers, do not provoke your children to anger by the way you treat them. Rather, bring them up with the discipline and instruction that comes from the Lord.
EPHESIANS 6:4

Send an E-mail to Yourself

For two weeks in a row, I wrote out e-mails that I wanted to send but knew I shouldn't. They were defensive, came from frustration, and would have led to greater friction had I sent them to their intended recipients. So, do you know what I did with them? I sent them to myself.

This proved to be fruitful because, when we did discuss the matters at hand, I had framed up some key talking points. Additionally, not sending them to anyone but myself allowed me to rest, reflect, and put some space between the emotions I was feeling and what was really necessary to move the ball down the field.

One of the worst ways to handle conflict is by sending an e-mail. Written communication doesn't allow for the recipient to see the nonverbal communication that may soften the message. The recipient may hear emotion that you did not intend, and the offense can grow deeper and wider because of this poor approach to communication.

Don't be hasty. If you find therapy in hitting Send, write an e-mail to yourself. This will help eliminate strife and pride. Take some time to process the situation and discern what really needs to be said, but do it with a level head. I promise you that you will be glad you took this approach. Proverbs 13:10 states, "Pride leads to conflict; those who take advice are wise." Take out the pride and see peace come.

Pride leads to conflict; those who take advice are wise.　　　PROVERBS 13:10

Putting on That Green Jacket

The green jacket is the coveted prize of the Masters Golf Tournament, one of golf's four major tournaments. It is held in Augusta, Georgia, each spring. The one who masters "Amen Corner" and bests the rest of the field after four days of competition is the one who has the privilege of being adorned with the green jacket that declares him to be the Masters champion.

The green jacket is given only to those who have mastered both the game of golf and themselves. They have not only perfected their swing, but they have kept their mind and emotions intact in the midst of vast pressure. You see, it is a matter of both swing control and self-control.

Proverbs 25:28 states, "A man without self-control is like a city broken into and left without walls" (ESV). I think this applies to us in many ways—financially, physically, morally, and emotionally. Where do you lack self-control? Is it in your diet? Ask the Lord for strength, and commit to it. Is it in your finances? Seek help, get on a plan, and stick to your budget. Is it a moral issue? Confess your sin to the Lord and to a brother so that you can be restored and set free.

I want to challenge you to realize the necessity of self-control and to ask the Lord to show you where you need to master your mind and emotions. It may be painful at first, but if you stay at it, you will be amazed at the change that is born in your life.

A man without self-control is like a city broken into and left without walls.
PROVERBS 25:28, ESV

The Weight of Anxiety

Professional sports is a huge global industry. Soccer is growing rapidly, and my children know the names of athletes on other continents because of the video games that they play and the Internet.

I have known many a professional athlete and pastored a few of them as well. What the public doesn't see is the weight of their performance and the uncertainty of where they will live and play in the coming season. The public doesn't see the truth that owners and management of these teams view these men and women as liabilities and assets in their business models. This can create anxiety and strain on their marriages, uncertainty for their children, and a weight in their hearts that people don't understand.

I am sure that there are things about what you do and pressures that you face that other people don't really understand until they walk in your shoes.

Listen to Proverbs 12:25. It states, "Worry weighs a person down; an encouraging word cheers a person up." If you live long enough, you are going to get weighed down with worry. How wonderful it is when someone gives you an encouraging word. Who in your life today needs that encouraging word from you? It only takes a second to send someone a text or an e-mail saying, "I prayed for you today. God is with you!" So when you see someone weighed down with the worries of life, bless him and show your appreciation with your words. Take just a moment to make him glad.

Worry weighs a person down; an encouraging word cheers a person up.
PROVERBS 12:25

Tired of Being Tired

What you do with your frustration determines your future. I have no doubt that you have heard someone say, "I got tired of being tired." This is often said about lingering frustration someone may have had. It's what four-time World Series champion Darryl Strawberry felt about his life before he really got his addictions under control. Now God is taking his mess and making it his ministry.[20] When you are tired of being tired, you are at a great point for change. You see, frustration is a great catalyst for change.

While doing Insanity Max:30, an intense Beachbody workout, I got frustrated with myself for putting ten pounds back on and allowing myself to go backward in my fitness once again. For the majority of my life I have struggled with carrying more weight than I should. I commit myself to hard work for six or even eight months, but then, through stress, bad choices, and a lack of accountability, I fall away from focused fitness. You may be like me, or you may struggle with other frustrations that get you back in the exact same place. Whether your struggle is with your weight, alcohol, or pornography, when you are tired of being tired, look up, seek help, and get moving in the right direction once again.

God is not done developing you. Philippians 1:6 says, "I am sure of this, that he who began a good work in you will bring it to completion at the day of Jesus Christ" (ESV). If you stay the course, God will take your mess and turn it into your ministry! Remember, what you do with that frustration determines your future.

I am sure of this, that he who began a good work in you will bring it to completion at the day of Jesus Christ. PHILIPPIANS 1:6, ESV

---

[20] You will want to check out more of Darryl Strawberry's ministry at www.strawberryministries .org, as he is now living a life of purpose, sharing the good news of Christ, and helping people break free from their addictions.

Accurate Praise

Legendary football coach Bill Walsh once said, "Nothing is more effective than sincere, accurate praise, and nothing is more lame than a cookie-cutter compliment." Coach Walsh didn't mince words there, did he?

Stop and think for a moment about the amount of accurate praise you actually give. Do your children hear you affirming them for a job well done when they receive their report cards or when they execute their chores?

The Bible declares that Jesus was the perfect mixture of grace and truth. John 1:14 states, "The Word became flesh and made his dwelling among us. We have seen his glory, the glory of the one and only Son, who came from the Father, full of grace and truth" (NIV). In my experience, rarely do you meet someone full of both grace and truth. Most people are full of one or the other, but few people are full of both. Think about the ebb and flow of life for a moment. There are times when what we need most is truth. But keep in mind, truth is best received in an environment of grace. At other times, especially when we know we have made a mistake, we desperately need grace. The last thing we need is someone coming along and saying, "I told you so."

As you interact with those in your life, I want to challenge you to be full of both grace and truth. Ask God to help you grow in each of these areas.

The Word became flesh and made his dwelling among us. We have seen his glory, the glory of the one and only Son, who came from the Father, full of grace and truth.
JOHN 1:14, NIV

Bella and Alexa

There are two females in my house who I can give orders to without question. The other two, my wife and daughter, often question what I say. But Bella and Alexa know better.

Bella is our best-friend golden doodle, who has all sorts of personality. She loves to be in the middle of things, and she can't wait to load up in the truck to get the kids off to school. Bella is getting better about obedience the older she gets and the more established our patterns become.

Alexa is an Amazon Echo that my wife and kids gave me for Christmas. Alexa is special. I tell her to play music, and she dials in something perfect for me. I ask her to give me the weather forecast, and without batting an eye, she immediately tells me our local weather forecast. If she is too loud, I don't have to ask her to be quiet; I just say, "Alexa, volume three," and she turns it down. If I want to add something to the shopping list, I give her the command, and it gets done.

But neither Alexa nor Bella gives perfect obedience. Alexa doesn't always understand my inquiry, so she sometimes tells me that she doesn't have an answer to my question. Bella, the three-year-old canine, has a will of her own that often disregards the request of her master. Though she is growing in obedience, Bella often struggles to get it right.

I am familiar with Bella's conflict. I, too, struggle to get it right before my master, the Lord Jesus Christ. I am thankful for the apostle Paul's honest admission at the end of Romans 7 where he speaks of his own struggle to obey, and his opening words of Romans 8: "There is therefore now no condemnation for those who are in Christ Jesus" (verse 1, ESV). Though I struggle, Christ's amazing grace abounds!

There is therefore now no condemnation for those who are in Christ Jesus.
ROMANS 8:1, ESV

Value vs. Importance

Hunter Smith and Darrin Gray, in their book *The Jersey Effect*, unpack the crisis that we have in sports. They state, "Athletes . . . are raised to believe they're important. . . . Importance, however, is performance-based. Importance doesn't last. Importance is empty."[21]

The result is that as a society, we are raising up people who are important but don't see themselves as valuable. When their performance stops, their identity goes away, and they often struggle. Smith and Gray cite a statistic that nearly 78 percent of all former NFL players, two years after being finished with football, are either bankrupt, divorced, or unemployed.[22]

Such negative effects don't happen just in sports. They happen every day in the marketplace. They happen in marriages. All of this because we don't know who we really are.

Much of the book of Ephesians deals with understanding the identity of the Christian. Several times, the apostle Paul says to the church in Ephesus, "Formerly you were . . . now you are. . . ." Then in Ephesians 4:1 we see this challenge: "Therefore I, a prisoner for serving the Lord, beg you to lead a life worthy of your calling, for you have been called by God."

In chapter 4, Paul explains how to live in light of having your identity grounded in Christ. The word *called* means being issued a summons. In essence, Paul is saying, "Because you have been summoned to God through Christ, live in a manner responsible to that summons." You see, when we learn that we are valuable because of our union with Christ, our identity gets settled. We realize that we have been chosen by God to be his children, and we stop worrying about the opinion of others and having to perform for them.

I, a prisoner for serving the Lord, beg you to lead a life worthy of your calling, for you have been called by God. EPHESIANS 4:1

---

21 Hunter Smith and Darrin Gray, *The Jersey Effect*, with Stephen Copeland and Ken Turner (Bloomington, IN: WestBow Press, 2012), 18.
22 Ibid., vi.

Winning and Losing . . . Teaching and Learning

The great Tom Landry once said, "When you want to win a game, you have to teach. When you lose a game, you have to learn." Well, when I played sports growing up, I did a lot of learning. I don't know if I was the common denominator for being on losing teams, but I sure did seem to learn a lot during those times of disappointment.

One of my hardest seasons was playing Little League baseball at the senior-division level. This age group went right up to eighth grade. I was a tad overweight and didn't move very fast. As a matter of fact, my own team would pretend to clock me on my way to first base by chanting, "January, February, March, April . . ."

In that season, I was the tenth player on a nine-player field. I would get my mandatory two innings in by playing right field, and then I would get my one at bat. Needless to say, it was a long season, and I didn't do too well.

Looking back, I wish I had really evaluated my abilities. But my love and zeal for baseball clouded my judgment. Going into eighth grade, I chose not to return to football so that I could continue to play fall baseball. This was a mistake that I look back on with regret.

When disappointment comes, it is important to stop and learn as much as you can. I wish today that someone would have been honest with me and said, "Roger, you were built for football, not baseball." I wish I would have looked back over that frustrating Little League season and realized that my days were numbered in that sport. Now that I am a man, I've learned the benefit of seeking advice before making significant decisions. Proverbs 11:14 states, "There is safety in having many advisers."

When the game does not go your way, take a step back and listen to the advice of others. There, you will find wisdom so you can make adjustments or change directions altogether.

There is safety in having many advisers.　　　　　　　PROVERBS 11:14

Just Take Another Step

Have you ever watched an Ironman competition? Maybe you have participated in one. These extreme races involve a 2.4-mile swim, a 112-mile bike ride, and a full marathon run of 26.2 miles. My brother Troy did an Ironman, and finishing was the realization of a big goal in his life. I have known a few other guys who have done this race as well. It is incredible to see the endurance of these athletes. I wonder at what point in that race they thought and even how frequently they had to say to themselves, "Just take another step."

I was once out on a run during a vacation. I had taken a break from running for a week or so because of injury. Now I was running in a different climate with a strong headwind, and I quickly came to the point of telling myself, "Just take another step."

You may be in a season that feels like running a marathon, or even competing in an Ironman race, and you are ready to throw in the towel. It may be your job, a struggle with your children, or a deep wound in your marriage. There is a strong headwind in your face, you are coming off an injury, and the temperature is on the rise. Friend, I want to encourage you to take another step.

Romans 5:3-4 states, "We can rejoice, too, when we run into problems and trials, for we know that they help us develop endurance. And endurance develops strength of character, and character strengthens our confident hope of salvation." In the sufferings of this trial, if you keep going, you will see endurance develop that will lead to hope. But remember, to get that hope, you have to take another step today.

We can rejoice, too, when we run into problems and trials, for we know that they help us develop endurance. And endurance develops strength of character, and character strengthens our confident hope of salvation.

ROMANS 5:3-4

An Honest Admission

In his book *Racing to Win*, Hall of Fame football coach Joe Gibbs talks about his quest to get his first head coaching job. After a random conversation with a stranger in an Arkansas airport that was too coincidental to be coincidence, he writes, "I thought about how I had been trying to manage my own career, calling my own shots and trying to make things happen. My quest for a head coaching job had consumed me, affecting my relationships and every decision I made. Even though I was a Christian, God was not in charge of my life. I was."[23]

What an honest admission! Have you ever been there? Maybe you are there today. It is easy to take Christ as your Savior but not surrender all of the areas of your life to his leadership. Every one of us will have to wrestle with this temptation at one time or another. If you are wrestling with it now, I want you to see a promise of God about his leadership for your life. Proverbs 3:5-6 says, "Trust in the LORD with all your heart; do not depend on your own understanding. Seek his will in all you do, and he will show you which path to take."

He promises to show you which path you should take! I want to encourage you to put your trust in God. When Coach Gibbs did this, something happened. Gibbs states, "An overwhelming peace washed over me."[24]

Friend, when you trust the Lord, peace comes. Don't wait another day.

Trust in the LORD with all your heart; do not depend on your own understanding. Seek his will in all you do, and he will show you which path to take.   PROVERBS 3:5-6

---

23 Joe Gibbs, *Racing to Win* (Sisters, OR: Multnomah, 2002), 69.
24 Ibid.

Vowing to Stay the Course

It happens all too often in my life. I start out strong, motivated to lose weight and get moving. Somewhere along the way, I get stressed, busy, and hungry. I fail to prepare for the day, and I sabotage my diet. That day gets parlayed into a few days, and the next thing I know, I have gone a month, not caring or thinking about what I put into my body.

When I start the journey back, I eagerly go for a run or step on the elliptical machine, only to get three-fourths of the way through and ponder quitting. At this point, it is time to have a hard talk with myself. When that moment creeps up, I say to myself, "Roger, if you quit before you are done, you are finished." Seeing quitting as failure is a truth I must grasp, lest I ride the yo-yo of weight gain and loss the rest of my life. Though I am tempted to quit, I need to vow to stay the course.

In biblical times, people often made vows to God. These weren't regulated and required, but they were voluntary choices people made because of their faith in the Lord and their hopes for this life. In essence, they made the decision once and then stewarded that decision every day. What vow do you need to make to God? Mine involves the way I steward my weight. When you do make that vow, remember the words of Psalm 61:8, which states, "I will sing praises to your name forever as I fulfill my vows each day."

I will sing praises to your name forever as I fulfill my vows each day.

PSALM 61:8

Crock-Pot or Microwave

I was talking to a mom of a junior high student, and in her few words I could hear both hope and despair regarding her son. Hope because of the young man that she longed for him to become, and despair because she wasn't seeing it yet.

In a culture that screams, "Microwave it!" we have got to be willing to take the longer path of the Crock-Pot. Yes, we can eat pot roast from a microwave. It comes out of the freezer, has all types of preservatives, and can be consumed right out of the plastic container. But we all know that pot roast from a frozen dinner is a far cry from the way our moms made it. The longer, harder path is to work with fresh ingredients, take our time, and really see the flavor come to life as it simmers and cooks.

I have learned that when God grows us, he prefers to use the Crock-Pot over the microwave because he wants the changes in us to be permanent and lasting. Even Jesus took the natural course of time to grow into the great man that he became. Luke 2:52 declares, "Jesus grew in wisdom and in stature and in favor with God and all the people."

Don't rush your child's development. Keep working with the freshest ingredients, and consistently pour into your children the wisdom of God and a vision for what they could be as they grow. Be consistent, persistent, and resilient, and may your children grow as Jesus did!

Jesus grew in wisdom and in stature and in favor with God and all the people. LUKE 2:52

The Root of Happiness

Shelly-Ann Fraser-Pryce is a two-time Olympic gold medalist, five-time world outdoor-track champion, and 2014 world indoor-track champion. With all that recognition, you would think she would have always been happy, but she says, "In 2008 I went to the Olympics and I won. I had the money, and I had everything that I really wanted, but I wasn't contented. I wasn't happy. In 2009 I won again, and I still wasn't happy. . . . And I knew something was missing. . . . It was time for me to start living for Christ."[25]

Her faith is what finally brought her the peace and happiness that she was seeking. Many Christians are happy to take Christ as their Savior, but they relegate him to the background of their lives instead of truly living for him. I've witnessed many men reverting back to the values of the world to find their esteem. I would argue that they have never completely understood the fullness of their redemption and God's plan for their lives.

When Christ is Lord and is guiding the passions, priorities, and pursuits of a man, things are ordered. Christ is more valuable than anything that the world has to offer. After having tremendous success, Saul of Tarsus, who became the apostle Paul, learned this lesson. He said in Philippians 3:8, "Yes, everything else is worthless when compared with the infinite value of knowing Christ Jesus my Lord. For his sake I have discarded everything else, counting it all as garbage, so that I could gain Christ."

Where are you today? Are you trying to find happiness in accomplishment, acknowledgment, and approval from the world? Are you hoping to have your heart filled from all that this world has to offer? Or have you truly tasted and seen that the Lord is good? Place him on the throne of your heart, and allow him to shape you in every way.

Yes, everything else is worthless when compared with the infinite value of knowing Christ Jesus my Lord. For his sake I have discarded everything else, counting it all as garbage, so that I could gain Christ.   PHILIPPIANS 3:8

---

25 Brett Honeycutt, "Life in the Fast Lane," *Sports Spectrum*, June 30, 2014, http://www.sportsspectrum.com/articles/2014/06/30/life-in-the-fast-lane/.

Get Up and Lay It Down

Legendary NBA coach Phil Jackson once said, "Like life, basketball is messy and unpredictable. It has its way with you, no matter how hard you try to control it."

When moments or even seasons like this hit, they can overwhelm you and cause you to lose sleep. So when you are tossing and turning and replaying the difficulty that you are facing, get up and lay it down.

That's right, get out of bed, get on your face, and ask God to hear your prayer. Tell him your worries, lay the problem at his feet, and thank him for hearing you. When you take your burdens to the Lord instead of tossing and turning all night, you will be able to find rest. So many people choose to drink or even medicate for sleep, but I am convinced we are far better off getting up and laying it down.

Jesus said in Matthew 11:28-29, "Come to me, all of you who are weary and carry heavy burdens, and I will give you rest. Take my yoke upon you. Let me teach you, because I am humble and gentle at heart, and you will find rest for your souls." So after you have gotten up and laid it down, go to bed and enjoy your rest. You will be amazed at how well you sleep.

Remember this promise from the apostle Peter today! First Peter 5:7 says, "Give all your worries and cares to God, for he cares about you."

Give all your worries and cares to God, for he cares about you.   1 PETER 5:7

Hurry Up and Slow Down

At eleven years of age, my son Cooper has completed only two or three full rounds of golf. When we have the opportunity to golf together, it is great one-on-one time. He enjoys the game and has the potential to be good, but at this point, he is limited by his lack of patience for the pace of the game.

This lack of maturity leads to some interesting shots. We keep it fun, but often I have to tell him, "Hurry between shots, and slow down for the shot." Right now, it's the other way around. He takes all sorts of time getting to the next shot. He laughs, jokes, messes with the dogs in the backyards of homes lining the fairway. But when he gets to his ball, he gets right up on it and fires away.

If we aren't careful, our spiritual lives can be a lot like Coop's golf game. When it comes to Scripture reading or prayer, we take our time between shots, but when we get to that important moment to open the Bible and lift our hearts to the Lord in prayer, we fly right through it. We lack the maturity to hurry up between our quiet times and slow down when we get there.

Listen to the words of the psalmist as he writes of slowing down in his time with God. Psalm 119:15 states, "I will study your commandments and reflect on your ways." Remember, hurry to your time with the Lord, and slow down when you get there.

I will study your commandments and reflect on your ways.   PSALM 119:15

Models or Critics?

Hall of Fame coach John Wooden once said, "Young people need models, not critics." If we believe that the coming generation is to have success, we might sit up and listen to Coach Wooden.

In the arts or in sports, the critics are a dime a dozen. They get paid to diagnose what is wrong and point it out. Critics have no responsibility to fix the problem or to even care why a problem exists in the first place.

When it comes to the next generation of our youth, it is easy to be a critic. Their habitual use of technology, the way they wear their clothes, the music they listen to, and their political ideology can easily make you cynical. But remember, anybody can be a critic.

Models, on the other hand, say, "Hey, kid, look at me. If you follow my lead, you can make something of your life." Models don't judge offhand. They draw near. Models don't discard; they invite you to come close.

In a day and time when nearly 50 percent of the children in America grow up in a one-parent home, there is a desperate need for people who will serve as models for the next generation. This is what Solomon did when he wrote the book of Proverbs to his sons. Proverbs 2:1 declares, "My child, listen to what I say, and treasure my commands." In other words, "Boys, you can look to me, and I will show you how to become a man."

Why not spend a couple of minutes each day in the book of Proverbs equipping yourself with wisdom? Then choose to model that wisdom and change that day.

My child, listen to what I say, and treasure my commands.   PROVERBS 2:1

Attention to the Details

When I was in my late teens, I had the chance to apply for a management position with the Pappas Restaurant Company, a large, family-owned restaurant chain based in Houston, Texas. I interviewed with Harris Pappas, one of the three brothers who owned the company. I remember that interview distinctly because Mr. Pappas revealed to me what I already knew about myself. He showed me through various aptitude tests that I didn't really like paying attention to the details. I remember he challenged me by saying something like "Your future success will be determined by how well you master the details." The older I get, the more I realize Mr. Pappas was right.

For me it was noticing the details, but for you it might be the ability to multitask, or to be persuasive. We all have areas where we need to be challenged. There is one area where each of us needs to be challenged if we are to excel in this life. It has to do with our hearts and our speech. Proverbs 22:11 states, "Whoever loves a pure heart and gracious speech will have the king as a friend."

You see, when you attend to the details of keeping the heart from being polluted, your speech will be gracious. But if you allow the heart to get bitter, everyone will know. This will keep you from progressing.

Remember Jesus' words from Matthew 12:34, "Whatever is in your heart determines what you say." There is a direct correlation between your heart and your mouth.

Whoever loves a pure heart and gracious speech will have the king as a friend.   PROVERBS 22:11

No E-mail until Lunchtime

Interruptions interrupt intentionality. I find that my most productive times of the day are in the early mornings. I am more eager to pray, more eager to exercise, and more eager to get the most important tasks done when I focus on those things before anything else. I am striving to live by the rule to tackle the biggest and hardest things first. As a result, I am learning to wait on checking e-mail until lunchtime.

E-mail beckons, doesn't it? It screams, "Check me! Read me! Reply to me!" It has become an all-access, all-hours-of-the-day interruption to my work instead of being a great tool for my work. Yet it is a necessary part of my work, so I must check it, send it, and reply to it.

Whether it is by e-mail, fantasy football, or Facebook, we are more distracted in our day-to-day lives than we have ever been. Being a disciplined, productive employee involves my willingness to look at every area of my day and ask, "How can I do it better? Is there a practice that will bring me greater focus, create greater reliability, and generate greater outcomes?" I have concluded that for me, being disciplined, even in my e-mail usage, will make a big difference.

When it comes to your work, think about working as unto the Lord. Psalm 128:1-2 declares,

> How joyful are those who fear the LORD—
>   all who follow his ways!
> You will enjoy the fruit of your labor.
>   How joyful and prosperous you will be!

When we fear the Lord, we honor him in the way we work. Enjoy the fruit of your labor as you make adjustments that maximize your productivity.

How joyful are those who fear the LORD—all who follow his ways! You will enjoy the fruit of your labor. How joyful and prosperous you will be!

PSALM 128:1-2

What It Takes to Win

Championship dynasties like the San Antonio Spurs, the San Francisco 49ers, and the New York Yankees amaze me with their ability to continually compete for championships. Through the years, these clubs have consistently been competing for national titles. It is truly amazing what people can accomplish when working together.

For anything great to last, it must have strong leadership and a system that sustains it. The quality that keeps these championship teams competing for the title year after year is the leader's awareness that things change and that what was true last season isn't necessarily true this season. Additionally, the leader must create a system to take direction and input from others. He must be humble enough to know that sometimes his subordinates see clearer and further than he does.

Whether you're thinking of your challenges in the marketplace, in marriage, in church, or in parenting, note these words of Solomon: "The wise are mightier than the strong, and those with knowledge grow stronger and stronger. So don't go to war without wise guidance; victory depends on having many advisers" (Proverbs 24:5-6). Victory in any area of your life comes with the manifold wisdom of a broad, diverse team. It comes when they challenge you, share from their experience, or bring faith and inspiration to the group. Do you have wise counselors around you? If not, why not? Remember, even Solomon, the wisest man in the Bible, needed advice.

The wise are mightier than the strong, and those with knowledge grow stronger and stronger. So don't go to war without wise guidance; victory depends on having many advisers.　　　　　PROVERBS 24:5-6

Being Unshakable in a Shaky World

Have you watched the news lately? Things that were once stable seem to be shaking up. From 9/11 in 2001, to the financial crisis in 2008, to the Arab Spring in 2010, to the recent emergence of ISIS . . . our world seems to be coming unhinged.

How do you parent your children with stability in a world of instability? How do you find certain peace in the midst of an anxious world? Many people turn to the false promise of having more stuff to insulate them from uncertainty. Others turn to substances to help alleviate the anxiety, only getting temporary respite from that which concerns them. But I want to point you to the Scriptures and to Jesus Christ, the only source of true peace.

You see, in Jesus Christ, we have one whom we know will bring stability and an entirely new order of things one day. Our stability today springs from our hope for tomorrow. Revelation 21:3-4 says,

> I heard a loud shout from the throne, saying, "Look, God's home is now among his people! He will live with them, and they will be his people. God himself will be with them. He will wipe every tear from their eyes, and there will be no more death or sorrow or crying or pain. All these things are gone forever."

My friend, in Christ you can find certainty in an uncertain world. He is coming again to bring stability forever, so be sure that you have put your hope in him!

Look, God's home is now among his people! He will live with them, and they will be his people. God himself will be with them. He will wipe every tear from their eyes, and there will be no more death or sorrow or crying or pain. All these things are gone forever. **REVELATION 21:3-4**

Learning to Say Yes

You and I live in a culture that constantly cries out to us to get more, hoard more, and consume more for ourselves. Learning to live with an open hand is scary for many. But a life of generously sharing our income will give us, as described in the Bible, "the life that is truly life" (1 Timothy 6:19, MSG). We can say yes to being generous with our money, whether at home or at church.

There is great joy in the homes of those who intentionally seek to bless their wives and children through being generous with their money. These gifts don't have to be big-ticket items; a surprise coffee drink from her favorite coffee shop or a bouquet of flowers will show your wife that you care about her and want to bless her. When I can, I try to treat my children, too.

Another way you can be generous is by joining others in God's church to resource its mission, vision, and operations. Jesus never invalidated the tithe introduced in the Old Testament, and the first fruits offering is a proclamation of his death and resurrection. Begin with giving the first tenth of your income, and grow in the grace of giving. This discipline is a fundamental aspect of being a Christian.

Second Corinthians 9:7-8 states, "'God loves a person who gives cheerfully.' And God will generously provide all you need. Then you will always have everything you need and plenty left over to share with others." Say yes to your family and the church, and enjoy taking the first steps toward "the life that is truly life."

"God loves a person who gives cheerfully." And God will generously provide all you need. Then you will always have everything you need and plenty left over to share with others.   2 CORINTHIANS 9:7-8

Staying Hydrated

One of the most important foundations of athletic performance is hydration. If an athlete is not hydrated properly, his or her performance will suffer. Some college-level coaches go so far as to test their athletes' urine to see if they are hydrating properly.

While on a jog, I noticed I wasn't hydrated enough. I had been drinking too many diet sodas and not eating the best foods. I woke up that morning, had some coffee, did some writing, then set out on a forty-minute jog. I wasn't too far into that jog when I knew I wasn't hydrated enough. My body let me know.

Just as we need to stay hydrated in the physical realm, we need to be hydrated in the spiritual realm. Scripture calls us to be filled with the Holy Spirit. This isn't some sort of out-of-body religious experience, but a simple request of the Lord to fill you up.

Ephesians 5:18 states, "Don't be drunk with wine, because that will ruin your life. Instead, be filled with the Holy Spirit." When I preach, I say, "Lord, fill me up so that you can pour me out." But beyond preaching, I ask the Lord to fill me so that I can live each day sensitive to my reactions and the Spirit's leading.

If we are going to live according to God's Word, we must be filled with the Holy Spirit. Stay hydrated by asking the Lord to fill you, and strive to walk in his way.

Don't be drunk with wine, because that will ruin your life. Instead, be filled with the Holy Spirit.   EPHESIANS 5:18

Customer Service and Organizational Silos

After opening their new gaming system Christmas morning, my kids were excited to download the latest version of one of the most popular football games on the market. This game was part of a bundle you could download to the system over the Internet. All we had to do was peel off the sticker that covered the twenty-five-digit code included with the gaming system, enter the code, and watch the icon spin until the download was complete.

But there was a problem with this scenario. My eleven-year-old son took off the sticker that covered the twenty-five-digit code. He brought the code to me with thirteen of the twenty-five numbers and letters missing and asked, "Dad, can you fix this?"

Christmas Day customer support is nuts! After waiting on hold for two hours, I gave it my best effort, but the people on the other end didn't know what to do. They recommended I contact the manufacturer, a third-party provider of the software. But the manufacturer sent me back to the gaming system company. The gaming company recommended we contact the company that we had purchased the system from, which happened to be their parent company. After many calls, I finally reached someone who took care of the problem for us. Unfortunately, I learned that customer satisfaction wasn't the company's goal. Instead of working together, these companies operated as silos, and their clients were suffering for it.

The truth is that silos within an organization or network will turn people away. Instead of a silo mentality, collaboration is the key, and good relationships among leaders to foster that collaboration are mission critical.

When Paul and Barnabas parted ways, it was because of a breakdown in a relationship. Acts 15:37-38 states, "Barnabas agreed and wanted to take along John Mark. But Paul disagreed strongly, since John Mark had deserted them in Pamphylia and had not continued with them in their work." Even great missionary work is hampered when leaders can't agree.

Barnabas agreed and wanted to take along John Mark. But Paul disagreed strongly, since John Mark had deserted them in Pamphylia and had not continued with them in their work. ACTS 15:37-38

When Opportunity Knocks, Walk This Way

When opportunity knocks, how do you know where to go? Do you stay in your current situation or go to another place of employment? Do you uproot your family, or do you deepen your roots right where you are?

How do you know where to go and when to go? I don't believe there is an easy answer to that question. But I do know that you can have confidence when you arrive at your answer. Proverbs 2:9 says, "Then you will understand what is right, just, and fair, and you will find the right way to go."

We want to know what is right, just, and fair, as well as the right way to go, don't we? But did you notice that the verse starts with the word *then*? It doesn't simply say, "You will know." It says, "Then you will know."

When will we know the right way to go? I have come to conclude that it is after we have done the heavy lifting of looking for wisdom, as described before this verse, in Proverbs 2:1-8. This section of Scripture depicts a true search as if one is a student who is eager to learn, a pirate who is digging for buried treasure, or a lost person who is desperate to find directions. These verses describe an aggressive hunt for the answer.

Having had to walk in this uncertainty myself, here is what I have come to discover. Whether you stay or go, deepen your roots or chart a new course, God wants to use the opportunities before you to strengthen your relationship with him. After he gives you wisdom through your search, "Then you will understand. . . ."

Then you will understand what is right, just, and fair, and you will find the right way to go. PROVERBS 2:9

MAY

Getting Fit

Did you know that May is National Physical Fitness and Sports Month? That means it's time to get fit. Your health and fitness can be two of your biggest assets or worst liabilities. They will affect how you interact with your family, how you perform at work, and how you enjoy your overall life.

Having vision for your life isn't just a matter of spiritual principles or applications. Having vision for your life entails thinking long term and making practical changes along the way to get to your destination. Pat Williams, an executive with the Orlando Magic, has a goal to live to be one hundred years old and write two hundred books in his lifetime. To do this he exercises an hour each day and eats right. He has survived cancer, has run many marathons, and is striving toward writing those books every single day.

Today is an opportunity to make progress. Ephesians 5:15-17 states, "Be careful how you live. Don't live like fools, but like those who are wise. Make the most of every opportunity in these evil days. Don't act thoughtlessly, but understand what the Lord wants you to do."

What goals are you hoping to accomplish that require you to be healthy and fit? How are you training your body so that you can be present for the big moments in your life and your children's lives? Get moving in the right direction, and seek to be fit in every area of your life.

Be careful how you live. Don't live like fools, but like those who are wise. Make the most of every opportunity in these evil days. Don't act thoughtlessly, but understand what the Lord wants you to do. EPHESIANS 5:15-17

500,000 Hugs

Reunions can be sweet. Reunions that come after great dissension and grief, even sweeter. Those that come after deployment to war are the sweetest. Fort Hood, in Killeen, Texas, lost a great lady in December 2015. Elizabeth Laird, known to those at Fort Hood as the "Hug Lady," died after a battle with breast cancer.

Ms. Laird was called the Hug Lady because she gave an estimated 500,000 hugs while attending every single deployment and homecoming at the base since 2003. What an amazing testimony and legacy. I wonder what it was like for her when she found out that someone she knew, someone she'd hugged when he or she was sent off to war, didn't return. I would imagine that living that vulnerably caused her to cry many a tear as some soldiers returned while others did not. Ms. Laird was honored by the First Cavalry Division Commander Major General Michael Bills with a plaque in recognition of her service to soldiers.

A good hug is a powerful statement of love, support, and unity. When Jacob and Esau were reunited, there were no words, but there was a great hug. Genesis 33:4 states, "Esau ran to meet [Jacob] and embraced him, threw his arms around his neck, and kissed him. And they both wept." I believe that God uses a hug to say what words can't say. I believe he uses a hug to declare deep sadness and regret, joy, and love. Who do you need to go hug today?

Esau ran to meet [Jacob] and embraced him, threw his arms around his neck, and kissed him. And they both wept.   GENESIS 33:4

A Fifteen-Round Fight

Floyd Mayweather and Manny Pacquiao fought in the fight of the century in May 2015. These two legends of the boxing world were finally squaring off, and the match was hyped beyond belief. Unfortunately, the hype was greater than the fight, as the two older boxers didn't give the show that many had hoped for.

Some fights are over quickly; some last for what seems an eternity. Nehemiah, a leader in Jerusalem, found himself in the fight of his life, one with heavyweight punches being thrown. You see, Nehemiah was fighting to rebuild and reestablish the walls and the city of Jerusalem, the City of God.

Nehemiah was fighting for the Lord's glory and the people's safety, and this took time. It also brought angst and fear and demanded sacrifice. As the people worked on rebuilding the wall, a guard kept watch day and night, and the people labored day after day. Nehemiah inspired the people to stay in Jerusalem, keep battling for their future, and take the threat seriously. By fighting for their future, Nehemiah shows us how to fight for ours.

You may find yourself fighting for your marriage, your teenager's future, or the integrity of your name. Every move you make matters. Nehemiah 4:22 states, "I also told everyone living outside the walls to stay in Jerusalem. That way they and their servants could help with guard duty at night and work during the day." Don't underestimate the deception and harsh tactics of the enemy. Stay prayerful, fighting on your knees at night, and focused, being ever alert and vigilant during the day. May the Lord be your banner as you fight today!

I also told everyone living outside the walls to stay in Jerusalem. That way they and their servants could help with guard duty at night and work during the day.
NEHEMIAH 4:22

Four Ways to Be Generous

When my oldest son, Brady, turned thirteen, I wrote him a short book about things I wanted for him. One of the things that I want for him is to learn to be generous with what God gives him. So to instruct him in stewardship, I shared these four principles for cultivating generosity in his own life:

1. Give 10 percent of your earnings to the Lord, through the church. This is the beginning of learning to give. You and God can do more with 90 percent of your income than you can do with 100 percent. When you make money, set aside a "tithe," or one-tenth of your income, to honor the Lord and experience his promise to you from Proverbs 3:9-10: "Honor the LORD with your wealth and with the best part of everything you produce. Then he will fill your barns with grain, and your vats will overflow with good wine."

2. Look for ways to be generous with your time. You should not only give your money to God's work, but you should also give your time to God's people and to those God is longing to use you to reach. Successful people say yes and then figure out how to get it done.

3. Be generous toward your wife and kids. I long to run a house where the word *yes* is prevalent. Generosity starts in your own home. Be generous to your family first with your money and your time. If you can, spend money on great vacations, and make special memories with your family.

4. Call others in your circle of influence to a generous life. Lead others to give by inviting them to join you in your journey of generosity. Do this by creating moments that are bigger than what you can facilitate on your own.

When you experience grace, you want others to find the same. Go be generous today!

Honor the LORD with your wealth and with the best part of everything you produce. Then he will fill your barns with grain, and your vats will overflow with good wine. PROVERBS 3:9-10

From Fighter to Trainer

If you follow the Rocky movies' plotlines, you will see a progression of wisdom being passed down from old to young. Mickey poured into Rocky and helped him defeat the likes of Apollo Creed. Apollo then became the trainer and helped shape the less experienced Balboa, who then defeated Clubber Lang. When Creed passed at the hands of the Russian fighter Drago, there was no dominant figure to pour wisdom into the heavyweight, and the moviegoer could feel the absence being played out on the big screen.

In the final Rocky movie, *Creed*, Adonis Johnson, the son of Apollo Creed, seeks the wisdom of an old Rocky Balboa to help him go to the next level as a fighter. There is something powerful to consider when we see this ancient practice of the fighter becoming the trainer and pouring into the next generation. It mirrors fathering and coaching. It is the picture of the student growing up to become the teacher.

Mentoring and apprenticeships have been the standard way of training the next generation for centuries. Notice the observations of the Queen of Sheba when she journeyed to see King Solomon. She was evaluating for herself what she had heard of his teaching and the vast wisdom he possessed. Notice how she noted the impact that she saw. She said, "Happy are your men! Happy are your servants, who continually stand before you and hear your wisdom!" (1 Kings 10:8, ESV). Students who seek to grow find mentors who can benefit them with the principles that nourish them today and prepare them for tomorrow. Mentors who have a genuine interest in their students' well-being, who delight in seeing their growth and success. May we reclaim this lost ancient discipline of passing wisdom down from age to age!

Happy are your men! Happy are your servants, who continually stand before you and hear your wisdom! 1 KINGS 10:8, ESV

Handling Disappointment

Longtime head coach of the New England Patriots Bill Belichick isn't known for his oratory skills. He has a stoic, unemotional approach to communicating with the media. This is the case when his team wins and when they lose. After the Patriots lost the 2015 AFC Championship game in Denver, Belichick noted that he was disappointed that they didn't accomplish everything they had set out to do. When asked about how he would evaluate the team for the following year, Belichick, in true form, said, "We will evaluate the team this year the same way we have in years past."

Thirty-one of thirty-two teams will end the NFL season disappointed. It is a fact of all athletic competition that only one team can come out on top as the champions. Evaluating the team to get better for next season is a disciplined process of analyzing strengths and weaknesses and seeing where improvement can come through the draft and free agency.

Handling disappointment in life isn't as simple or clean. A lot of emotion can spill out when they're probably better left contained. Oftentimes, we express our disappointment to others who have no power to resolve things, but we never speak directly to the decision makers who can get things done if they know how disappointed we are. Matthew 18:15 instructs us well here: "If another believer sins against you, go privately and point out the offense. If the other person listens and confesses it, you have won that person back." Hard conversations can be fruitful if we handle them well, but we must handle ourselves first so that our message to those who have disappointed us can be heard.

If another believer sins against you, go privately and point out the offense.
If the other person listens and confesses it, you have won that person back.
MATTHEW 18:15

Home Phone—What's That?

Do you answer your home phone? Do you even have a home phone any longer? We live in a day and age when nearly everyone in the household has his or her own personal number for a cell phone. Family members who are too young to have their own phones will answer the home phone when it rings, but the rest of us see who it is first via caller ID or simply ignore it, believing it to be a telemarketer. We think, *If this is important, they would know to call my cell number. I'm not answering that.*

How often do you think we do the same when God is trying to bring us his wisdom? Like the home phone, we ignore it.

Wisdom actively calls to us, and yet we often disregard its call. Even though we have ears to hear, we don't always want to know the truth, so we avoid it, ignore it, or act as if it isn't even calling out to us.

The Bible describes an active call that wisdom brings to us. It says in Proverbs 1:20-23:

> Wisdom shouts in the streets. She cries out in the public square.
> She calls to the crowds along the main street, to those gathered
>   in front of the city gate:
> "How long, you simpletons, will you insist on being simpleminded?
>   How long will you mockers relish your mocking? How long
>   will you fools hate knowledge?
> Come and listen to my counsel. I'll share my heart with you and
>   make you wise."

Don't ignore the wisdom of God. By engaging in the practice of a "proverb a day" by reading a chapter of the book of Proverbs every single day, you will find yourself growing in wisdom, knowledge, and understanding.

Wisdom shouts in the streets. She cries out in the public square. She calls to the crowds along the main street, to those gathered in front of the city gate: "How long, you simpletons, will you insist on being simpleminded?"

PROVERBS 1:20-22

How Should I Ask?

The Jump Rope for Heart annual school fund-raiser has been around for many years. Benefiting the American Heart Association, the event gives schoolkids an opportunity to raise money, raise awareness, and raise their fitness level when they participate by jumping rope at their schools.

When my daughter, Carson, came home with one of the forms, she showed me some of the "Pups," little puppy figurines that she would personally receive for different levels of money raised. Since I had to take her to the church for her piano lesson, I decided to let her loose on the office.

While going up the stairs, I asked her, "What are you going to say? How will you ask for the money?" She said, "I don't know. How should I ask?"

I gave her some pointers, suggested a few things, and then said, "Okay, go ahead. Go ask Ms. Becca." Carson then responded, "I want to think about it first." A few minutes later, she was off.

After her first request, she came back with a ten-dollar bill from Ms. Becca. Then she went on to Ms. Jennifer and got a twenty-five-dollar check. The more success she had, the more emboldened requests she made.

Our prayer lives are that way as well. Sometimes we are hesitant at first to say anything to God. We don't know what we will say or how we will say it. After thinking about it, we make our requests known to him. After we see him answer, it picks us up, and we ask again and again and again.

Psalm 34:8 states, "Taste and see that the LORD is good. Oh, the joys of those who take refuge in him!" Remember this verse when you go to him to make your request.

Taste and see that the LORD is good. Oh, the joys of those who take refuge in him!   PSALM 34:8

A Hall of Fame Dad

Hall of Fame quarterback Steve Young, in the foreword to *Dad's Playbook*, says, "If there were a Hall of Fame for husbands and dads, I'd make it my number one goal to get there. On the day I was inducted into the Pro Football Hall of Fame, just before I concluded my speech . . . I made a statement that I hope I can live up to. I said, 'I sincerely love my family and know that being a Hall of Fame husband and dad is what will eventually define my life.'"[26]

Guys, what goals do you have for your family or your legacy? Does the way you are living your life today lead to those goals? Many men strive for money. Being successful is important, and working to leave an inheritance is very honorable. But I have seen many a man lay his children on the altar of sacrifice for victory in the marketplace. Remember, you can't take it with you.

Others strive for fame, recognition, or popularity among their peers. They will rearrange their schedules to be with someone important, to the detriment of their children. Keep in mind that the concern of man's opinion is a trap according to Proverbs 29:25: "Fearing people is a dangerous trap, but trusting the LORD means safety."

Will you follow God's plan or man's plan for success? What will define your life? May it be the success of being a Hall of Fame husband and father!

Fearing people is a dangerous trap, but trusting the LORD means safety.

PROVERBS 29:25

---

26 Steve Young, foreword to *Dad's Playbook: Wisdom for Fathers from the Greatest Coaches of All Time*, by Tom Limbert (San Francisco: Chronicle Books, 2012), 9.

I'll Sign You a Copy

"What are you doing?" my daughter asked me. "I'm writing my book," I replied. "When will you be finished?" she then asked. "Very soon," I replied. Carson continued, "Will it be a real book?" I smiled and said, "Yes, and I'll sign you a copy." Carson promptly looked at me and said, "No thanks, I like Junie B. Jones books." All I could do was laugh at the sweet, honest, heart-breaking innocence of my six-year-old. She finally looked at me and said, "Sorry, Daddy," to which I replied, "That's quite all right."

I love how God has a way of using the closest people in our lives not just for us to enjoy and do life with but to also speak truth to us. Peyton Manning, the only quarterback in NFL history who has taken two different teams to the Super Bowl and won, shares that the only way he has been able to improve in his career is by being willing to receive feedback from those closest to him. He names Coach David Cutcliffe, his former coach at Tennessee, as one of those men.

Here are a few verses to keep in mind when those closest to you are speaking the truth. First, Proverbs 1:5 states, "Let the wise listen to these proverbs and become even wiser. Let those with understanding receive guidance." Second, Proverbs 27:5-6 states, "An open rebuke is better than hidden love! Wounds from a sincere friend are better than many kisses from an enemy." You see, God has a way of allowing those who are near us to add value to us, if we would but listen. Seek to learn from what they have to offer, and continue to grow.

Let the wise listen to these proverbs and become even wiser. Let those with understanding receive guidance.
PROVERBS 1:5

The Influence of a Mom

Tim Brown, Hall of Famer and Heisman Trophy winner, talks about the influence his mom had on his life in his book *The Making of a Man*. Tim writes, "Every mother is special. I have great admiration for all moms. Each is a full-time doctor, psychologist, pastor, teacher, chef, taxi driver, and police officer, all rolled into one. Mothers love their children with a fierce devotion that no one else on the planet can match. And even though we sometimes pretend otherwise, we—their sons—need them."[27]

I remember a moment as a child when I thought, *My mom must really love me!* We were on a vacation to Branson, Missouri, going down a multicolored slide at a carnival. It was the type of slide where you sit on a potato sack and slide down multiple levels. I was having the time of my life. Somehow, I had run out of tickets and my siblings still had some. I saw sacrificial love in action the moment my mom said, "Here, honey, take my ticket and go again." To a five-year-old, that is what sacrificial love looks like.

Aren't you glad your mom loves you like she does? If you have children, aren't you thankful for the way their mother serves your kids? Moms aren't perfect, but they are some of the first people who teach us what faithfulness to another looks like.

Remember the fifth commandment, the first one with a promise: "Honor your father and mother. Then you will live a long, full life in the land the LORD your God is giving you" (Exodus 20:12). Don't just honor your mother on Mother's Day. That is when it is expected most. Do it on an ordinary day, and turn that ordinary day into an extraordinary one for your mom.

Honor your father and mother. Then you will live a long, full life in the land the LORD your God is giving you. EXODUS 20:12

---

[27] Tim Brown and James Lund, *The Making of a Man: How Men and Boys Honor God and Live with Integrity* (Nashville: W Publishing, 2014), 18.

Learning When You Can

It seems that during every off-season, a handful of athletes get themselves into real trouble. Sports radio hosts say out loud what we're all thinking, wondering when these guys will ever learn their lesson.

The Duke of Wellington once said, "Wise people learn when they can. Fools learn when they must." There is a fine line between the wise and the foolish, and I believe it all boils down to our ability to learn.

Life is definitely going to be a teacher. The question that really matters is, When will you learn? The wise learn on the go, as they evaluate their lives, as they see the struggles of others, and as the opportunities for growth present themselves. The wise approach life as students, ever learning, ever growing.

Fools learn when they have no other options. They are described as fools because of the one key decision they have already made—the decision to fail to learn and be instructed. Fools think they already have the answers, and as a result, they fail to listen, fail to heed caution, and fail to grow when they see others making mistakes.

Proverbs 10:17 states, "People who accept discipline are on the pathway to life, but those who ignore correction will go astray." How about you? Are you learning when you can, or only when you must? Every day is an opportunity for personal, physical, and spiritual growth. Mistakes will be made, grace extended, and life will go forward. But when others make mistakes, learn from them. When you make your mistakes, quickly take inventory of what you can do differently, and make the changes necessary so that you don't repeat your folly.

People who accept discipline are on the pathway to life, but those who ignore correction will go astray.   PROVERBS 10:17

Life Requires Grit

Seattle Seahawks coach Pete Carroll is known for bringing in motivational speakers, professional golfers, authors, and sports psychologists to teach and challenge his team on how to get that extra edge. In his journey, he encountered a trait called "grit" that captured his attention. It is a term coined by Angela Lee Duckworth, a psychologist and associate professor from the University of Pennsylvania, who states, "In all those very different contexts, one characteristic emerged as a significant predictor of success. And it wasn't social intelligence. It wasn't good looks, physical health, and it wasn't IQ. It was grit."[28]

She defines *grit* as "a passionate perseverance toward a long-term goal." You see, it takes grit to be successful in this life. Your talent isn't enough. Your opportunities aren't enough. Your resources aren't enough. Those things are important, but it takes grit, a passionate perseverance toward your long-term goal, to be what God wants you to be.

Proverbs 28:20 speaks of this type of faithfulness. It says, "The trustworthy person will get a rich reward, but a person who wants quick riches will get into trouble." Don't take shortcuts, but passionately persevere in doing what God has called you to. Remember, if it was easy, you wouldn't be needed. Be trustworthy, determined, and unrelenting, and persevere to the finish line.

The trustworthy person will get a rich reward, but a person who wants quick riches will get into trouble.   PROVERBS 28:20

---

28 Angela Lee Duckworth, "Grit: The Power of Passion and Perseverance," *TED: Ideas Worth Spreading*, https://www.ted.com/talks/angela_lee_duckworth_grit_the_power_of_passion_and_perseverance/transcript?language=en.

A Proverb a Day

Have you ever discovered your propensity to be both wise and foolish? I have. You see, I have figured out that there are moments when wisdom has danced in my heart, and there are moments when folly has streamed forth from my lips. I wish I were only wise.

Proverbs 14:16 states, "One who is wise is cautious and turns away from evil, but a fool is reckless and careless" (ESV). I have been both cautious and reckless, wise and foolish, in the same day, and I hate the inconsistencies! But here is what I have also discovered through the years: "A proverb a day keeps the fool at bay."

You may have noticed that a lot of the daily devotionals in *A Minute of Vision for Men* have come from the book of Proverbs. I find its thirty-one chapters very practical and applicable. It seems to be written especially for men, as it is short, pithy, memorable, and to the point. Its teaching is rich and lasting. For each day of the month, there is a chapter in Proverbs full of wisdom just for me. If today is the fourteenth day of the month, I read Proverbs 14. If tomorrow is the fifteenth, then I will read Proverbs 15.

Proverbs will challenge you in your finances, your relationships, your business practices, and your view of life and death. Open the book of Proverbs each day, and you will see, "A proverb a day keeps the fool at bay."

One who is wise is cautious and turns away from evil, but a fool is reckless and careless.
PROVERBS 14:16, ESV

Constant Innovation

When I began my job as a waiter for the Pappas Restaurant Company at Pappadeaux Seafood Kitchen, I was given a training manual that I would be tested on at each and every training shift. It was thick, and it required that I work hard and study it if I was going to succeed as a waiter. I still remember the three touchstones of the Pappas Restaurant Company: (1) superior product, (2) superior service, and (3) constant innovation.

I was reminded of this third touchstone, constant innovation, when I stayed at the Hilton Palacio del Rio on the San Antonio River Walk. This hotel's construction was completed in only 202 days in preparation for the "HemisFair," the Texas World's Exposition of 1968. The H. B. Zachry Company pioneered the modular construction, with already fully furnished rooms put in place with an elaborate crane system.

A plaque in the hotel lobby gives tribute to H. B. "Pat" Zachry by quoting his philosophy, which begins with, "I do not choose to be a common man. It is my right to be uncommon if I can. I seek opportunity—not security." It continues with words that speak of having a zeal for life and work, and for being a person who makes something of his life. I was inspired as I read it, thinking, *Here is a man, made in the image of God, who lived his life ruling, reigning, and exerting dominion. That is a life well lived.*

You, too, were made to rule, reign, and exert dominion. Genesis 1:26 states, "God said, 'Let us make human beings in our image, to be like us. They will reign over the fish in the sea, the birds in the sky, the livestock, all the wild animals on the earth, and the small animals that scurry along the ground.'"

It is a liberating day when we learn that God created us to rule, reign, and exert dominion. God, who rules, reigns, and exerts dominion, has given us the same privilege. But the key is to do it God's way.

God said, "Let us make human beings in our image, to be like us. They will reign over the fish in the sea, the birds in the sky, the livestock, all the wild animals on the earth, and the small animals that scurry along the ground."

GENESIS 1:26

Passing the Test

Have you ever wondered how you would do on the Wonderlic Cognitive Ability Test? The "Wonderlic" is given by the NFL to the incoming potential draftees as they go through all kinds of assessments in preparation for the draft. It measures aptitude for problem solving, and an average score is twenty. Ryan Fitzpatrick, a Harvard graduate, scored a forty-eight on the test, which research shows correlates with an IQ around 150. What kind of score would you get—below average, average, or above average?

Quite often in our spiritual walks, we test ourselves against others around us. We feel average or above average when someone we know is really struggling, or we feel below average when someone we know always seems to have it all together and we know we don't.

There are two problems with assessing ourselves against others. First, the standard changes all the time as people come in and out of our lives. Second, we see ourselves both as the one on trial and the judge making the ruling.

We are to be discerning about those around us, but the righteous standard that has been set for us never changes. Proverbs 17:3 states, "Fire tests the purity of silver and gold, but the LORD tests the heart."

Remember, it is the Lord who sets the standard and tests the heart. Live in light of the fact that he is the one we should please. But also know that you can't meet his standard apart from Christ. That is why we need the grace that Christ brings. Ephesians 2:8-9 declares, "God saved you by his grace when you believed. And you can't take credit for this; it is a gift from God. Salvation is not a reward for the good things we have done, so none of us can boast about it."

As you rely on his grace, ask his Spirit to be at work in you so that when you are tested, you are found to be faithful.

Fire tests the purity of silver and gold, but the LORD tests the heart.

PROVERBS 17:3

Taking Time to Laugh

Someone once said that laughter is the best medicine. That person knew intuitively what scientists have learned. Dr. Paul McGhee says, "Your sense of humor is one of the most powerful tools you have to make sure that your daily mood and your emotional state support good health. As a matter of fact laughter relaxes the whole body. It boosts the immune system; laughter triggers the release of endorphins and protects the heart."[29]

More than being good for your health, laughter is one of the best ways to keep a relationship healthy. One of the things I love to do is laugh with my family. It brings joy to me to hear them laugh a deep belly laugh. Whether it's about something that the dog does or something one of them says, we love to just laugh together.

I want to encourage you to develop a strategy for laughter. Take the family to a show, rent a comedy that the whole family can enjoy, or sit with your kids and watch *AFV*. Watching peoples' mistakes on video with a good setup and music in the background is a sure way for us to laugh together.

Proverbs 15:30 states, "A cheerful look brings joy to the heart; good news makes for good health."

Enjoy your day today, and never be so serious that you can't laugh.

A cheerful look brings joy to the heart; good news makes for good health.

PROVERBS 15:30

---

[29] "Laughter Is the Best Medicine," *Help Guide*, http://www.helpguide.org/articles/emotional -health/laughter-is-the-best-medicine.htm.

Breaking Trust

Many athletes have been disgraced because of their actions off the field or because they cheated and lied to get an edge or steal a victory. We have seen that disgrace clearly in cycling, track and field, baseball, and football. The irony in the vast majority of these scenarios is that when the athletes were confronted, they responded with lies.

During his fifth-grade year, my son Cooper had a little conflict on the playground. I asked him if he started it or if he was defending himself. I was thankful to hear him say he was defending himself. I told him then, "That is what I hoped to hear. But listen, if I find out you are lying, your punishment is going to be much worse than if you had just owned your actions."

Breaking trust is a big deal to the health of our relationships. Breaking trust is also a big deal to our Lord.

Proverbs 12:22 states, "The LORD detests lying lips, but he delights in those who tell the truth."

For some of these athletes who we felt have lied to us, we will never look at them the same. That is because you can't trust a liar. Remember, once you break trust, it is nearly impossible to get it back. Although it is painful, speak the truth and keep trust. If you have done wrong, admit it, because the consequences of being found out as a liar can be far greater than your original mistake.

The LORD detests lying lips, but he delights in those who tell the truth.

PROVERBS 12:22

The Golden Rule of Leadership

Have you heard of "The Golden Rule of Leadership"? When it comes to leading teams, Coach Lou Holtz says, "Do right. Do your best. Treat others as you want to be treated."

Unfortunately, one of the first places where kids hear adults screaming, hollering, and cutting them down is on the athletic fields. What if we coached our kids in the manner we would want to be treated? What if we did this not only with our children but also with our spouses and our employees? How much more valued would we be as leaders?

In other words, what if we actually heeded the Golden Rule? It isn't just something we learned in grade school. These are actually Jesus' words: "Do to others whatever you would like them to do to you. This is the essence of all that is taught in the law and the prophets" (Matthew 7:12).

I don't know if I have ever thought about that sentence after the Golden Rule. It declares that if you live life this way, you are living out all that God was trying to convey as he declared his character through the law and as he forecasted his love through the prophets about the coming Messiah.

I love how Jesus keeps it so simple. Let's do the same. If you want to prosper in leading a team, in your relationships and interactions with people, and in life in general, do to your fellow humans as you would have them do to you.

Do to others whatever you would like them to do to you. This is the essence of all that is taught in the law and the prophets.　　MATTHEW 7:12

There's Nothing like It

Winning a Little League championship was one of the best experiences I had while coaching my sons' baseball teams. I've only won one, but I'll never forget it. That season was machine-pitch baseball, and the boys were in second and third grade. I have a picture in my office of the moment, just after the championship game, when as a team, we gathered under the scoreboard with locked arms and big smiles on our faces. The scoreboard read, "Visitor 17, Home 12."

That season was one of ups and downs. I had some really talented players who came together at just the right time for us to go on a run. I had solid players who stepped up and contributed to keep the momentum going. But I also had a few players on that team who had significant behavioral issues, and I wasn't sure that they would get to stay on the team. My patience was tried like never before. One of the lowest episodes was when an opposing coach shot his middle finger at me and my assistant coach, in front of all the kids.

That season had drama that caused me to shake my head in frustration and disgust and say, "There's nothing like it." Then there were a few moments leading up to and including the championship where I said to myself, "You know, there's nothing like it."

It reminds me of the local church, who when sick and struggling is the least attractive of all entities on the planet. Truly, there is nothing like it. But when the church is strong and healthy and functioning as she is supposed to, I also confess, "There's nothing like it!" No church is perfect, just as no team or season is perfect. But when she is working right, it is the most beautiful entity on the earth. May we never lose sight of Ephesians 3:21, which states, "Glory to him in the church and in Christ Jesus through all generations forever and ever! Amen."

Glory to him in the church and in Christ Jesus through all generations
forever and ever! Amen.   EPHESIANS 3:21

Can I Have a Do Over?

A pastor tells the story of the shortest play ever. It opened and closed on the same day in London in 1875. On opening night, the director was disgusted with the first act and informed the audience that the play would not continue. Initially excited for the play to open, the director had ordered champagne and served the actors before the play began. Apparently a number of the cast had a few too many drinks, resulting in the horrible first act. I am sure the director wanted a do over.

If you're like me, I'm sure that there are times when you wished you had a do over. We can't undo anything we've said or done, but when we receive God's grace through faith, we receive a pardon for our sins. The Scripture calls this "justification" and describes it in Romans 3:23-25:

> Everyone has sinned; we all fall short of God's glorious standard.
> Yet God, in his grace, freely makes us right in his sight. He did
> this through Christ Jesus when he freed us from the penalty for
> our sins. For God presented Jesus as the sacrifice for sin. People
> are made right with God when they believe that Jesus sacrificed
> his life, shedding his blood.

If you have yet to put your faith in Jesus, make today the day. God's grace is our do over. Through Jesus' death on the cross, you can be forgiven for all your mistakes. Pray this prayer with me to receive Christ as your Savior:

> Heavenly Father, I need a do over. I have sinned and have fallen short
> of your standard. Please forgive me. Thank you for making me right
> in your sight, God, because I have put my faith and trust for my
> salvation in the Lord Jesus. I pray this in Jesus' name, amen.

Everyone has sinned; we all fall short of God's glorious standard. Yet God, in his grace, freely makes us right in his sight. He did this through Christ Jesus when he freed us from the penalty for our sins. For God presented Jesus as the sacrifice for sin. People are made right with God when they believe that Jesus sacrificed his life, shedding his blood. ROMANS 3:23-25

Perception vs. Reality

In his book *The One Year Uncommon Life Daily Challenge*, coach Tony Dungy says, "Perceptions don't win ball games. No team can rely on its reputation. . . . After all it may not even be accurate—perception is not the same as reality."[30]

You know, sometimes uncovering reality from our perception can take work. Coach Dungy says that to develop a good game plan for life, we need to know who we really are versus how others perceive us. We need to be rooted, not in the image of what we want to be, or who society says we should be, but in who God made us to be.

Author Brad Lomenick challenges his readers to build a habit of self-discovery into their lives. He states, "Developing a habit of self-discovery means creating intentional rhythms whereby one observes who he is, listens to his life, and strives to define himself apart from his professional assignments."[31]

Lomenick, the former leader of the "Catalyst Movement," found that he had lost his sense of identity outside his work because he didn't know how to separate himself from it. This can lead to big mistakes and bad habits.

The habit of self-discovery is something that effective leaders do on a regular basis, seeking the sense to know what is at work in their hearts. For some it looks like a weekly Sabbath, journaling about what is in their hearts and minds, and connecting with other men in authentic community. Don't let your career or others' perception of you define who you are. The psalmist in Psalm 119:73 says to God, "You made me; you created me." Be faithful to who God made you to be.

You made me; you created me. PSALM 119:73

---

[30] Tony Dungy and Nathan Whitaker, *The One Year Uncommon Life Daily Challenge* (Carol Stream, IL: Tyndale, 2011), January 12.
[31] Brad Lomenick, *H3 Leadership: Be Humble, Stay Hungry, Always Hustle* (Nashville: Nelson Books, 2015), 5.

Do They Hurt or Heal?

Did you know that one of the strongest muscles in your body is your tongue? It doesn't wear down over time and through excessive use like the other muscles in our body. We use it to speak, to drink, to chew, and some people like Michael Jordan and my younger son, Cooper, use it when they are driving to the basket.

As a strong muscle, the tongue has great power. Scripture declares that the tongue has the power to hurt and the power to heal. Proverbs 12:18 states, "Some people make cutting remarks, but the words of the wise bring healing." The English Standard Version translates verse 18 as, "There is one whose rash words are like sword thrusts."

Pastor Rick Vasquez says that his father gave him the nickname "Feo," which is Spanish for "ugly," when he was a kid. Rick said that he then tried to live up to that name. Rick lived an ugly life. He made many poor choices and ended up being incarcerated for his crimes. In jail, Rick's name was changed to "Chamuco," which means "demon," and once again, he lived up to his name. Rick was placed in solitary confinement because he was considered a threat to the prison's security staff.

The words we use set the trajectory of the lives of our children. They set the climate of our relationship with our wives. Our words will influence the quality of the contribution of those we work with make to our team.

How are your words? Are they like the thrust of the sword, piercing and damaging flesh, or are they like a salve that brings healing? You get to choose whether your words will hurt or heal. Let's use our words to heal.

Some people make cutting remarks, but the words of the wise bring healing.
PROVERBS 12:18

When a Bully Pokes You in the Chest

Have you ever been bullied? I would assume that as kids we all experienced a bit of bullying. But what about as adults? As an adult, I have experienced times of being poked in the chest—times when someone tried to push me around or spoke falsely about me in public in order to get his or her way.

When people try to use pressure to oppress you so that they can have their way, what should you do? For many of us, our first instinct is to react out of anger and set things right by fighting back.

But if we are not careful, it can only get us into greater trouble. You see, reacting to bullying is being like the second guy throwing a punch on the field. The referees never see the first violation. They only see the reaction, and that's when the yellow flag comes out.

Scripture gives us another way when someone pushes us around:

> Dear friends, never take revenge. Leave that to the righteous anger of God. For the Scriptures say, "I will take revenge; I will pay them back," says the LORD. Instead, "If your enemies are hungry, feed them. If they are thirsty, give them something to drink. In doing this, you will heap burning coals of shame on their heads." Don't let evil conquer you, but conquer evil by doing good. (Romans 12:19-21)

This is a hard ethic, I know. But the call of the Lord is to conquer evil with good. When we make this tough choice to bless those who curse us, we will resemble Christ the most.

Don't let evil conquer you, but conquer evil by doing good.   ROMANS 12:21

The Ministry of Presence

Have you ever been around someone suffering, and you didn't know what to say? It happens to pastors a lot, as we walk into hospital rooms or intensive care units, or worse, meet with families for funeral preparation. As I prepare people for the viewing and funeral, I often tell them that they need to come to the service with grace in their hearts for what people will say. You see, we aren't terribly comfortable with those who are suffering or grieving, so sometimes, in our discomfort, we will say things that are awkward, rude, or not theologically sound. I have heard some grieving people say, "Yeah, someone told me that if I had more faith, he wouldn't have died." What a tragedy!

As a pastor, I have learned the importance of what is called the ministry of presence. It isn't terribly vocal, and it isn't always looking for the right words to say. As a matter of fact, more often than not, the ministry of presence is absolutely silent. It is simply being present. When someone is suffering in a deep way, your presence will do more good than your words.

You see, your presence communicates to that person that he or she is a priority to you. Your presence declares you care. Your simple presence at that person's side during a time of loss or grief communicates that he or she is not alone.

Notice the example of the ministry of presence in Job 2:11 and 13: "When three of Job's friends heard of the tragedy he had suffered, they got together and traveled from their homes to comfort and console him. . . . Then they sat on the ground with him for seven days and nights. No one said a word to Job, for they saw that his suffering was too great for words."

Don't force the words when you don't know what to say. Be present, and be confident that your presence is enough.

When three of Job's friends heard of the tragedy he had suffered, they got together and traveled from their homes to comfort and console him. . . . Then they sat on the ground with him for seven days and nights. No one said a word to Job, for they saw that his suffering was too great for words.

JOB 2:11, 13

Choose Your Coach

Hall of Fame Coach Tom Landry once said, "A coach is someone who tells you what you don't want to hear, who has you see what you don't want to see, so you can be who you have always known you could be." You don't always get to choose your coach in athletics. As a matter of fact, it is usually the other way around.

Yet in our spiritual walks, Scripture challenges us to choose wisdom as our coach. Proverbs 8 is an invitation to join wisdom's team. From verse four to verse thirty-six, wisdom is personified as a woman speaking in the first person, essentially extending a personal invitation to learn from her.

Wisdom will tell you what you don't want to hear and help you see what you don't want to see, so you can become the man you want to be. Here is her invitation:

> My children, listen to me, for all who follow my ways are joyful. Listen to my instruction and be wise. Don't ignore it. Joyful are those who listen to me, watching for me daily at my gates, waiting for me outside my home! (Proverbs 8:32-34)

There is so much in Proverbs 8 I would love to share with you. But the best thing I could say today is to go and read the rest of the chapter with this thought in mind: choose your coach by choosing the very wisdom of God.

My children, listen to me, for all who follow my ways are joyful. Listen to my instruction and be wise. Don't ignore it. Joyful are those who listen to me, watching for me daily at my gates, waiting for me outside my home!

PROVERBS 8:32-34

Sidelined because of Injury

At rookie minicamp, Dante Fowler Jr., the number-three overall draft pick in the 2015 NFL draft, tore his ACL in his very first practice. How devastating it could have been for him, his team, and his financial future! You see, he didn't yet have a contract with the Jacksonville Jaguars but instead had an agreement of a contract range if he were to get injured before signing.

Life can be so unpredictable, can't it? We like to think that we are in control. We feel as if we can dictate all that will take place in our lives, so we work hard for our future. We should be working hard for our future, but we must recognize our limits, because none of us knows what tomorrow holds.

As a matter of fact, there are so many reminders of our lack of control that we would be wise to look to the Lord of all and yield our spirit of control to him. In Matthew 6:25 and 33, Jesus said, "That is why I tell you not to worry about everyday life—whether you have enough food and drink, or enough clothes to wear. Isn't life more than food, and your body more than clothing? . . . Seek the Kingdom of God above all else, and live righteously, and he will give you everything you need."

Our life is a journey as stewards. I want to challenge you as a fellow steward of talent that God has bestowed upon us, to trust the Lord for your future and steward well what is before you. Go give it your best today, and trust that he is in control.

That is why I tell you not to worry about everyday life—whether you have enough food and drink, or enough clothes to wear. Isn't life more than food, and your body more than clothing? . . . Seek the Kingdom of God above all else, and live righteously, and he will give you everything you need.

MATTHEW 6:25, 33

The Emptiness of Importance

Have you ever heard of Peyton Manning or Tim Tebow? These men have experienced both the thrill of celebrity and the crush of defeat. In the book *The Jersey Effect*, Hunter Smith and Darrin Gray help us understand just how empty being important can be. Their fundamental assertion is that we live in a day where people are cultivated based on how well they perform, making them feel important.

But as Smith and Gray state, "Everything that man accomplishes can easily be undone. Peyton Manning, arguably the best quarterback to play the game—cut. Tim Tebow, the best thing that happened to Denver in 2011 . . . traded and forgotten."[32]

Knowing your value, outside of what you do, can be a powerful and liberating experience. True worth of the individual is given to us by God. The Declaration of Independence proclaims, "We hold these truths to be self-evident, that all men are created equal, that they are endowed by their Creator with certain unalienable Rights, that among these are Life, Liberty and the pursuit of Happiness."

We often allow the pursuit of happiness to lead us to decide what we will do with our lives. We derive so much importance from our success. But the biblical perspective is that we were made for life and liberty in a relationship with Christ. This leads to our happiness. The Bible declares our importance to God by showing us how much we are really worth to him.

John 3:16 tells us, "This is how God loved the world: He gave his one and only Son, so that everyone who believes in him will not perish but have eternal life." Don't let success define your importance. Let your importance be defined by the one who sent his only son to stand in your place.

This is how God loved the world: He gave his one and only Son, so that everyone who believes in him will not perish but have eternal life. JOHN 3:16

---

[32] Hunter Smith and Darrin Gray, *The Jersey Effect*, with Stephen Copeland and Ken Turner (Bloomington, IN: WestBow Press, 2012), 18.

Frustrated? Look in the Mirror

The great slugger Ted Williams once said, "There has always been a saying in baseball that you can't make a hitter, but I think you can improve a hitter. More than you can improve a fielder. More mistakes are made hitting than in any other part of the game."

When a hitter begins to make mistakes, it often leads to a hitting slump. Slumps are frustrating—for the player, the team, and the fans. Lengthy slumps can get players sent down to the minor leagues to work out the kinks and get reestablished.

In moments of frustration, we usually have negative reactions. But if we are self-aware and take inventory of our thoughts, words, or actions, we often will see that a small, simple adjustment in those thoughts, words, or actions can make all the difference in the world. You see, if we allow it to, frustration can serve as a mirror that shows us the truth of our ways, bringing us understanding. When we slow down and ask why, we can get to the truth.

Proverbs 3:13 states, "Joyful is the person who finds wisdom, the one who gains understanding."

When we see why we are frustrated with our jobs, our finances, or our relationships, it can cause us to see clearly the path forward to bring about the change necessary for our lives. So if you are frustrated, know that your frustration can be a powerful force. Use it for good by asking God to show you the best way forward. When you are frustrated, look in the mirror.

Joyful is the person who finds wisdom, the one who gains understanding.
PROVERBS 3:13

Blisters and Forgiveness

Toward the end of her kindergarten year, there was a day when my daughter, Carson, failed to put on her socks with her shoes. By the time we got to her school, her shoes had irritated the blister on her small toe, which had come from wearing her new church sandals earlier that week.

After dropping Carson off at school, I told her I would bring her socks to her. I got home, picked up a pair of socks, put them in a bag with her name and the teacher's name on it, set the bag down, and left it there the rest of the day.

When I picked up my daughter from school that afternoon, I realized my error. I was disappointed in myself because I knew I had disappointed her. I said, "Carson, I am so sorry. I set them aside. I just didn't leave the house with them." Do you know what this mature little girl said to me?

She said, "That's okay. I forgive you, Daddy." What a blessing to hear!

Colossians 3:13 states, "Make allowance for each other's faults, and forgive anyone who offends you. Remember, the Lord forgave you, so you must forgive others." We need to hear "I forgive you" when we disappoint someone else. We also need to say those words to others who have disappointed us. There is power in your words, and when you receive and extend the words of forgiveness, the sting of the blister subsides.

Make allowance for each other's faults, and forgive anyone who offends you. Remember, the Lord forgave you, so you must forgive others. COLOSSIANS 3:13

Peace That Passes Understanding

I once had a chance to have dinner with author, speaker, and former US Army ranger Major Jeff Struecker when he spoke at a fund-raising event for our church's clinic, Casa El Buen Samaritano, which serves the most impoverished of the southwest part of our city with world-class healthcare. There are few people I respect more than Jeff Struecker.

You see, Major Struecker fought in the Battle of Mogadishu, and the book and movie *Black Hawk Down* are based off his and three others' firsthand testimonies. He has an amazing story, as you may already know if you have read the book or seen the movie.[33]

One of the things Jeff said during our conversation that really stuck with me was, "Although men were dying all around me, and though I was in the fight of my life—gun fights that were happening ten feet from me, I felt a remarkable peace because of God's presence with me." He said, "The Scripture calls it the peace that passes all understanding."

That's quite a thought—to be in a life-or-death situation and yet feel peace because you know the presence of Almighty God is with you.

Psalm 23:4 says, "Even when I walk through the darkest valley, I will not be afraid, for you are close beside me. Your rod and your staff protect and comfort me." Is there a valley you are walking through that is covered in shadows and causing you to fear? I want to encourage you to look up, trust in the presence and the power of the God who created you and loves you, and enjoy his peace that passes understanding.

Even when I walk through the darkest valley, I will not be afraid, for you are close beside me. Your rod and your staff protect and comfort me.

PSALM 23:4

---

[33] To hear his full firsthand account of the story, you can read Jeff's book *The Road to Unafraid*.

JUNE

From Coach to Consultant

Dad, have you ever felt you might be in the way of your kids? It was a tough day when I realized I needed to take a step back from being the play-calling influencer that I normally am to being a sideline observer. It was a difficult realization, but one that I had to come to if my oldest son was going to stand on his own.

That is the aim for our children, isn't it? Isn't it our desire for our kids to become the men and women who are able to stand on their own two feet?

For that to happen for my son Brady, I had to stop being the coach all the time, and I had to shift to the consulting role. I am still present and am still challenging him, but I am also mindful that I am no longer calling all of the plays. Notice I used the word *all*. I still call some of the plays, but as he gets older, it will be less and less.

By the time he leaves my house, I need him to be able to call his own plays. My hope, and my job going forward, is to make sure he knows who to listen to. The best thing I know to do is point him to the Lord, because that is where he will find the wisdom and knowledge that he needs.

Proverbs 1:7 says, "Fear of the LORD is the foundation of true knowledge, but fools despise wisdom and discipline." If you are shifting from the role of coach to consultant, point your son or daughter to the Lord for the insight that he or she is going to need.

Fear of the LORD is the foundation of true knowledge, but fools despise wisdom and discipline.   PROVERBS 1:7

Fundamentals Are Fun

My son Cooper is a huge Houston Rockets fan. He even has James Harden and Hakeem Olajuwon socks—the kind where the player's likeness is printed on them. When Cooper had the chance to go to a Rockets summer basketball camp, he asked me, "Dad, what do you think we will cover at the Rockets camp?"

I quickly replied, "Fundamentals." He then said, "Those aren't fun." I said, "Maybe so, but they lead to fun."

Like Coop, many people believe that the fundamentals aren't all that fun, and rehearsing them over and over seems to be drudgery. But in all disciplines, including relationships, when things break down, it is because the fundamentals have been abandoned. When you step back and examine the situation, it becomes clear that everything seems to work its way back to fundamentals.

The most fundamental aspect of the Christian faith is love. First Corinthians 13:7-8 states, "Love never gives up, never loses faith, is always hopeful, and endures through every circumstance. Prophecy and speaking in unknown languages and special knowledge will become useless. But love will last forever!"

As a result, I try to start every day with an action of love toward my wife and children. I find that when the smallest, simplest, most rudimentary action, like making my wife a cup of coffee, is practiced, it sets the tone for the entire house. Then I can truly say, "Fundamentals really are fun."

Love never gives up, never loses faith, is always hopeful, and endures through every circumstance. Prophecy and speaking in unknown languages and special knowledge will become useless. But love will last forever!
1 CORINTHIANS 13:7-8

My Favorite Coffee Mug

I love a good cup of coffee. I especially love a good cup of coffee at a nice restaurant after a good meal. There is a richness to the drink that I truly enjoy. At various times through my years of drinking coffee, I have adopted favorite coffee mugs.

One of my favorite mugs at home was cracked. It was a nice, everyday pattern that somehow splintered but never fell apart. As Sunday morning would roll around, I would intentionally use this mug before preaching, reminding myself that I am just a cracked vessel and praying that God would use me.

Then I bought a mug on vacation from Seaside, Florida, that simply says, "Seaside." What a glorious place! When I drink out of that mug, I remember the great times we had on that family vacation, my long runs at the beach, and the beauty of the Emerald Coast.

For Father's Day one year, Brady got me an extra-large coffee mug that reads, "My Dad Is a Big Deal." Being funny, he taped over some of it so that when I opened it, it would read, "My Dad Is Big." Considering I'm six feet five inches and over 250 pounds, he thought he was being hilarious.

But my favorite mug of all time is one I have to wash by hand. My daughter, Carson, who loves to do artwork, went to a pottery store and decorated it for my birthday when she was five or six years old. The mug reads, "I (heart) Dad." It is blue with yellow dots, the words on it are raised off the side of the mug, and the heart is colored red. On the bottom is her handwritten name. It is a treasure that I hope I will never break or lose.

Ecclesiastes 3:12-13 states, "I concluded there is nothing better than to be happy and enjoy ourselves as long as we can. And people should eat and drink and enjoy the fruits of their labor, for these are gifts from God." I am trying to appreciate the simple things, like coffee mugs, a bit more, seeing them as gifts from God.

I concluded there is nothing better than to be happy and enjoy ourselves as long as we can. And people should eat and drink and enjoy the fruits of their labor, for these are gifts from God. ECCLESIASTES 3:12-13

A Quiet Impact

In today's culture, awards mean a lot. So much of what we do is in order to get accolades and praise from friends, coworkers, family members, or even people we do not know. During his years in college, Tim Tebow received practically every award that a football player can get. While helping him move out of his apartment, Tim's dad peeked in a box that was full of trophies and awards that he knew nothing about. Not only were the awards not displayed in Tim's apartment, but his parents were often surprised by the people who would call and tell them that they had received a call or a visit from Tim.

His father noted, "To Tim it is not about the fanfare. He genuinely cares about people. He keeps those things private because it's not about the accolades."

When I hear this story, I am reminded of Matthew 6:1, which says, "Watch out! Don't do your good deeds publicly, to be admired by others, for you will lose the reward from your Father in heaven." When you do the good God has put in your heart to do, don't do it for recognition by others, because their praise is empty. Do it for the recognition of your Father in heaven. He'll be sure to reward you, and that reward will last for all eternity.

What good will you do today? Is there someone at your office who is going through a hard time? Is there a homeless person in your community whom you see often but have failed to think about helping? Consider being a blessing to others, but keep it between you and the Lord.

Watch out! Don't do your good deeds publicly, to be admired by others, for you will lose the reward from your Father in heaven. MATTHEW 6:1

Either Way, You Are Going to Pay

It seems hard to believe, but nothing of value in life is free. As a matter of fact, if someone helped you and footed the entire bill, chances are you wouldn't appreciate it like you would if you had some of your own skin in the game.

One of the most challenging lessons for young athletes to grasp is the need to pay the price to improve in the off-season. Some off-season programs are quite regimented, while others are fairly relaxed. The players who embrace a challenging off-season see significant improvement because they pay the price a little bit every day. This is the pain of discipline.

Other players, who assume that all is well and unchanged, often stroll into the off-season lacking discipline, focus, and effort. As a result, when camp rolls around, they are unprepared for what lies ahead. Their pain level is intense because they are both physically and emotionally unready for what they are experiencing. Because they chose to play instead of pay, they come to the new season in debt, unable to keep up with the progress that others have made. As a result, much of the game passes them by and keeps them on the sidelines. This is the pain of disappointment.

There is a pain associated with making right choices and a pain associated with wrong ones. Proverbs 2:21-22 states, "For only the godly will live in the land, and those with integrity will remain in it. But the wicked will be removed from the land, and the treacherous will be uprooted."

Choose your pain—discipline or disappointment. Remember, you can pay now or pay later, but either way, you are going to pay.

Only the godly will live in the land, and those with integrity will remain in it. But the wicked will be removed from the land, and the treacherous will be uprooted.

PROVERBS 2:21-22

Serving in the Box, PART I

One look at a tennis court, and the boundaries are obvious. You must serve into the small, square box in order to even begin play. You must stay inside the narrow lines to play singles; you must stay inside the outside lines to play doubles. Even though anything touching a line is fair, anything outside the line, no matter how minute in distance, is out—a fault.

God has given us a similar framework for our lives—his commandments. When you stay within the lines, you are in fair ground. Journey outside of them, and it's a fault. Our Father has even provided our own "Hawk-Eye" system that alerts us when we are out of bounds—the Holy Spirit. We, too, can know when we are even one millimeter outside of the boundaries he has set for us, if we attend to the voice of this ever-present guide.

Joshua 22:5 states, "Be very careful to obey all the commands and the instructions that Moses gave to you. Love the LORD your God, walk in all his ways, obey his commands, hold firmly to him, and serve him with all your heart and all your soul."

Stay within the lines, and enjoy playing this game of life. Listen to the voice of the Holy Spirit, so that when you fault, you can quickly confess it and resume play.[34]

Be very careful to obey all the commands and the instructions that Moses gave to you. Love the LORD your God, walk in all his ways, obey his commands, hold firmly to him, and serve him with all your heart and all your soul.

JOSHUA 22:5

---

[34] Today's devotional was written by Jan Whitehead, the mother of professional golfer Michael Whitehead and NCAA tennis coach Daniel Whitehead.

JUNE 7

Serving in the Box, PART II

The game of tennis has strict, unbending lines that signify what is in and out of bounds. Outside the line, there is no forgiveness or appeal, no chance for success. But inside the lines, great freedom exists.

Variety in the game of tennis is critical. The service game includes big serves up the tee, serves out wide, kick serves, and off-speed serves. Great tennis matches include the serve and volley, baseline play, playing the net, and drop shots, as well as overhead slams and lobs. No player has the same game or strategy as the next. This is part of the excitement and beauty of the game of tennis.

It is so, also, with the body of Christians. While God calls us all to live within the lines, he calls us all to life in the body that is unique to us. The variety of the talents and calls given to God's saints is part of the excitement and beauty of this Christian life.

First Corinthians 12:4-7 states, "There are different kinds of spiritual gifts, but the same Spirit is the source of them all. There are different kinds of service, but we serve the same Lord. God works in different ways, but it is the same God who does the work in all of us. A spiritual gift is given to each of us so we can help each other."

Let us celebrate the different styles of "serves" that our brothers and sisters exercise. Let us support the "net play" as well as the "baseline game" in our journey together. Let us develop our own style of play based on the talents and calls God places on us, and allow the body around us to do the same. Let us enjoy the spiritual gifts bestowed to all for the common good![35]

There are different kinds of spiritual gifts, but the same Spirit is the source of them all. There are different kinds of service, but we serve the same Lord. God works in different ways, but it is the same God who does the work in all of us. A spiritual gift is given to each of us so we can help each other.

1 CORINTHIANS 12:4-7

---

[35] Today's devotional was written by Jan Whitehead, the mother of professional golfer Michael Whitehead and NCAA tennis coach Daniel Whitehead.

The Jaguar That Ate the Crocodile

While I was checking my Facebook account one day, I came across a cool video of a jaguar pulling a crocodile out of a river. The jaguar was crouching over the water on the edge of a rock. The next thing you know, the jaguar jumps into the murky water below the surface, brings up a crocodile, and hauls it off for a meal. Immediately following that video, I watched a house cat stare down an alligator and make it go running. Immediately after that, in another video, I heard the bleating of a deer and saw it struggling to escape the death grip of a grizzly bear. Yeah, that last one I could have done without. You can see some crazy videos on Facebook!

How often do you want to click on that "viral video" just to see some street brawl, to hear about the latest celebrity scandal, or to watch nature take its course when a bear eats a deer for dinner? There is something captivating about it that causes us to wonder, *Why did I want to watch that?*

Gossip has the same effect on us. Unverified accusations about a friend, coworker, or family member have an initial appeal that we can't escape. Proverbs 18:8 says, "Rumors are dainty morsels that sink deep into one's heart." But after a while we wonder why we were so engrossed in the story, realizing we would have been better off had we ignored the mess entirely. Scripture challenges us to avoid gossip and the gossiper. Proverbs 20:19 states, "A gossip goes around telling secrets, so don't hang around with chatterers."

A gossip goes around telling secrets, so don't hang around with chatterers.

PROVERBS 20:19

Abundant Crops Are Messy

St. Josemaria Escriva said, "Jesus did not say you would not be troubled, you would not be tempted, you would not be distressed, but he did say you would not be overcome."

The year 2014 was one of great abundance in my work, yet with that abundance came times when I felt overcome. I wasn't, but it sure did feel that way. One of the challenges I faced that year was the fact that demands on my time had increased. I knew how to manage the church to see our needs met, and that took work. But when being part of a significant harvest started to feel really messy to me, I began to rethink how I was using my time, as abundance created its own set of opportunities, challenges, and responsibilities.

Proverbs 14:4 says, "Without oxen a stable stays clean, but you need a strong ox for a large harvest." This word tells me that it gets messy when you are successful. It tells me it can flat out stink sometimes. But I have got to be willing to deal with the ox if I want the harvest. The truth is, the mess is what helps produce the harvest.

So here is my prayer: "Thank you, Father, for the way you bring in your harvest. Your Word tells me it is worth the extra work." I hope in your life you are willing to work through the mess and the overwhelming circumstances to see the blessing and abundance on the other side.

Without oxen a stable stays clean, but you need a strong ox for a large harvest.
PROVERBS 14:4

The Legacy of the Father

Have you ever used the expression "Like father, like son"? It speaks to the various qualities that sons pick up from their fathers. Ken Norton Jr. picked up his athletic ability from his father, former heavyweight champion Ken Norton Sr. These two men had an unbreakable bond, as Norton Sr. raised his son through some very difficult and hard times, all on his own. Norton Jr. played linebacker at UCLA and then played a number of years in the NFL.

Their split from one another became a big surprise to many in the media and to those who knew them well. Norton Jr.'s high school football coach, who had always admired the father that Norton Sr. was to his son, couldn't fathom a scenario that would drive the two apart. After a few years of estrangement, they reconciled because Angela, the wife of the former NFL linebacker, took it upon herself to bring the two proud and stubborn heavyweights together.

What attributes did you pick up from your father? It is probably a mix of his strengths and his weaknesses. Even if you didn't know him, you may carry his name and nature. As followers of Christ, we have a heavenly Father who has put his name and nature on us. As a result, we are to seek to live in a way that is pleasing to him. Ephesians 5:1 challenges us with these words: "Imitate God, therefore, in everything you do, because you are his dear children." May it be said of us, in relationship to our heavenly Father, "Like Father, like son!"

Imitate God, therefore, in everything you do, because you are his dear children.
EPHESIANS 5:1

The Action after the Action

Has your temper ever caused you to act like a fool? I bet every single one of us can relate to being hotheaded. In the 2014 NBA play-offs, Indiana Pacer Lance Stephenson did everything he could to get into LeBron James's head. He even went so far as to blow in his ear, trying to elicit a foolish response. James kept his emotions intact, and he and his Heat continued to dominate the Pacers to make it to the NBA finals. After the game, when James was asked what he thought about Stephenson's tactics, he said, "I'm just here to play basketball. . . . I don't get into all of the extracurricular activities."

It is easy to see a foolish reaction from a quick temper on the football field or basketball court. All you have to do is watch the action after the action. This extra action is the quick-tempered response that causes an entire team to be penalized because one of their players couldn't handle his emotions.

Proverbs 14:17 says, "Short-tempered people do foolish things." There are so many opportunities to lose your temper. Whether you are sitting in traffic and someone cuts you off, or you are disappointed by a friend or family member, it is easy to do and say things that you regret. Do you have control of your temper? If you don't, rest assured that those on your team—your family, church, or coworkers—will also be penalized when you act like a fool.

Short-tempered people do foolish things.   PROVERBS 14:17

Bacon-Wrapped Jalapeños

Just saying "bacon-wrapped jalapeños" takes you to a good place, doesn't it? It may remind you of a tailgate party or of a special appetizer served at a gathering of friends. It isn't every day that I get to enjoy this amazing man-food!

Instead, most days are filled with a good bit of effort, work, and obligation. The demands of this fast-paced world can take the sense of joy right out of you. But today, when I wrote this, those amazing bacon-wrapped jalapeños I ate brought back the joy.

Have you hit a wall recently? Have you wondered if there has got to be more than this? You can spend only so much time in the rat race before you get discouraged. When we get too extended, it is easy to disappoint those we care about the most.

I want to remind you to make sure you rest. Make sure you take a Sabbath break each week. Set aside time to worship, relax, and renew relationships. By setting this time aside, you are taking a stand against overscheduling yourself. This is your time to rest and enjoy what you have been blessed with. First Timothy 6:17 states, "Teach those who are rich in this world not to be proud and not to trust in their money, which is so unreliable. Their trust should be in God, who richly gives us all we need for our enjoyment." What God has given to you is for your enjoyment. Slow down, put some bacon-wrapped jalapeños in the oven, and enjoy the blessings of the Lord.

Teach those who are rich in this world not to be proud and not to trust in their money, which is so unreliable. Their trust should be in God, who richly gives us all we need for our enjoyment.   1 TIMOTHY 6:17

Setting and Achieving Goals

The number of people who lack a strong sense of purpose is astounding. They have few goals and no plan of execution for the ones they do have. Jim Rohn said, "Discipline is the bridge between goals and accomplishment."

Goals are a natural part of our growth process. They help us stay focused, give us a sense of accomplishment, and help give us direction in life.

There are a few things to consider when it comes to setting and achieving goals. One, make sure your goals align with God's purpose for your life. Two, know that all goals come with the possibility of failure. It is here that we ask God for faith to live without fear and to move us to the next level. As we take these steps, we will start to see the plans God has for us come about. The third thing I know is that accomplishing anything of significance takes longer to achieve and requires more effort than was ever estimated. Accomplishing something great takes tenacity as well as talent.

But here is an encouraging word for you about the details of your life and the goals that you have that will honor God. Psalm 37:23 states, "The LORD directs the steps of the godly. He delights in every detail of their lives."

If we are trusting God with our goals, he promises to make our steps firm. As a matter of fact, seeing us rule, reign, and exert dominion in his image brings him great delight. Keep at that goal you've set, and do it for the glory of God.

The LORD directs the steps of the godly. He delights in every detail of their lives.   PSALM 37:23

Disappointing Losses

Baseball great Connie Mack once said, "You can't win them all." Mack knew that if he was going to be successful in baseball, he had to learn to deal with disappointment and loss. Losing stinks. Not getting what you want when you want it after working so hard to get it feels even worse. But losing is unavoidable. If you are going to be successful in life, you must develop a plan for handling disappointment.

Here are three tips to help you when you face the disappointment of losing:

1. Keep fighting. Don't quit on yourself, your family, or your team. Those who quit fail every time. If you keep fighting, the tide may turn.
2. Learn all you can from your loss, and find ways to correct your course. This will help you prepare for the next opportunity to help your family, team, or company get a win. Learning from the disappointment of a loss is paramount if you are going to make progress personally and professionally.
3. Stay ready by guarding your heart. In other words, keep discouragement at bay. Discouragement settles in as depression if you let it linger. Take your discouragement to the Lord, and put it on him.

Galatians 6:9 states, "Let's not get tired of doing what is good. At just the right time we will reap a harvest of blessing if we don't give up." Keep doing good, and prepare for the harvest. Giving up doesn't produce a crop.

Let's not get tired of doing what is good. At just the right time we will reap a harvest of blessing if we don't give up.　　　　　GALATIANS 6:9

The Summer of Responsibility

Legendary Hall of Fame coach Tom Landry once said, "The secret to winning is constant, consistent management." This principle applies in leadership, in business, in marriage, and in parenting.

That is why we designated one summer as the "Summer of Responsibility." We have been teaching our kids responsibility all through their lives. But in this particular summer, we upped our management, set clear expectations, and stayed on top of our kids to take their responsibility to the next level. From washing the dishes and taking out the trash to reading and exercising before playing video games, they were learning that it takes discipline to set yourself apart.

Do you know what we found? We didn't find rebellion, frustration, or too many arguments. We found that our kids embraced the discipline. With a clear schedule, timeline, and reward, along with labeling the season "The Summer of Responsibility," the kids rose to the occasion and embraced the discipline. One friend told me, "People are looking for clear leadership, and this applies to our kids as well." Looking back, I now wish I would have called it "The Summer and Fall and Winter and Spring of Responsibility."

Proverbs 10:5 states, "He who gathers in summer is a prudent son, but he who sleeps in harvest is a son who brings shame" (ESV). The summer months are a great time to rest, slow down, and get a vacation. The season is also a great time to teach our kids about working hard and utilizing the time off from school to take responsibility for themselves. I would encourage you to build a theme around each summer. Be consistent, clear, and fun. When you do, your kids will rise to the occasion.

He who gathers in summer is a prudent son, but he who sleeps in harvest is a son who brings shame. **PROVERBS 10:5, ESV**

The Greatest Gift a Father Can Give

Jim Valvano, the national champion head basketball coach from North Carolina State, once said, "My father gave me the greatest gift anyone could give another person: he believed in me."

I think that is the greatest thing my dad ever did for me as well. I remember that when I was a kid, he would put me to bed, and we would say my prayers. After praying, he would tell me, "Roger, you can do anything you want to in this life. Just make sure you ask God what he wants you to do, then go do that."

It is a powerful thing for young children to hear from their fathers that they can do anything they put their minds to. Let's release the potential of our children by truly believing in them and letting them know it. Do you need an example of how to do it? Look to the eternal Father who spoke a blessing to the eternal Son.

Matthew 3:16-17 states, "After his baptism, as Jesus came up out of the water, the heavens were opened and he saw the Spirit of God descending like a dove and settling on him. And a voice from heaven said, 'This is my dearly loved Son, who brings me great joy.'"

Do you hear the blessing of the heavenly Father? At this big moment in Jesus' life, the Father publicly declares his love.

Now think about this. If the eternal Father chose to bless the eternal Son with his words, how much more should we as earthly fathers do the same for our children?

If you didn't have a dad who spoke these gifts into your life, look to your heavenly Father. He thinks so highly of you that he would place his Son on the cross to pay for your sins. When you realize how much the heavenly Father believes in you, anything is possible.

After his baptism, as Jesus came up out of the water, the heavens were opened and he saw the Spirit of God descending like a dove and settling on him. And a voice from heaven said, "This is my dearly loved Son, who brings me great joy."
MATTHEW 3:16-17

Trust . . . Walk . . . Learn

Ropes courses are a trip. High-ropes courses are designed to get you up in the air on top of a telephone pole, harnessed and secured by a cable, doing things you would never do on your own to learn something about yourself and your team.

I remember the first time I did a high-ropes course. I thought I was going to fall to my death. I then thought that there was no way humanly possible I could walk from the top of one telephone pole to another a few feet away, twenty or more feet in the air. But once you step out on the rope and complete the station, you are amazed by your abilities, humbled by your team's faith in you, and thankful for making it safely across.

Sometimes life puts us up high on a telephone pole with a large number of people surrounding us, looking up to see what we will do and how we will respond. Here, in this place, we must learn to trust, walk, and learn.

- Trust the promises of Scripture. Proverbs 11:23 says, "The desire of the righteous ends only in good" (ESV).
- Walk by faith. Hebrews 10:39 states, "But we are not of those who shrink back and are destroyed, but of those who have faith and preserve their souls" (ESV).
- Learn that God has a plan. Proverbs 16:9 says, "The heart of man plans his way, but the LORD establishes his steps" (ESV).

When you trust, walk, and learn, you will be amazed by God's abilities, humbled by his faith in you, and thankful for his protection in the midst of difficult circumstances.

The heart of man plans his way, but the LORD establishes his steps.

PROVERBS 16:9, ESV

Bringing Your Best

Watching athletes in their prime is spectacular. When they have been injured and yet continue to perform at a high level through the pain, it is almost miraculous. There is something special about seeing them at their best.

Do you remember when you had the most satisfaction in your work? How about in your relationships? Do you recall what it felt like to possess victory even after tremendous adversity? I bet you got a sense of real satisfaction after you brought your best to the table.

President Theodore Roosevelt once said, "Do what you can, where you are, with what you have." That's great stewardship. President Roosevelt was challenging us to bring our best to each and every day of our lives.

In athletics, a coach will say, "Leave it all on the field" or "Give it everything you've got." In the story of Cain and Abel, "Abel also brought a gift—the best portions of the firstborn lambs from his flock. The LORD accepted Abel and his gift" (Genesis 4:4). Cain's gift was rejected, but Abel's was accepted because he brought his best. You see, God wants nothing less than our best.

So before you call that divorce attorney, give your marriage your best. Before you publish your résumé, give your work all you've got. Before you quit again on that weight-loss plan, take another step onto that treadmill. Bring your best and live with the satisfaction that you did what you could, where you were, with what you had.

Abel also brought a gift—the best portions of the firstborn lambs from his flock. The LORD accepted Abel and his gift.　　　　　　　　GENESIS 4:4

In the Front of the Line

Did you know you are in the front of a line? In an episode of his weekly audio challenge, "Monday Morning Cup of Inspiration," Dr. Kevin Elko challenged his listeners to consider this metaphor. He stated, "If the world were represented metaphorically, and one hundred people stood for the entire population of the world with the most blessed at the front of the line, and the ones starving to death and not making it through the day in the back of the line, everyone hearing this message would be at the very front of the line, probably even first."

Elko went on to challenge his listeners to do something with what they have been given. The apostle Paul does the very same thing in his letter to the Ephesians.

Fundamental to the Christian life is the calling to live our lives with purpose, because God has placed us here on the earth with a purpose. The apostle told the believers in Ephesus, "We are God's masterpiece. He has created us anew in Christ Jesus, so we can do the good things he planned for us long ago" (Ephesians 2:10). It is safe to conclude that we have not been saved to sit, but saved to serve.

So what are you doing with your prestigious position in the front of the line? Unfortunately, many people found at the front of the line are found complaining. Yet, as Elko said, "We should all realize that we should stop complaining, because God put us in the front of the line to take care of the back of the line." Now that's living with real purpose.

We are God's masterpiece. He has created us anew in Christ Jesus, so we can do the good things he planned for us long ago. **EPHESIANS 2:10**

The Multi-Generational All-Pro Dad

In a text conversation with my friend Darrin Gray, one of the leaders at All Pro Dad, I praised him for living out what he and his entire organization embody. You see, Darrin was taking his son Zach on a special trip for his thirteenth birthday. On that trip he was going to share with Zach some big ideas about being a man, being responsible, and being accountable.

When a boy reaches thirteen, something happens in his father's heart. It is then that a father realizes his time with his children is short and it's time to impart crucial life lessons. When I wrote the book *Thirteen Going on Eighteen: Becoming a Man of Influence* for my oldest son, Brady, I saw the clock ticking and knew that my time with him was limited. I always wanted him to have my words.

I haven't met Darrin's dad and don't know his story, but I sent Darrin this text message before they departed: "Look at Proverbs 23:24 today. I trust your dad is happy today as you are cultivating wisdom in the life of your son. #Allprodad."

Listen to the multigenerational impact of being an all-pro dad. Proverbs 23:24 states, "The father of godly children has cause for joy. What a pleasure to have children who are wise." This verse doesn't necessarily convey three generations rejoicing at the same time, but allow me to make an assumption for a minute. I assume that there is joy in the grandfather who sees his son being wise by seeking to pour wisdom and truth into his children.

The father of godly children has cause for joy. What a pleasure to have children who are wise. **PROVERBS 23:24**

Pulling into the Pits

NASCAR driver Brad Keselowski made headlines in the summer of 2015 when he pulled in for a pit stop on lap 58 of a 160-lap race at Pocono Raceway. As Keselowski approached his crew, his brakes locked, and he collided with a few of his crew members. Fortunately, no one was seriously injured. Keselowski also suffered a penalty because of a sprawling tire that halted the race, but his team was so proficient that he was able to overcome this setback and finish the race in second place.

As a husband or father, a lot is expected of you—work, coaching your children's teams, honey-dos around the house. . . . Life is demanding and has a way of taking from you on a daily basis, unless, of course, you have a way to refuel and refresh.

Hebrews 12:1 states, "Since we are surrounded by such a huge crowd of witnesses to the life of faith, let us strip off every weight that slows us down, especially the sin that so easily trips us up. And let us run with endurance the race God has set before us."

The race of life isn't a sprint but a long and winding endurance race. As a result, one of the things I tell my team often is, "You can't give out what you don't have." You see, at some point your contributions become detrimental to the team if you aren't fueled up and sharing out of what is fresh in your life.

So when you need to refuel in life, you have got to have a pit stop. Find a way to pull over and take the respite necessary to replenish what has been spent. Fill up again, and make sure you value those in your pit crew who help you go out and finish the race. A daily practice of refueling for me involves Scripture reading. Consider the Psalms and Proverbs as a beginning point.

Since we are surrounded by such a huge crowd of witnesses to the life of faith, let us strip off every weight that slows us down, especially the sin that so easily trips us up. And let us run with endurance the race God has set before us.
                                                              HEBREWS 12:1

What Your Words Say

In 2005, Major League Baseball, mired in the scandal surrounding performance-enhancing drugs, saw some of its players appear before Congress to give testimony. It was a frustrating day for all involved. Many of the players refused to answer direct questions. One noted that he wasn't there to talk about the past. But if you get subpoenaed, isn't that exactly what you are expected to do? Another player made a mockery of the situation, pretending not to be able to speak English. Clearly out of their comfort zone and believing that if they just bluffed enough the problems would go away, many of these players lost all credibility with the fans who had held them in such high honor for their accomplishments. These men embarrassed both the game of baseball and Congress.

The scandal reminds us that our words mean something. As a pastor who uses a lot of words to teach and lead my congregation every Sunday, I am acutely aware that it only takes a bit of poor communication to get in trouble. I speak from experience but pray that I have grown in my ability to use words for good and that others would see wisdom in what I have to say.

Proverbs 18:4 states, "Wise words are like deep waters; wisdom flows from the wise like a bubbling brook." May we use words that are full of wisdom, knowing that what we say, when we say it, and how we say it says a lot more about us than we realize!

Wise words are like deep waters; wisdom flows from the wise like a bubbling brook.   PROVERBS 18:4

Sometimes the Best Deal Is No Deal

"Sometimes the best deal is no deal at all." Those were the words of my attorney and dear friend, Arty Howard. Arty had walked with me and a team of six others through a long nine-month negotiation process with our church's next-door neighbor, our city government. We each had land contiguous to the other, and we were considering an exchange that could have been mutually beneficial. At the eleventh hour, though, we chose to back away from the table. This was a hard moment after all that we had invested in the negotiation process.

But this moment was one I am thankful for because I believe with all of my heart it was the right decision. Walking away from something after giving an entire season of your life to it seems hard, and maybe even foolish. But forcing something because of being shortsighted certainly is foolish. I believe that many young couples force marriages because neither person in the relationship has the courage to disappoint the other. Years later, they finally verbalize what they believed during the engagement period—they should have called it off.

Sometimes it takes more courage to pull away from something than it does to continue down a road because of what you have invested to get to this point. Forced relationships, business partnerships, or land exchanges aren't advisable if what lies before you ends in disappointment for all parties.

Proverbs 14:8 states, "The prudent understand where they are going, but fools deceive themselves."

Have the courage to pull the plug. Know where you are going, and remember, as my buddy Arty says, "Sometimes the best deal is no deal at all."

The prudent understand where they are going, but fools deceive themselves.

PROVERBS 14:8

Can I Ask You a Favor?

When was the last time you asked someone for a favor? Asking for a favor is asking for a special grace from someone else that will inconvenience that person but benefit you. Asking for a favor is akin to asking someone to take money out of his or her account knowing it may not be returned. No wonder it's often difficult to ask!

Have you ever wondered if God could do you a favor? Many people fail to share their requests with God because they feel it may inconvenience him. They also know that they really can't pay him back for answered prayers. If that is your approach to prayer, then you don't truly understand God. He is not bound. Our Lord owns the cattle on a thousand hills (see Psalm 50:10). He can answer any prayer request. Many people think, *I'll pray for others, but I don't want to bother God with these little things.* That perspective views God as having limited funds to pay his bills instead of as the God who can do anything.

Listen to wisdom as she speaks in Proverbs 8:35: "Whoever finds me finds life and receives favor from the LORD." So let me ask you this question: Did you know that as you seek, find, and walk in God's wisdom, he already favors you every day? Do you need a favor? Ask him.

Imagine your life being lived where God is daily doing favors (bestowing his divine blessing) for you through his gracious wisdom. He is not a genie in a bottle who will act as if your wish is his command, so that you can name it and claim it. But in walking with him and listening for his leading, you will find the gracious, profound blessings that only he can bestow. Seek his wisdom, and you will enjoy his favor.

Whoever finds me finds life and receives favor from the LORD.   PROVERBS 8:35

No Regrets

In his self-titled autobiography, legendary football coach Bum Phillips says, "You don't want regrets at my age—when there is no time left in the game."[36] We would be wise to listen to Phillips. His autobiography is filled with all the life lessons he learned, from his time fighting in World War II to his years as coach of the Houston Oilers. The biggest lesson Coach Phillips learned was when he became a Christian, taking Jesus Christ as his Lord and Savior.

Phillips didn't become a Christian until later in life, after years of living for himself. He states, "Christianity became a big part of my life—and thus a big part of my story—even if I steered away from it until I was 76 years old."[37] Have you, like Coach, steered away from becoming a follower of Christ? If so, why? What is holding you back?

Second Corinthians 6:2 states, "God says, 'At just the right time, I heard you. On the day of salvation, I helped you.' Indeed, the 'right time' is now. Today is the day of salvation." If you are not a follower of Christ, I want to encourage you to take the time today to examine the Christian faith and ask the hard questions. Do the hard work, for the last thing you want is to be in the fourth quarter of life with time running out and to be standing there with a life full of regret instead of the peace that is available to you in Christ.[38]

God says, "At just the right time, I heard you. On the day of salvation, I helped you." Indeed, the "right time" is now. Today is the day of salvation.

2 CORINTHIANS 6:2

---

[36] Bum Phillips and Gabe Semenza, *Bum Phillips: Coach, Cowboy, Christian* (Brenham, TX: Lucid Books, 2010), 14.

[37] Ibid.

[38] If you need a good resource to help you, Lee Strobel's *The Case for Christ* is an excellent treatment of some of the hard questions that people ask about Christianity. Strobel, a former atheist and reporter for the *Chicago Tribune*, shares his journey from atheist to fully devoted follower of Christ. If you have hard questions or have a friend with hard questions about the faith, turn to Strobel's work for guidance and answers.

The Difference between Demolition and Construction

At the end of the 2015–16 NFL season, with Peyton Manning eyeing retirement and Brock Osweiler a free agent, many speculated that the Denver Broncos were going to be content to tear down their championship team and begin the rebuilding process. With the cost of Manning and Osweiler together, it would be too expensive for Denver to keep other key elements of their championship team. In the end, Manning retired and Osweiler accepted an offer from the Houston Texans, leaving the Broncos with the opportunity to rebuild part of their team.

Every summer our church deploys people all around the world to do missions ministry. We do this because it's a great exercise in sharing and living out our faith, it catalyzes our partners in other countries, and it grows the faith of the missions teams, which impacts the church body at home. We encourage families to sign up so they can experience ministry together. Usually we have some sort of project that involves some construction that even kids can do. The part the kids like the most is demolition, because they get to rip into stuff and tear it apart.

Now, anyone can do demolition. The Broncos didn't need their general manager, John Elway, to oversee the demolition of their team, because no skill is required in demolishing something. In fact, Manning and Osweiler helped with the demo when they left the team. The Broncos do need Elway to build the team, because it takes great skill to build.

Proverbs 14:1 states, "A wise woman builds her home, but a foolish woman tears it down with her own hands." I want to encourage you to invest in yourself and in your home. Learn the skills it takes to be wise, and build something that will last. Remember, anybody can tear something down. If you are not yet married, be sure the woman you marry is a wise woman who will help build your home.

A wise woman builds her home, but a foolish woman tears it down with her own hands.

PROVERBS 14:1

183

A Person of Influence

So often we limit our scope of influence, and we do not realize that we have the opportunity to make a difference in the lives of everyone with whom we come in contact. We are all leaders, because someone is always looking up to us no matter who we are. People today are desperate for leadership. I believe every one of us has influence; we will use it either positively or negatively.

In his book *The One Year Uncommon Life Daily Challenge*, former NFL coach Tony Dungy shares his experience growing up and visiting his uncles and aunts in Detroit. The impact they made in his young life through their leadership can be seen in Dungy's accomplishments and character as an adult.[39] We need to broaden our vision and realize the influence that we can have on our extended family, friends, and coworkers—even the people we just pass throughout our day.

In Matthew 5:14-16, Jesus says, "You are the light of the world—like a city on a hilltop that cannot be hidden. No one lights a lamp and then puts it under a basket. Instead, a lamp is placed on a stand, where it gives light to everyone in the house. In the same way, let your good deeds shine out for all to see, so that everyone will praise your heavenly Father." We encounter so many people each and every day, and Jesus has called us to be a good influence on them. We need to be mindful of them, seek to serve them, and be a blessing to them. This is the way to cultivate our influence.

You are the light of the world—like a city on a hilltop that cannot be hidden. No one lights a lamp and then puts it under a basket. Instead, a lamp is placed on a stand, where it gives light to everyone in the house. In the same way, let your good deeds shine out for all to see, so that everyone will praise your heavenly Father.
MATTHEW 5:14-16

---

[39] Tony Dungy and Nathan Whitaker, *The One Year Uncommon Life Daily Challenge* (Carol Stream, IL: Tyndale, 2011), March 13.

The Field of Selfishness

If we aren't careful, our successes can tempt us to become filled with pride and forsake those who helped get us to that very place. Indianapolis Colts tight end Ben Utecht learned this lesson at the pinnacle of his career, Super Bowl XLI. When it was time to take the field, Utecht's father was at the top of the tunnel, crying out with all of his might for his son to hear him. Utecht turned, saw his father, went up to him, and said, "Dad, not now." As Utecht began to run on the field, he was convicted that he was forsaking the one who had helped get him to this point in his career. He says, "The playing field had become my field of selfishness."[40]

Ephesians 6:1-3 states, "Children, obey your parents because you belong to the Lord, for this is the right thing to do. 'Honor your father and mother.' This is the first commandment with a promise: If you honor your father and mother, 'things will go well for you, and you will have a long life on the earth.'"

Sometimes this honor is given to a parent we may have never met. A friend of mine, Antonio Armstrong, who neither knew his father nor shared his last name, won all Southwest Conference honors as a linebacker for Texas A&M's Wrecking Crew with the name Antonio Shorter. After winning these honors and making a name for himself, Antonio chose to honor his father by taking his dad's last name. Antonio's dad passed away before he ever met him, but Antonio told me that he feels God would have him honor his dad by carrying his last name, because he is the man he is today thanks to his mom and dad.

Remember, no matter your success, you didn't get there alone. Take the time to appreciate those who helped get you where you are today.

Children, obey your parents because you belong to the Lord, for this is the right thing to do. "Honor your father and mother." **EPHESIANS 6:1-2**

---

40 Hunter Smith and Darrin Gray, *The Jersey Effect*, with Stephen Copeland and Ken Turner (Bloomington, IN: WestBow Press, 2012), 37.

Eric's Seven Men

New York Times bestselling author Eric Metaxas tells the story of seven great men in history, including George Washington, William Wilberforce, Eric Liddell, and Dietrich Bonhoeffer, in his book *Seven Men: And the Secret of Their Greatness*. Metaxas says of these men, "I was looking for seven men who had all evinced one particular quality: that of surrendering themselves to a higher purpose, of giving something away that they may have kept."[41]

Do you know what makes a man great? Greatness in men comes from a willingness to sacrifice for the sake of others. In John 15:13, Jesus says, "There is no greater love than to lay down one's life for one's friends." Jesus serves as an excellent example of this sacrificial love. How can you follow his lead? Begin at home by serving your wife and children. Then find ways to serve in your community, sitting on boards and volunteering as a tutor or coach. This sacrificial love should also be evident in your work or service to the country.

In an era of masculinity being under assault, we desperately need men who will stand, serve, and sacrifice for a greater good and a greater cause. Men, let's stand and be the men we were created to be, laying down our lives for those around us!

There is no greater love than to lay down one's life for one's friends.

JOHN 15:13

---

[41] Eric Metaxas, *Seven Men: And the Secret of Their Greatness* (Nashville, TN: Thomas Nelson, 2013), xxii.

Model Your Expectations

In the 2014–15 season, the Houston Rockets played spectacular basketball, eventually making it to the Western Conference Finals. Houston fans were excited about their hometown team that year as the Rockets continued to rack up wins. When I had a chance to take my family to a game during the regular season, we were excited to see our team play well. But we found ourselves a bit disappointed. You see, the performance that night didn't live up to the hype around town, as they played a sloppy brand of basketball that resulted in a loss.

Expectations are a powerful force that can lead to joy or disappointment. The great Dallas Cowboy running back Tony Dorsett once said, "To succeed you need to find something to hold on to, something to motivate you, something to inspire you." Dorsett was saying that good coaches articulate what they expect from their athletes.

Good parents do the same. So what is it that you expect from your children? Remember, your children will look to you to motivate and inspire them. Help your children live up to your expectations by modeling those expectations. If you want your children to do their best, then do the same yourself. If you want your children to be caring and thoughtful, then model this same carefulness and thoughtfulness. If you want them to be polite, then by all means, show them what it is to be polite.

Model your ideals, and your team will follow. In his book *Dad's Playbook*, Tom Limbert says, "Just as a coach outlines plays and defines goals, it's up to you to create a game plan and provide explanations."[42] As you lead your children, remember this promise from Proverbs 22:6: "Direct your children onto the right path, and when they are older, they will not leave it."

Direct your children onto the right path, and when they are older, they will not leave it.   PROVERBS 22:6

---

[42] Tom Limbert, *Dad's Playbook: Wisdom for Fathers from the Greatest Coaches of All Time* (San Francisco: Chronicle Books, 2012), 19.

JULY

Aruba, Jamaica, We Ain't Gonna Take Ya

I love the beach, and I love the music of the Beach Boys. I especially love the beach when it is just Julee and me there. Don't get me wrong—I love playing in the sand with my kids, but I truly love just sitting oceanside with my wife.

For our twentieth anniversary, Julee and I planned a trip to Aruba. We had been there sixteen years earlier, but we hadn't returned and thought this milestone in our lives was a good time to go back.

As we were preparing for the trip, our kids kept saying, "We want to go! Take us!" Someday we hope to, but we have found one thing that fuels our marriage and our love for one another is to strategically get away at least one time a year, just by ourselves. Two times a year is ideal, but we must have at least one getaway with just the two of us. So when they would say, "Take us!" my wife would sing out, "Aruba, Jamaica, we ain't gonna take ya."

We enjoyed nearly a week together on the beach. We rented a jeep and toured the island. We went to a beautiful place to relax together and renew our love.

Proverbs 5:18 says, "Let your fountain be blessed, and rejoice in the wife of your youth" (ESV). Kiss your kids good-bye, get out of town, and go drink deeply of your love for each other! This intentional time will strengthen your marriage in a special way as you make new memories together.

Let your fountain be blessed, and rejoice in the wife of your youth.
PROVERBS 5:18, ESV

The Same Old Mistakes

Do you remember when your coach would throw his biggest tantrums? He would stomp his foot, raise his voice, and pinch all of his blood supply in such a way that his face would turn red with frustration. My coach would do that when we would make the same old mistakes.

Name the sport, and you can name the mistakes that send the coach into orbit. In football, it is mistakes in blocking assignments or snap counts. In basketball, it is traveling and neglecting the hustling and passing.

What I have found in my life is that when I forsake some simple fundamentals like getting enough sleep, spending time in prayer and studying Scripture, and having time for my family, I make the same old mistakes that cost me. I end up being short with my wife, frustrated with my kids, and rude to my colleagues. The smallest things become irritants because I am not executing on the simple fundamentals that are essential to my life.

I introduced the idea of Sabbath a few weeks ago. Let me ask you to reflect on this Scripture and the principle behind it again: "God blessed the seventh day and declared it holy, because it was the day when he rested from all his work of creation" (Genesis 2:3).

Have you started taking a Sabbath? If God rested after his work, we must as well. Take one day a week to lay down your work and dedicate it to worshiping God. Relax with your family, and be renewed.

God blessed the seventh day and declared it holy, because it was the day when he rested from all his work of creation. GENESIS 2:3

Who's in Your Huddle?

A sportswriter wrote in 2015 that the "Big D" in Dallas stood for dysfunction.[43] This was written midseason after Jerry Jones, the Cowboys owner, affirmed the actions of his troubled defensive tackle, Greg Hardy. On the field, Hardy had gotten into the face of the special teams coach and unit because of their botched play that gave up the team's lead.

Though a tremendous force to be reckoned with on the defensive line, Hardy has also had serious trouble off the field concerning violence toward women. When asked about Hardy's conduct on the field, Jones called it real leadership and stated that he loved Hardy's intensity. He even referenced how Hardy warmed up, which seemed to be so out of place at the time.

What surprises me, though, is that anyone would be surprised by Hardy's conduct on the field, based on what is known about him off the field. Proverbs 20:11 states, "Even children are known by the way they act, whether their conduct is pure, and whether it is right." "Big D" didn't just get to Dallas on that play in the middle of the season.

In my opinion, there has been "Big D" in Dallas for years. If you are a playmaker, a shutdown corner, or able to wreak havoc in the backfield, your off-the-field character really is overlooked.

But here is the lesson that I believe we should take away from this: when you put people in your huddle who have a past filled with folly, you ought to expect it to come out on the field, which will cost your team greatly. As a leader, you must know who is in your huddle and pick those with good reputations.

Even children are known by the way they act, whether their conduct is pure, and whether it is right.
PROVERBS 20:11

---

43 Jenny Vrentas, "The Cowboys' Greg Hardy Experiment Has Gone Awry," *Sports Illustrated*, October 27, 2015, http://mmqb.si.com/mmqb/2015/10/27/nfl-dallas-cowboys-greg-hardy -jerry-jones-jason-garrett.

Can a Virtuous Man Hesitate?

As we celebrate our nation's independence today, let us recall that our liberty was not simply handed to us. American husbands and fathers left the warmth of their beds to fight the British invasion at Concord and Lexington. In his book *Seven Men: And the Secret of Their Greatness*, Eric Metaxas highlights George Washington's impact as a great leader of our nation in its infancy. Upon hearing of the hundreds of casualties on both sides of the fight, George Washington penned these words to his friend George Fairfax:

> Unhappy it is though to reflect, that a Brother's Sword has been sheathed in a Brother's breast, and that, the once happy and peaceful plains of America are either to be drenched with Blood, or Inhabited by Slaves. Sad alternative! But can a virtuous Man hesitate in his choice?[44]

In that moment, Washington decided to stand up and fight for the liberty of this land. One of the things we need most in this day and time is virtuous men to stand up and fight for our families, for our faith, and for our future. In our liberty, we must remember our responsibility.

First, we should pray for our leaders. First Timothy 2:1-2 states, "I urge you, first of all, to pray for all people. Ask God to help them; intercede on their behalf, and give thanks for them. Pray this way for kings and all who are in authority so that we can live peaceful and quiet lives marked by godliness and dignity." No matter what side of the aisle you are on, as a follower of Christ, you have a responsibility to pray for those in authority. Pray that they would possess God's wisdom and govern for the common good of the people.

I urge you, first of all, to pray for all people. Ask God to help them; intercede on their behalf, and give thanks for them. Pray this way for kings and all who are in authority so that we can live peaceful and quiet lives marked by godliness and dignity.   1 TIMOTHY 2:1-2

---

[44] Eric Metaxas, *Seven Men: And the Secret of Their Greatness* (Nashville: Thomas Nelson, 2013), 13.

Be Careful

New York Giants defensive lineman Jason Pierre-Paul injured his right hand when he was playing with firecrackers during an Independence Day celebration in 2015. Pierre-Paul lost an index finger and fractured his thumb in the accident. Initial reports said that his actions might cost him some of his $15 million contract for the upcoming season, if he was able to continue playing. There were concerns about his ability to play his position effectively, because so much of the combat in the football trenches is done with your hands.

As a parent, I often tell my children, "Be careful," because I know my kids can get injured by their own foolish decisions or by the actions of other people who act carelessly. I look back on some of my decisions as a teenager and those of my friends and am thankful that the Lord spared me any real troubles. His hand was upon me, and I am convinced it was because of the prayers of my parents.

Our heavenly Father also tells us to be careful and to do so by obtaining wisdom. Wisdom says, in Proverbs 8:36, "Those who miss [wisdom] injure themselves." Self-inflicted injury is probably the worst type of injury because you know in your heart of hearts that it could have been avoided. I want to encourage you today to be careful by seeking, finding, and acting on the wisdom of God. If you are a parent, seek to point your children to this wisdom, and begin each day covering them in prayer.

Those who miss [wisdom] injure themselves.　　　　　　PROVERBS 8:36

More Joy

In my interview with four-time World Series champion Darryl Strawberry, or D-Straw, as he is called, he told me he was so miserable before he found Christ that when he signed a $20 million contract, he found no joy in it. You may remember Darryl's story. It begins with abuse from an alcoholic father, a rebellion and hardening of heart as a teenager, and a gifted athletic background that lifted him out of that world and drove him to prove his father wrong.

Darryl's story continues as one embattled with the trappings of success. On his first road trip in the big leagues, veteran players exposed him to the fast life of Major League Baseball, which included cocaine, strip clubs, and lots of wild parties. As a result, Darryl became addicted to women, alcohol, and drugs. Darryl got into great trouble and lost his family, his career, and even his freedom when he served time in prison.

Yet Darryl Strawberry found true joy when he turned it all over to the Lord. He submitted everything to the lordship of Christ and committed to growing in his relationship with Christ. Darryl found the truth of Psalm 4:7, which states, "You have given me greater joy than those who have abundant harvests of grain and new wine."

Now full of joy, Darryl preaches the gospel that saved him to crowds all over the United States, and he helps others recover from addiction. Do you have the joy that Psalm 4:7 describes? Remember, nothing that has been made was designed to satisfy your heart. That place is reserved for the Lord.

You have given me greater joy than those who have abundant harvests of grain and new wine.

PSALM 4:7

Pay Now, Play Later

Vince Lombardi is quoted as saying, "Mental toughness is many things, and rather difficult to explain. Its qualities are sacrifice and self-denial. Also, most importantly, it's combined with a perfectly disciplined will that refuses to give in."

The words "perfectly disciplined" are so strong. Self-discipline involves acting on a decision you have already made, instead of responding to how you feel in the moment. It often involves sacrificing the pleasure and thrill of the moment for what matters most in life and the greater reward that is to come.

Jesus teaches us to pay now so that we can play later. Self-denial and self-discipline are acts of self-leadership. When Jesus was tested, he was tempted three different times with things that would bring him instant gratification—that which would satisfy his appetite physically, that which would test God's love and care for him, and that which would bring him earthly possessions and honor. But Jesus resisted the lure of instant gratification. Each time the devil tempted him, he responded with the Scriptures. In his first temptation we see Jesus' response in Matthew 4:4: "No! The Scriptures say, 'People do not live by bread alone, but by every word that comes from the mouth of God.'"

When we are surrounded by a world of instant gratification, we need to stand firm in our convictions that are fueled by God's Word. We need to see the bigger picture around us, as Jesus did. He saw that his journey led to a cross and a grave so that he might be exalted and we might be seated with him in glory. Jesus modeled it for us. Let us, too, learn to pay the price now so we can play later.

Jesus told him, "No! The Scriptures say, 'People do not live by bread alone, but by every word that comes from the mouth of God.'"   MATTHEW 4:4

Owning Your Mistakes

Through the years there have been all sorts of scandals in sports—from "Shoeless" Joe Jackson throwing the World Series to Tonya Harding authorizing an assault on Nancy Kerrigan. Some athletes remain infamous while others are able to make a comeback in their sport.

The athletes who have humbled themselves and admitted their mistakes are ultimately given grace and an opportunity to come back and prove themselves again. Think of the baseball steroid scandal that began in 2005. There were many players who were suspended at one point or another. The Yankees had a handful of high-profile players who were accused of using some sort of performance-enhancing drug to assist them in either their performance or recovery.

One in particular, Andy Pettitte, quickly admitted his mistake and asked for the fans to forgive him. He went on to pitch at a high level and ultimately had his number retired by the New York Yankees during the 2015 season. Others who have continued to deny the accusations have placed a wedge between themselves and the public because the public doesn't like being lied to.

Proverbs 28:13 states, "People who conceal their sins will not prosper, but if they confess and turn from them, they will receive mercy." Pettitte owned his mistakes and is a good example of how we can do the same. When you have made a mistake, don't dig in and deny. This strategy will lead to a diminishment of your influence and effectiveness. Instead, humble yourself, apologize for your error, and learn from your mistakes. Over the long haul you will preserve your influence and even possibly see your influence grow. Remember, humility leads to honor, and pride to disgrace.

People who conceal their sins will not prosper, but if they confess and turn from them, they will receive mercy.　　　　　PROVERBS 28:13

Way Too Fast

I looked up the other day and saw my six-year-old daughter swinging on the trapeze bar on the swing set. In an instant the truth that I can't stop the hands of time hit me square between the eyes. She has grown so much lately, and before I know it, she will be headed off to college. Trying to keep her at this age is like trying to grasp oil in the hand.

After a moment, my thoughts of her growing up too fast were interrupted with the words, "Dad, can you come get me? This hurts my bottom." After a chuckle, I said, "Absolutely," and went to help her get down. I took her in my arms and asked her to not grow up. I asked, "Would you stay this age forever?" She laughed and said, "No, silly, my birthday is in April."

You know, I can't control time, but I can strive to maximize the moments I have been given. This is a gift from God. Ecclesiastes 3:10-11 states, "I have seen the business that God has given to the children of man to be busy with. He has made everything beautiful in its time" (ESV).

I am grateful that the Lord often reminds me to soak in the moment I have been given. Pretty soon, this season will be over, and Lord willing, I'll be walking my little girl down the aisle. That will be beautiful, just as this season is beautiful. I want to be found faithful in each season of her life and not take the days we have together for granted.

Enjoy the moments of today, because you can't get them back.

I have seen the business that God has given to the children of man to be busy with. He has made everything beautiful in its time. ECCLESIASTES 3:10-11, ESV

Being a Dad by Being a Teacher

As a father of three, I have found that my greatest role is that of being a dad. I am constantly thinking of ways to better fulfill this God-given responsibility, and I am convicted to not just teach others in my role as a pastor, but to also proactively teach my children.

One of the things that I commonly see in believers is that they aren't prepared for suffering. One of the lessons I wanted to teach my son Brady through *Thirteen Going on Eighteen: Becoming a Man of Influence*, the book I wrote for him, was the value of persevering through suffering. Here is what I wrote:

> To persevere in faith, you will also have to reconcile suffering in your heart and mind. Suffering is a part of this "old order" of things. . . . The ultimate fulfillment of Christ's kingdom will be the new heaven and new earth where there is a complete eradication of suffering. The Scripture declares,
>
> > Look, God's home is now among his people! He will live with them, and they will be his people. God himself will be with them. He will wipe every tear from their eyes, and there will be no more death or sorrow or crying or pain. All these things are gone forever. (Revelation 21:3-4)
>
> When Christ establishes his Kingdom, he will make "everything new" (Revelation 21:5). . . . Suffering is a result of sin and man's choices. . . . No one is exempt from it. Don't expect not to suffer, or your faith won't sustain you when you do.

I want to encourage you to take the time to prepare your children for the sufferings of this age.

[God] will wipe away every tear from their eyes, and there will be no more death or sorrow or crying or pain.　　　　　　　REVELATION 21:4

A Hard Word

Do you want to know whether a person, culture, or nation is for or against God and his ways? Consider how the person, culture, or nation values human life.

Scripture says that there are a few things that are never satisfied, including man's desires, fire, and the grave (see Proverbs 27:20; 30:16). There will always be death on this earth, and there will always be people who support it. The people who advocate taking the life of the unborn and encourage medically assisted suicide and the disintegration of the home as the cornerstone of culture, love death.

It's a hard word, and it may sound harsh to put it that way, but please listen to how Proverbs 8 ends. Verse 36 states, "All who hate me love death." Those who tear down the very foundations of life and society for their right to seek pleasure as they see fit embrace a culture of death that exalts itself against what God has declared to be good.

There seem to be only two choices. Either we make the wisdom of God the standard by which we live our lives, invest in our communities, and govern our nation, or we reject it to our own demise. Those who hold power will strive to retain power. With God's absolute standards of justice and righteousness, we have a foundation for law and order. With God as our Creator, we confess we are endowed by him with certain inalienable rights.

Unfortunately, in our world today, the wisdom of God is despised. Take a look around at the affection for death, and you will see that the wisdom of God has been ignored by many. Let's not travel down the road to death.

All who hate me love death.   PROVERBS 8:36

The Impact of Influence

In his book *Game Plan for Life*, three-time Super Bowl and NASCAR champion Coach Joe Gibbs says, "I've come to realize that despite everything nice that's come with my career . . . the most important thing Pat and I are going to leave on this earth is the influence, good or bad, we've had on others."[45]

Coach Gibbs brings up a few points we should consider:

1. We have influence . . . the ability to direct and inform others.
2. Influence will be positive or negative. It is never neutral.
3. What we do with our influence is our legacy.

If Coach Gibbs is right, then we all have some sort of influence. If I understand the Scriptures correctly, we will be called to give an account of our influence. As a husband, father, and pastor, I try to influence others to discover Christ and his plan for their lives. I challenge them to develop in their faith and deploy their influence for God's purpose and glory.

In Matthew 5:13, Jesus says, "You are the salt of the earth. But if the salt loses its saltiness, how can it be made salty again?" (NIV). We have been given the responsibility to influence those around us.

In Matthew 25, we see two different responses to the master's inquiry when he comes to inspect what his servants have done with what they have been given. To the first servant, who fulfilled his responsibility, the master says, "Well done, good and faithful servant!" (verse 23, NIV). To the servant who did nothing with what he'd been given, the master says, "You wicked, lazy servant!" (verse 26, NIV).

What will you hear when you are called to give an account of your stewardship of influence?

You are the salt of the earth. But if the salt loses its saltiness, how can it be made salty again?
MATTHEW 5:13, NIV

---

[45] Joe Gibbs, *Game Plan for Life: Your Personal Playbook for Success* (Carol Stream, IL: Tyndale, 2009), 18.

Stretching to Strength

Heisman Trophy winner Marcus Mariota strives to live a life that glorifies God. He says, "Going all in . . . is being motivated to always set the bar higher and never get complacent. We do that with His power and for His glory."[46]

Complacency is the easy path of comfort. All too often, we choose that path and look back at our average seasons with regret. You see, we know that God is longing to work in and through our lives both individually and also corporately through his church. But we must leave the complacency behind and go all in.

We must allow God to stretch us to strength. This "all in" life is one where we are intentional about growth and maturity because we don't want to leave anything on the field. We embrace discipline, we strive to get stronger, and we put ourselves in places of weakness so that the Lord can stretch us. We are striving to live a life that glorifies God.

First Corinthians 9:26-27 states, "I run with purpose in every step. I am not just shadowboxing. I discipline my body like an athlete, training it to do what it should. Otherwise, I fear that after preaching to others I myself might be disqualified." The apostle Paul was very intentional to live what he professed with his words. This wholeness and integrity isn't always easy, and I have learned that it will not happen unless I am intentional about being stretched to strength.

Are there areas of sin where you continually struggle? Are you giving of your resources so the Kingdom can advance? Are you under the teaching of a pastor in a local body of believers where you can grow, serve, and deploy your gifts? These are just some questions to prod you to address areas where you need to grow intentionally. Run with purpose in every step!

I run with purpose in every step. I am not just shadowboxing. I discipline my body like an athlete, training it to do what it should. Otherwise, I fear that after preaching to others I myself might be disqualified.   1 CORINTHIANS 9:26-27

---

46 "All In," *FCA Magazine* (November/December 2014), 12, http://www.fca.org/digitalmagazine /fcamagvol56issue6.

When the Bible Calls You Stupid

The off-season for professional athletes can be a time when they find trouble. With money to spend and time on their hands, a few of them will invariably make the news for actions that seem to the rest of us to be really, really stupid. When you look up the definition of the word *stupid*, it says, "Lacking intelligence or common sense."

As a parent, I tell my children not to call each other stupid, and as a kid I was prohibited from calling my siblings stupid, even though I sometimes felt they deserved it.

But I found a verse in Scripture that uses the word I was prohibited from using. Why would the Bible call someone stupid? When does Scripture tell someone they lack sense? The answer is pretty simple. Proverbs 12:1 states, "To learn, you must love discipline; it is stupid to hate correction."

There it is. Hating correction is stupid. I have found that this is the very fine line between life as a fool and life as a person of wisdom. Being teachable is the determining factor between wisdom and folly. Is someone trying to correct you at work or home, or while coaching at the ballpark? Is the Lord trying to bring correction into your life so you will walk the right path? The fact that the Lord is willing to correct you and discipline you is evidence of his love. Don't be stupid. Heed this word.

To learn, you must love discipline; it is stupid to hate correction.

PROVERBS 12:1

A Walk-On Coach

Dabo Swinney, the Clemson Tigers head football coach, describes himself as a "walk-on coach." A walk-on wide receiver for the Crimson Tide, the Pelham, Alabama, native has worked hard for his success on the football field. Playing under receivers coach Tommy Bowden and head coach Gene Stallings at Alabama, Swinney had to work double duty to earn a spot over a recruited scholarship player.

After graduation, Swinney was given a graduate assistant role and then earned a job on the Alabama coaching staff. After being out of football for a time, Coach Swinney rejoined Coach Bowden at Clemson as his wide-receivers coach. Swinney was known for his recruiting prowess and his personal connection to his players. His work ethic stood out to the then athletic director, Terry Don Phillips, who made a coaching change midseason, releasing Coach Bowden and naming Swinney as the interim head coach. The only thing that changed after that was that the interim tag was removed.

I had the privilege of interviewing Coach Swinney before the 2014–15 season, when he shared his faith journey with me. From a broken home with an alcoholic father, to a time when he and his mom were homeless, to walking on at Alabama, Coach Swinney has had to overcome tremendous adversity and learn to persevere through great difficulty. God has done a work in his life, and his zeal for the Lord, his family, his players, Clemson University, and others is very clear.

When I think of Coach Swinney, I think of Proverbs 14:23, which says, "Work brings profit, but mere talk leads to poverty!" You know, there is so much beyond our control, but when we focus on what we can control and dedicate it all to the Lord, anything is possible. Go work hard today, and enjoy the profit that comes!

Work brings profit, but mere talk leads to poverty!　　　　PROVERBS 14:23

Myths, Mistakes, and Failures

NFL Hall of Fame football coach and four-time NASCAR champion Joe Gibbs writes in his book *Game Plan for Life* about winning championships with the Redskins while struggling horribly with financial mistakes: "Maybe I've got a nice résumé and have created some really special memories, but the best—and hardest—lessons I've learned in my life have come from failures, my own shortcomings, and buying into some of the biggest myths our modern society has to tell."[47]

One of those myths he bought into is the belief that to be happy, you have to be rich. Our culture idolizes wealth, and if we are not careful, we can quickly worship the god of Mammon, the idol Scripture identifies as the competition for our heart's allegiance. Matthew 6:24 says, "No one can serve two masters. For you will hate one and love the other; you will be devoted to one and despise the other. You cannot serve God and be enslaved to money."

Today, Coach Gibbs is a very wealthy man. But he tried to use his wealth from the position he held as the head coach of the Washington Redskins to become rich. This led to many bad investments that almost brought about his financial ruin. Once Coach Gibbs got his house in order by submitting his finances to the Lord and God's plan for his wealth, he was better able to handle the increase that his experience and abilities enabled him to earn.

No one can serve two masters. For you will hate one and love the other; you will be devoted to one and despise the other. You cannot serve God and be enslaved to money.

MATTHEW 6:24

---

47 Joe Gibbs, *Game Plan for Life: Your Personal Playbook for Success* (Carol Stream, IL: Tyndale, 2009), 4. Joe Gibbs writes about having a game plan for your finances in his book and has many resources to give you guidance and counsel. You can find out more at www.gameplanforlife .com/finances.

More Renewal

It's summertime. Time to hit the beach, the mountains, the lake, or the theme park. There is something about taking a vacation that renews us. It is a chance to retreat, to sleep late, and to be with friends and family.

Renewal is a critical part of our spiritual lives too. But how are we made new?

Ephesians 4:22-24 tells us "to put off your old self, which belongs to your former manner of life and is corrupt through deceitful desires, and to be renewed in the spirit of your minds, and to put on the new self, created after the likeness of God in true righteousness and holiness" (ESV).

Spiritual renewal involves being renewed in the spirit of our minds (see Ephesians 4:23). We are renewed when we do three practical things:

1. Practice the Presence of God: The call of Jesus is a call to abide or dwell in him. John 15:5 states, "Yes, I am the vine; you are the branches. Those who remain in me, and I in them, will produce much fruit. For apart from me you can do nothing." We can approach God's throne through prayer and praise.

2. Park in God's Word: Colossians 3:16 says, "Let the word of Christ dwell in you richly, teaching and admonishing one another in all wisdom, singing psalms and hymns and spiritual songs, with thankfulness in your hearts to God" (ESV). We are to read God's Word and let it saturate our hearts and minds.

3. Ponder Eternity: Colossians 3:2 states, "Think about the things of heaven, not the things of earth." We are called to set our minds on eternal things.

Putting on the new man is an exercise in seeking more of what God offers. To get spiritual renewal, though, you have to hunger and thirst for it. As you seek personal refreshment this summer, seek spiritual refreshment as well.

Put off your old self, which belongs to your former manner of life and is corrupt through deceitful desires.   EPHESIANS 4:22, ESV

The Concussion Shed

The Texas Tech Red Raiders under head coach Mike Leach were a high-scoring machine that went to ten straight bowl games. All that Coach Leach and his staff had worked for started to unravel when wide receiver Adam James, son of former ESPN analyst Craig James, was isolated on two separate occasions after sustaining a mild concussion. After it was clear that James was suffering from a concussion, he was sent with a graduate assistant to a shed that kept all of the blocking dummies and other equipment necessary for practice. He was isolated there, in that dark place, while the rest of his team practiced.

Clearly this didn't sit well with the receiver, nor his father, who engaged the administration about how his son was being treated, and Coach Leach was eventually dismissed after an investigation into the allegations. In the end, Leach's isolation of James led to his downfall.[48]

Isolating ourselves can lead to our own downfall as well. Proverbs 18:1 states, "Whoever isolates himself seeks his own desire" (ESV). When you pull back from relationships, community, and accountability, it is because you are forsaking wise counsel, motivated by your own selfish ways. When you go to a dark place over and over again, there are going to be consequences. Combat your unfriendly isolation by living in the light. Stay in community with those who will challenge you to be the man you were created to be.

Whoever isolates himself seeks his own desire.　　　　　　PROVERBS 18:1, ESV

---

[48] In their book, *The System*, Jeff Benedict and Armen Keteyian share the details that ultimately led to Leach's dismissal.

The Power of Your Thoughts

Coach Vince Lombardi once said, "Life's battles don't always go to the stronger or faster man. But sooner or later the man who wins is the man who thinks he can." Your thoughts will set the trajectory of your life toward either a life that revolves around you and what you determine to be your purposes or a life that revolves around God and who and what he has created you to be.

What do you think about the statement that God has a plan for your life? Have you ever wondered what that plan is? Do you think that the Creator of the universe uniquely gifted you to do something extraordinary with your life? I do.

Ephesians 2:10 teaches us that we have been made as masterpieces of God, who has saved us for the purpose of doing good works that will bring him glory. You see, I believe that part of the mystery of the gospel is that the God of the universe actually invites us into a partnership with him to accomplish something spectacular. When you think about and understand this, it should challenge the way you live. It should inspire how you spend your time and invite you to serve the Lord with excellence.

Proverbs 23:7 in the King James Version states, "As [a man] thinketh in his heart, so is he." So what do you thinketh? I believe that winning in life begins by ordering your purposes and thoughts around the heavenly Father and what he thinks of your life.

As [a man] thinketh in his heart, so is he.　　　　　　PROVERBS 23:7, KJV

The Two-Minute Drill

In the foreword of Bum Phillips's biography, former Houston Oiler tight end Mike Barber says, "All of us come to a place and time when the clock is running out, it's the fourth quarter and we find ourselves about to make the biggest call of our life. That's when we find we need a coach."[49]

I haven't always seen the clock or known it was the fourth quarter, but the pressures of life have let me know when I've needed a coach. A "life coach" is a wise person who, like a sage, can teach in just a few words the applicable lessons that last us a lifetime.

This isn't the first time I have addressed this subject in *A Minute of Vision for Men*. But the Bible often repeats itself too. Good coaches glean from their experience and see beyond what is right before them. When we begin to visit with them about our struggles, our experiences, and our options, they often are able to hone in and diagnose the problem clearly. They are like an expert physician who can make a diagnosis over the phone, call in a prescription, and then say, "Now come see me tomorrow to confirm that diagnosis."

Proverbs 10:20 states, "The words of the godly are like sterling silver." If you feel like you are in the two-minute drill in life, look and listen for a godly person who has been where you are and has the wisdom that experience brings. Find the sage, and seek out his or her wisdom. An apt word can change everything.

The words of the godly are like sterling silver.　　　　　PROVERBS 10:20

---

[49] Mike Barber, foreword to *Bum Phillips: Coach, Cowboy, Christian*, by Bum Phillips and Gabe Semenza (Brenham, TX: Lucid Books, 2010), 9.

Consequences That Cleanse

After failing to live up to expectations and then finishing with a 2–14 record in the 2013 season, Coach Gary Kubiak was fired as the Houston Texans head coach. Kubiak was known as a player's coach, and there were reports that Kubiak had lost the locker room because of a lack of discipline.

When the Texans went out to replace Coach Kubiak, they looked for a "disciplinarian" who would hold players accountable. Because the Texans wanted a culture change, they turned to Bill O'Brien, the man known for chewing out future Hall of Fame quarterback Tom Brady when he was Brady's offensive coordinator in New England. O'Brien's strict coaching style gave the Texans hope for a better record.

Are you having the same struggles over and over with your children and those under your responsibility? Do you feel like there's a divisive culture in the team that you lead? If so, I want to challenge you to embrace that conflict that will lead to consequences that will cleanse. Many a supervisor or even a parent is afraid of confrontation. They will do whatever it takes to avoid conflict with those they supervise. The result is that they give up leadership to the ones they will not confront.

If we embrace the conflict that has positive consequences, there will be a cleansing that takes place. Proverbs 20:30 states, "Physical punishment cleanses away evil; such discipline purifies the heart." Don't be afraid to instill consequences that hurt. It will be for the betterment of the one who needs the discipline, and the others who are watching it unfold.

Physical punishment cleanses away evil; such discipline purifies the heart.

PROVERBS 20:30

Earning Their Respect

Peyton Manning learned a hard lesson at the University of Tennessee. He found himself unable to lead his new team, when as a freshman who started eight games, he couldn't get his teammates to respond to his verbal challenges. It took a while, but Manning learned that to get the team's respect, he had to earn it through hard work.

After fourteen seasons in the NFL, Manning found himself with a new team, the Denver Broncos. He indicated that it felt like a similar situation to that of going to Tennessee. As a result, Manning committed to earning the respect of his new teammates. He did this by getting to work early and hitting the weight room hard. He stayed humble and gave it his all so that his teammates could see his passion for the game and his commitment to the team. In his first season with the Broncos, he was voted team captain and ultimately led the team to the Super Bowl two times, winning it once, during his four years in Denver.

Just because you have a title doesn't mean you have respect. Respect is earned. It is given to the one who works harder, invests more, and cares the most. Romans 13:7 states, "Give to everyone what you owe them." When you invest with passion and hard work, you will see those around you begin to give you the respect you are due. So focus on what you can control, and you will have the respect that you need.

Give to everyone what you owe them.   ROMANS 13:7

I'll Try

NBA champion coach and executive Pat Riley once said, "There are only two options regarding commitment. You're either in or you're out. There is no such thing as life in-between." I think Riley is spot on with his assessment, and though we tend to agree with him, we often live our lives in the "I'll Try Zone." When we tell someone, "I'll try," we are actually saying, "I am not willing to commit."

How often do you respond with the words, "I'll try"? In other words, how often do you reply with a noncommittal response? Saying, "I'll try," actually communicates, "Don't count on me." It is better if we simply respond with a yes or a no. People who respond with a yes tend to find a way to get it done. People who reply with a no are at least being honest and can be respected. But those who say, "I'll try," and then back out at the last minute come across as flaky and unreliable.

When both our attitudes and words aren't established with yes and no, it weakens our homes, communities, and country. In your marriage, you are either in or out. At work, you are either in or out. With fitness, diet, and self-control, you are either in or out.

When Jesus was teaching on making vows, he said, "Just say a simple, 'Yes, I will,' or 'No, I won't.' Anything beyond this is from the evil one" (Matthew 5:37). In what areas have you been noncommittal? Remember, as Riley said, "There is no such thing as life in-between."

Just say a simple, 'Yes, I will,' or 'No, I won't.' Anything beyond this is from the evil one.   MATTHEW 5:37

Driving the Fairway

A long-flying, straight drive from the golf tee is a thing of beauty. People line fairways to get a glimpse of these amazing shots by the best golfers. Television cameras capture these beautiful shots over and over again for the fans tuning in from their living rooms. Many amateurs spend countless hours attempting to emulate these satisfying feats of athleticism.

Yet every golfer knows that one degree of error can turn the flight of perfection into a disaster. Over the length of a drive, a change that seems slight or insignificant at the tee creates a bad lie, or worse, an out-of-bounds drop. That simple degree of error is exacerbated over the length of a two- or three-hundred-yard shot.

Let us apply these same principles in our faith walk. It takes a conscious effort to maintain a "straight" faith, as it does to achieve a straight drive. Let us avoid bad habits that seem slight and insignificant so that we won't get off course in our lives, fearing this error more than we dread being out-of-bounds on the golf course. Let us focus on walking in the fair way of life, just as we seek to land our drives in the fairway of the golf course.

How are we to do it? Proverbs 11:5 says, "The godly are directed by honesty; the wicked fall beneath their load of sin." May we seek to walk blamelessly and straight before his righteousness, acknowledging him in all our ways![50]

The godly are directed by honesty; the wicked fall beneath their load of sin.

PROVERBS 11:5

---

[50] Today's devotional was written by Jan Whitehead, mother of professional golfer Michael Whitehead and NCAA tennis coach Daniel Whitehead.

Timing Is Everything

The West Coast Offense is an offense built on timing. Three steps and a hitch . . . five steps and get it out . . . five steps and a double hitch. In the West Coast Offense, timing is everything for a well-placed ball. Guys like Joe Montana and Steve Young made it appear poetic and effortless because they mastered the fundamentals of the well-placed ball.

A well-placed word can be as effective as a well-placed ball. Recently, one of my kids was hurt by the words of his peers when they criticized him for not being as skinny as they were. My son is not obese in the least bit. He has a thick frame, as I do, and will be very tall, as I am.

As young men do, my son gave them the impression that he blew it off and went about his day. But as soon as he got into the car with his mom, he let her know of the pain their comments caused him. The next day, his coach, not aware of the situation, encouraged him in this same area, declaring that my son was destined to excel with the power base the coach sees on him and telling him to use that for his advantage. My son's coach gave him encouragement at just the right time.

You know, encouragement is special when we are running low on hope. Encouragement is life-giving when we have been in a prolonged trial. And when someone who is totally unaware of our circumstances encourages us, we experience the love and support of almighty God because we know only God could prompt that person to say something.

Proverbs 15:23 states, "Everyone enjoys a fitting reply; it is wonderful to say the right thing at the right time!" This word is so true and so applicable. As you have received encouragement, give it. As you give it, so you, too, will receive it. Remember, timing is everything, and a well-placed word, like a well-placed ball, is a thing of beauty.

Everyone enjoys a fitting reply; it is wonderful to say the right thing at the right time!   PROVERBS 15:23

Run Another Play

When I launched *Vision for Life Radio: Where Faith & Sports Collide*, I had the privilege of interviewing former NFL great Randall Cunningham. Cunningham, who now pastors Remnant Ministries in Las Vegas, Nevada, was amazing to watch on the field in Philadelphia and Minnesota and was named the league MVP in 1998.

In June 2010, though, tragedy struck the Cunninghams when their young son Christian drowned in their backyard hot tub. It was the hardest moment of their lives. Cunningham described it as a sack so severe that he wondered if he would ever get up off the turf again. In his book *Lay It Down: How Letting Go Brings Out Your Best* Cunningham writes, "It's the hard times that can render us useless, forever on a downward spiral . . . or propel us forward. We can give up or we can stand up and determine in our mind and soul that we will go back to the huddle and run another play."[51]

I have to admit that my interview with Randall was one of my all-time favorites. It was evident through the joy he possessed that God himself had sustained Randall; his wife, Felicity; and the rest of the family. Never have I heard such strength after such tragedy!

Isaiah 12:2 declares, "See, God has come to save me. I will trust in him and not be afraid. The LORD GOD is my strength and my song; he has given me victory." As you face hard times, grief, and difficulty too severe to bear, I want to encourage you to get up, stand tall, and run another play. God will come to you and save you.

See, God has come to save me. I will trust in him and not be afraid. The LORD GOD is my strength and my song; he has given me victory. ISAIAH 12:2

---

51 Randall Cunningham and Tim Willard, *Lay It Down: How Letting Go Brings Out Your Best* (Brentwood, TN: Worthy Publishing, 2013), 5.

People Watching

It is amazing the things that you can see in big crowds these days. Whether you are at a mall, a theme park, or a sporting event, you are going to see some wild stuff. Sometimes what you see makes you laugh: you see the conflict of children in another family and think, *Okay, it's not just our family that struggles with our kids' behavior.* At other times, you will see things that disturb you, like the way a parent disciplines his or her children by scolding them and speaking curses upon them.

I don't get a lot of time to watch people, but when I do, I have to guard my own heart against poor judgment. You see, watching people can be very entertaining, but the problem with watching others is how quickly we can slip into prejudicial thoughts and feelings about an entire race or economic class of people. It is so easy to make uninformed judgments about others without giving any thought to whether they are true or not.

First Samuel 16:7 shows us how God looks at mankind: "The LORD said to Samuel [about David], 'Don't judge by his appearance or height, for I have rejected him. The LORD doesn't see things the way you see them. People judge by outward appearance, but the LORD looks at the heart.'" Before God, every person has value. Remember, Christ died for the entire world, and his death declared the Father's love for all. May we look at others as God does!

The LORD doesn't see things the way you see them. People judge by outward appearance, but the LORD looks at the heart.   1 SAMUEL 16:7

You've Got to Have a Quarterback

Many sports analysts and pundits have declared that to have a successful NFL team, you've got to have a quarterback. There are between 96 and 128 quarterbacks at any given time in the National Football League, if you count through the third string and the practice-squad players. I would assume that there is a large number of available quarterbacks that teams can sign off the street every year as well. Having a good quantity of quarterbacks to play the position isn't the problem. The problem is with having quality quarterbacks.

Just as the pundits say, "You've got to have a good quarterback," I would say that every young boy and girl truly needs a great father. It's easy to become a father. The problem isn't quantity. There are plenty of dads out there. The challenge before us is quality. Dads who get it—who lay down their lives for their children, who understand their responsibility, and who are present and accounted for in the lives of their children and family—are the dads we need. Quality dads are desperately needed today if we are going to have a chance as a family, a community, and a nation.

Second Samuel 13:21 states, "When King David heard what had happened, he was very angry." This verse is describing how David felt when he heard bad reports about his children. David did a lot of things well, but he struggled mightily as a father. The problem I see in 2 Samuel 13 is that David didn't do anything to deal with his children's actions. Don't be that father! Be in your kids' lives for the good and bad, thick and thin. Your children deserve a quality father.

When King David heard what had happened, he was very angry.

2 SAMUEL 13:21

Coldcocked Jets Face Another Hurdle

Headlines like the one above rolled off the presses the day after a Jets backup linebacker broke the jaw of their starting quarterback, Geno Smith, in 2015. When IK Enemkpali sucker punched Smith at training camp, the consequences were immediate. Smith's jaw was broken in two places, which resulted in undergoing surgery and sitting out for nearly ten weeks. Enemkpali was immediately released from the team, potentially ending his time in the National Football League. For Jets fans the consequences of another setback led *Sports Illustrated*'s Peter King to say, "It's always something with the Jets."[52]

Like organizations whose cultures suffer repeatedly, families and individuals are often plagued with setback and scandal as well. Trouble seems to have a way of finding certain folks over and over again, as if they stumble into it.

Proverbs 27:12 states, "A prudent person foresees danger and takes precautions. The simpleton goes blindly on and suffers the consequences." We would do well to heed this advice.

If you don't know how to spot danger, turn to the beginning point of wisdom and embrace the fear of the Lord. Proverbs 1:7 states, "Fear of the LORD is the foundation of true knowledge, but fools despise wisdom and discipline." Once you see danger on the horizon, don't go blindly on. Take precautions and make preparations so that you don't suffer unduly. When it is time to act, you will be ready.

A prudent person foresees danger and takes precautions. The simpleton goes blindly on and suffers the consequences.   PROVERBS 27:12

---

52 Peter King, "It's Always Something with the Jets," *Sports Illustrated*, August 11, 2015, http://mmqb.si.com/mmqb/2015/08/11/nfl-geno-smith-broken-jaw-new-york-jets.

JULY 30
Repetition, Repetition, Repetition

Bubba Crosby played Major League Baseball for the New York Yankees in the early 2000s. He was drafted out of Rice University by the Los Angeles Dodgers and was later traded to the Yankees. After his time in New York, his most successful time in the big leagues, Crosby went to Cincinnati and later retired in spring training with the Seattle Mariners.

When I had the chance to interview Crosby for my radio show, we talked about his time in New York and what it was like playing with guys like Johnny Damon, Alex Rodriguez, and Derek Jeter. He looked back on that time with great affection and then said something that surprised me. When I asked him to name one of the biggest lessons he learned when in New York, he answered, "The importance of fundamentals."

Crosby went on to note how Alex Rodriguez was a workhorse, daily hitting off the tee, then heading to the cage, and then going to batting practice. He said that Rodriguez took hours of ground balls day in and day out. Repetition, repetition, repetition.

We've all needed to have something repeated, whether it was because we didn't hear it or because it didn't sink in, or because it was so profound that we needed to hear it again. Repetition is a good thing for us. In reading Proverbs 14, I saw something repeated within the chapter, which had to do with a man's anger. Proverbs 14:29 states, "People with understanding control their anger; a hot temper shows great foolishness."

I saw this teaching in verse 16, but it didn't strike me until I saw it again in verse 29. The correlation of patience with understanding and wisdom, and the contrast of being quick-tempered and taking actions of folly was stressed through repetition.

Did it not sink in? Did I miss it? Or was it just that profound that I needed to hear it again? All of the above! Let's heed these fundamental matters and walk in wisdom.

People with understanding control their anger; a hot temper shows great foolishness.
PROVERBS 14:29

Seek Wisdom

Coach Gary Kubiak's Super Bowl win with the Denver Broncos had those of us in Houston wondering why it couldn't have been done here. Kubiak lost his job with the Texans after going 2–14 in the 2013 season. It was a season like none other in Houston, one that saw Kubiak collapse on the sidelines and get rushed to the hospital. The truth of the matter is that challenging seasons can make us or break us. I wonder if the challenges of 2013 prepared Coach Kubiak for the challenges of 2015.

How do you navigate challenging seasons? Have you ever been overwhelmed with what you were facing and wondered how you were going to navigate it so that you could come out better on the other side?

I walked through one of these seasons from August 2014 to August 2015. I have to admit, it was one of the most challenging seasons in my life. Because of my role as senior pastor, I was leading a team that found itself negotiating a land exchange with the city government. It was a complicated negotiation, and the political climate made it even more challenging. Every one of the council members was term limited, and a slate of candidates ran in opposition to this proposed exchange.

There aren't classes in seminary that cover these matters. Feeling as though I was on the outer edge of ignorance, I realized I needed to get some people around me who could help. So I surrounded myself with a team of wise counselors whose wisdom enriched me at every turn. I also spent a lot of time seeking God's direction. The end result was a good one for the church.

Proverbs 4:7 states, "Getting wisdom is the wisest thing you can do!"

Are you facing a season in your life that seems bigger than you can handle? Get wisdom! Do this by seeking out wise and godly counsel and by spending intentional time with God, seeking his leading.

Getting wisdom is the wisest thing you can do! PROVERBS 4:7

AUGUST

When Dad Disappoints

When I was a kid, I received a ten-dollar bill that was printed in 1935. I got the bill in 1980-something, and I believed this bill was worth well beyond the face value. I showed it to my dad and asked him to see if he would look into it for me. He said that he would and then proceeded to both forget about it and spend it. I was devastated. Surely he spent my fortune! To make me feel better and to amend for his transgression, he gave me a twenty-dollar bill.

Years later, I rolled up to the house with some breakfast from Chick-fil-A and told my son Cooper that I got him a chicken biscuit. I had already gotten his older brother off to school, via the drive-through, and I'd decided to bring Coop a chicken biscuit and Carson some Chick-n-Minis. Immediately, my wife told me that I had made a mistake, the same mistake I'd made three weeks ago. She said, "Don't you remember, he wanted the minis three weeks ago and you got on him for not being grateful?"

In all honesty, I didn't remember. This time, though, Cooper was hurt by my lack of recall. I had disappointed him, and although I was trying to serve him, I hadn't listened to what he really preferred. Graciously, he moved off to the side to hide his feelings, but I realized that I hadn't listened to his heart.

Dad, this is going to happen. My dad failed to listen to my heart and remember my request, and I failed to listen to Cooper's. We all make mistakes in this vein, and I am sure Cooper will do it with his kids too. But I want to remind you that your heavenly Father is always attentive and never forgets your requests.

At the end of a few other potent statements on prayer, James makes this conclusion: "The earnest prayer of a righteous person has great power and produces wonderful results" (James 5:16). Take your requests to your heavenly Father!

The earnest prayer of a righteous person has great power and produces wonderful results.
JAMES 5:16

AUGUST 2

Never Quit

One thing that neither Tom Landry nor Bear Bryant tolerated was having quitters on their teams. I don't know about you, but I know that these men wouldn't have allowed me to stay on their teams, because at various times in my life, I have given up. I know what quitting feels like.

Bear Bryant once said, "Never quit. It is the easiest cop-out in the world. Set a goal and don't quit until you attain it. When you do attain it, set another goal, and don't quit until you reach it. Never quit." I'm concerned that we have too many men quitting their most fundamental roles as husbands, fathers, and providers.

No matter what country I travel to, when I ask about the struggles of the communities there, every time, I get a report back that says the men have walked out on their families. I have heard this in Cuba, in Honduras, in Latvia, in the Dominican Republic, in Greece, and beyond. In every part of the world where society is breaking down, the breakdown can be traced directly to the fact that men quit on their most fundamental roles.

Maybe you've quit on your marriage, quit on your kids, quit on your job, or quit on God. Let me remind you that quitters fail every time. There's a way out and quitting is reversible. Malachi 4:5-6 states, "Look, I am sending you the prophet Elijah before the great and dreadful day of the LORD arrives. His preaching will turn the hearts of fathers to their children, and the hearts of children to their fathers. Otherwise I will come and strike the land with a curse."

If you found the quitter in you and you don't like that guy, turn to the Lord and ask him to help you repair this quality in your character. Repent and return to the fundamentals of love, nurturing, and provision that you are called to carry out. May the Lord return the hearts of the fathers to their children and the hearts of the children to their fathers!

Look, I am sending you the prophet Elijah before the great and dreadful day of the LORD arrives. His preaching will turn the hearts of fathers to their children, and the hearts of children to their fathers. Otherwise I will come and strike the land with a curse.
MALACHI 4:5-6

The Making of a Leader

The great Vince Lombardi once said, "Leaders aren't born, they are made. And they are made just like anything else, through hard work. And that's the price we'll have to pay to achieve that goal, or any goal."

I love the topic of leadership, probably more than leading itself. There is something about learning from the life experiences of other leaders and applying their principles to help us lead better. I enjoy reading about some of the great leaders of our country like George Washington and Abraham Lincoln. There are also many lessons about leadership found in the Bible from looking at Moses, King David, and Jesus. Each of these men embraced his calling to leadership and gave us so much to consider.

As a young man, I was eager to immerse myself in the writings about church leadership, but I came away frustrated. That is because no one was speaking directly to me, a subordinate. I wasn't leading much of anything to speak of, and when I would read leadership books by John Maxwell, Bill Hybels, or John Kotter, I would walk away knowing something was missing. I wasn't just frustrated in my study of leadership, I was frustrated that I didn't get to lead more aggressively at a younger age.

Then one day, in the midst of my "lack of leadership" frustration, God spoke to my heart and told me to follow my leader. In that moment everything changed. I found contentment, new purpose, and new opportunity. It was also in that season of following that I learned to lead. I wrote about what I learned during that time in my first book, coauthored with Mike Bonem, called *Leading from the Second Chair*.

Matthew 8:9 states, "I too am a man under authority, with soldiers under me. And I say to one, 'Go,' and he goes, and to another, 'Come,' and he comes, and to my servant, 'Do this,' and he does it" (ESV).

You see, it was when I learned to follow that God equipped me to lead.

I too am a man under authority, with soldiers under me. And I say to one, 'Go,' and he goes, and to another, 'Come,' and he comes, and to my servant, 'Do this,' and he does it.　　　MATTHEW 8:9, ESV

Leading with Balance

John Maxwell has been writing about and teaching on the subject of leadership for many years. My library is full of his works, and my life has been enriched because of his wisdom. Maxwell is a great communicator, and one of the things that I appreciate the most about him is that he makes it easy to remember his advice. For instance, Maxwell has various leadership sayings, or proverbs. The first I recall learning was "Everything rises and falls on leadership."

Not long thereafter I learned another one of his proverbs: "He that thinketh he leadeth, and hath no one following, is only taking a walk." When I digested this proverb I realized that sometimes leaders take their journeys too far too fast, leaving their people behind. Nehemiah, the great rebuilder of Jerusalem, was very sensitive to this concern. Look at Nehemiah 5:15-16:

> The former governors, in contrast, had laid heavy burdens on the people, demanding a daily ration of food and wine, besides forty pieces of silver. Even their assistants took advantage of the people. But because I feared God, I did not act that way.
>
> I also devoted myself to working on the wall and refused to acquire any land. And I required all my servants to spend time working on the wall.

Nehemiah was a wise leader. He knew that if he went too far too fast, he would overwhelm his people with what he was asking and seeking to accomplish. He found a way to get everything done that needed to be done without taking too much liberty in his role, and he led this way because he feared God. He walked this way for ten years.

As you lead, show care not to go too far too fast. Stay in proximity to those you lead so that you are aware of their ability and willingness to go where you feel led to go.

I also devoted myself to working on the wall and refused to acquire any land. And I required all my servants to spend time working on the wall.

NEHEMIAH 5:16

Timing Matters

Former Baylor University quarterback Bryce Petty said, "There were 1,786 days between my final high school start and my first start at Baylor. During that time, I learned that God has a purpose and plan for me, and it's not on my time. It's on his."

According to the law of timing, "The right thing at the wrong time is the wrong thing."[53] As a leader, I have dual processes going on as I make decisions. Process one is seeking the right answer to the problem or opportunity before me. Process two is looking for just the right timing of that decision.

I do this because I know that the right solution at the wrong time is going to cause me problems. But the right decision at the right time is going to fit like a glove. I believe that our heavenly Father leads in a similar way when he calls us to a task or vocation, but then has us wait. What we don't see in the moments of our impatience is the bigger picture of how he is going before us to prepare our way.

Psalm 37:5-7 declares, "Commit everything you do to the LORD. Trust him, and he will help you. He will make your innocence radiate like the dawn, and the justice of your cause will shine like the noonday sun. Be still in the presence of the LORD, and wait patiently for him to act."

Waiting on God is a very challenging thing. But what I can accomplish in my own striving cannot compare to what he can do when he moves. You see, there is nothing that I can do to make my life shine like the dawn and the purpose of my cause as if it were high noon. But he can! If you find yourself in a season of waiting, spend time with Psalm 37:1-11.

Commit everything you do to the LORD. Trust him, and he will help you.

PSALM 37:5

---

53 Joshua Harris, *I Kissed Dating Goodbye* (Colorado Springs: Multnomah, 1997), 75.

When Slow Is Better Than Fast

As I was preparing for our youth football draft one year, I reminded myself of how important fast players are for a football team. The previous season, I had a great group of young men, but we only got one victory, because we didn't have any speed.

We had size, but the size didn't help us, because the faster kids beat our boys to the hole. What I have learned from a few victories and a whole lot of losses is that in youth sports, it is all about speed. And, as Raiders coach Al Davis says, "You can't teach speed."

We may not have the speed of those few special athletes in sports, but many of us live our lives way too fast.

Here is what we need to understand about speed in our everyday lives. "Things of speed," as I once heard Bill Hybels say, "and things of the soul, move in opposite directions. They are at an inverse relationship to one another."

In other words, you can't cultivate the soul moving at Mach speed. God uses stillness to frame us and shape us. He uses nature to testify of his character. He uses stirring in the middle of the night to get us up to seek him in prayer. He whispers to our hearts his love for us.

What are you doing to cultivate the soul? The psalmist suggests being still: "Be still, and know that I am God! I will be honored by every nation. I will be honored throughout the world" (Psalm 46:10). In a time-constrained world, let's slow down so we can soak in the things of the soul.

Be still, and know that I am God! I will be honored by every nation. I will be honored throughout the world. **PSALM 46:10**

A Solid Directive

You have most likely heard the saying, "Fool me once, shame on you. Fool me twice, shame on me." While the core of the quote is to learn from our mistakes and not allow people in our lives to take advantage of us, I think there is even more we can learn from these words.

I am reminded of Proverbs 14:7, which says, "Stay away from fools, for you won't find knowledge on their lips." This simple, solid directive gives us great liberty to move on. As we are navigating life, we need to know that we should steer clear of those who are foolish.

Because there are a lot of fools out there, the book of Proverbs warns us of fools and gives us direction on how to handle foolish people. Proverbs 14:8 says, "The prudent understand where they are going, but fools deceive themselves." Proverbs 3:35 says, "The wise inherit honor, but fools are put to shame!"

Can you recognize a fool? Fools are loud, defiant, deceptive, manipulative, arrogant, and boastful. They don't care if they hurt others, and when confronted, they fail to admit that they were wrong.

If we are building our lives to praise God and serve God, we should actively be seeking wisdom and discernment and striving to identify the fools in our midst. When we can identify them, we can steer clear of them as well.

The prudent understand where they are going, but fools deceive themselves.

PROVERBS 14:8

Control Your Gap

Gap control is a large part of playing defensive line. A noseguard or defensive tackle can shut down an entire element of a team's running game with good gap control.

Being a Houston Texans fan, I love to watch J. J. Watt. Watt has a tremendous ability to control the gaps on his side of the line. He is a sack specialist, and even if he doesn't get the sack, he consistently puts quarterbacks on their backs by controlling his gaps and creating opportunities for his teammates. He also swats balls out of the air and consistently makes tackles for loss in the backfield.

One of the greatest testimonies about Watt is his zeal and effort for every single play. This hasn't always been the case in Houston on the defensive line. Another first-round draft pick was accused by the media of taking plays off and not being reliable. Eventually, this player signed with another team. But Watt has now won three Defensive Player of the Year awards because he won't allow himself to take any plays off. When Watt signed the $100 million contract, it was reported that he went to the Texans training facility at three in the morning to get in another workout. His drive to be the best and not get comfortable with what he has already achieved challenges every teammate around him to do the same.

How do our teammates view us? Are we taking plays off? When we do, we are seen as unreliable. Proverbs 25:26 states, "If the godly give in to the wicked, it's like polluting a fountain or muddying a spring." Don't give in! Zealously go out every single day and honor the Lord. Stand your guard and control your gap!

If the godly give in to the wicked, it's like polluting a fountain or muddying a spring.   PROVERBS 25:26

You've Got to Get Up

When former *Apprentice* winner Bill Rancic interviewed Peyton Manning, he asked, "What was the hardest hit you ever received while playing in the NFL?" Manning, without hesitation, recalled how he was hit repeatedly by one player in particular, Baltimore Ravens linebacker Ray Lewis. Manning laughingly reflected on the way that Lewis would use Manning's shoulders as a way to help himself up while whispering in his ear, "I'll be back in a few minutes, punk."

Rancic followed up by asking, "Do you let them know that they hurt you?" Manning responded, "You can't. You've got to get up. If they know that they have hurt you, they will come back and do it again." Manning made the decision before he ever took the field that if he got knocked down, he was going to get back up. In the moment, while lying on the turf, Manning had to manage that decision to get back up.

In business, marriage, finances, or in relationships, getting up when you get knocked down is mission critical if you are to go anywhere in life. Life has a way of knocking you down, but living a life pleasing to the Lord carries a promise with it. Proverbs 24:16 gives us this assurance: "The godly may trip seven times, but they will get up again."

Make a decision in advance to get up when you get knocked down, and then manage that decision because you have already made it. Remember, as Peyton Manning recalls, "You've got to get up," and as the Bible promises, "The godly . . . will get up again."

The godly may trip seven times, but they will get up again.　　PROVERBS 24:16

Greater Than the Stock Exchange

I love a good roller coaster, and as a kid I would often go down to our local Six Flags theme park, AstroWorld, with a season pass. My brother Troy and I, along with our friends Brad, Ted, and Rick, would ride all the rides late into the evening.

One of my favorite rides was also one of the quickest—Greezed Lightnin'. This roller coaster launched into a 360-degree loop, taking you all the way upside down and around. Coming out of the loop, it then rose up the track to a point where the coaster was nearly perpendicular to the ground. It would then begin to go backwards, back through the loop, and down the track going seventy or eighty miles per hour until the coaster would climb backward up the track, almost perpendicular again. When the back of the cars topped out at the end of the track, you were then facing straight down. It would swing through and come back to the starting point. This ride was the most fun when the park was empty and we didn't have to get off to ride it again.

The stock exchange and our various investments can often feel like a roller-coaster ride with all of its ups and downs. Yet we are drawn to it in order to financially advance in life. There is a greater exchange I want to ask you to consider—wisdom. Wisdom is an intentional exchange, but its returns are much more stable than the ups and downs of the stock market.

Proverbs 8:10-11 says, "Choose my instruction rather than silver, and knowledge rather than pure gold. For wisdom is far more valuable than rubies. Nothing you desire can compare with it." To really advance in life, choose the best exchange, because possessing the wisdom of God will help you identify life's true riches.

Choose my instruction rather than silver, and knowledge rather than pure gold. For wisdom is far more valuable than rubies. Nothing you desire can compare with it. **PROVERBS 8:10-11**

All In

Fellowship of Christian Athletes is an outstanding organization and a great way to engage with athletes of faith. Former Baylor University quarterback Bryce Petty was interviewed for *FCA Magazine* about his time at Baylor. Petty was asked, "In the game of football, what's it mean to go All In?"

Petty replied, "For me, I want to be the best in the nation on every play—whether that's a great handoff, a great pass, or being a good communicator on the field. When we compete like that on the field, it carries over to what we do off of it, too."[54]

Are you all in? Dr. Kevin Elko, in his *Monday Morning Cup of Inspiration*, admonishes his listeners to "be where your feet are." Because of the distractions of this digital age, it is easy to be somewhere else. The more we allow ourselves to be somewhere else, the more apt we are to disappoint those we love. There are so many distractions, challenges, and demands for our attention that it is hard to be all in on every play.

To be our best—as a parent, spouse, student, boss, or employee, we would learn well to focus on every play. Colossians 3:17 states, "Whatever you do or say, do it as a representative of the Lord Jesus, giving thanks through him to God the Father." I don't always remember that I am a representative of the Lord. Being my best begins with being where my feet are and serving those around me like Jesus serves me.

Whatever you do or say, do it as a representative of the Lord Jesus, giving thanks through him to God the Father.   COLOSSIANS 3:17

---

[54] "All In," *FCA Magazine* (November/December 2014): 9, http://www.fca.org/digitalmagazine/fcamagvol56issue6/.

Learning and Earning Your Way

After his first week in his high school's football program, my son Brady had a defining moment. In the midst of two-a-days in the August heat, his simple realization came out with angst in his voice as he told me, "Dad, this is hard." In that moment, Brady was facing the choice either to quit or to persevere despite his feelings.

No matter the setting, the culture of a new environment can break you or cause you to quit. During his first season, I watched my son move through the four sectors of experience, from ignorance, to knowledge, to mastery, to teaching others. Had I stepped in to help him, I would have weakened his resolve and only enabled his feelings of being defeated. Instead he learned what it took, made the choice to persevere, and then earned his way through it.

Philippians 1:6 states, "I am certain that God, who began the good work within you, will continue his work until it is finally finished on the day when Christ Jesus returns."

Moving to a new city, changing schools, or switching jobs brings about new challenges. When you go to that next new place, trust that the challenges that lie ahead will cultivate the work of God in you, if you cooperate. If you are tempted to withdraw, stay with it, even when it gets hard. You will be strengthened, grow in maturity, and come out better on the other side. Stay the course, because it will pay off.

I am certain that God, who began the good work within you, will continue his work until it is finally finished on the day when Christ Jesus returns.

PHILIPPIANS 1:6

One Man's Trash

With two games remaining in the 2015 NFL season, Jets quarterback Ryan Fitzpatrick needed just one more touchdown pass to beat the record Joe Namath had set for the number of touchdown passes thrown in one season as a Jet. Fitzpatrick, selected in the seventh round of the 2005 draft by the St. Louis Rams, had been on six teams by that point in his ten-season NFL career.

After moving to Houston and settling his family from Tennessee in 2014, Fitzpatrick contributed to the Houston Texans' nine-win season in Coach Bill O'Brien's first year as the Texans head coach. The 2014 season had its ups and downs, with Fitzpatrick being benched at one point and finishing 6–6 as a starter. Had he moved forward with the Texans, there would have been plenty of opportunity for improvement.

The Texans decided that they would go a different direction after the 2014 season, and they traded Fitzpatrick to the Jets. This reunited Ryan with his old coach, Chan Gailey. With Fitzpatrick's contract expiring at the end of his incredible 2015 season, there were reports that Fitzpatrick could get a significant raise, from $3.25 million a season to $12 million a season.

If you feel you've been passed on like Fitzpatrick was, remember that it only takes one leader to believe in you. When others discover about you what you already believe about yourself, the sky is the limit. Be encouraged by the words of Proverbs 22:29 today: "Do you see any truly competent workers? They will serve kings rather than working for ordinary people." Even if no one seems to notice you, be diligent with the talent you have been given.

Do you see any truly competent workers? They will serve kings rather than working for ordinary people.   PROVERBS 22:29

Why Training Camp Really Matters

Have you ever heard someone say, "I've got to go knock the rust off"? Training camp is an opportunity for athletes to do just that. Baseball, football, and basketball have times of training every year, and the first few days are the hardest. It is during those first few days when coaches are able to see what they have to work with and what they will need to focus on over the next few weeks.

Training camps are crucibles for athletes. It is there that their success or failure will be established. Many will be cut from the team, never to play the game they love again. Others will find their way and emerge as a starter, surprising the analysts, fans, coaches, and even themselves at times because they had such a good training camp.

We experience our own training camps as we go through challenging seasons. These seasons have a way to prune us so that they shape and mold our character. Scripture tells us that God doesn't waste these seasons. Proverbs 25:4 states, "Remove the impurities from silver, and the sterling will be ready for the silversmith." If you are in the midst of a season that feels like the first few days of training camp, remember that sometimes we have to have the rust knocked off so that God has something to work with.

Remove the impurities from silver, and the sterling will be ready for the silversmith.   PROVERBS 25:4

Standing in the Hall of Fame

I've always wanted to go to the Pro Football and Baseball Halls of Fame. There is something compelling in taking a trip through the halls of greatness, seeing the memorabilia and the busts of the best players in sports. These men are the most gifted, most competitive, and most determined athletes of their leagues.

What is the key to their long-term success? It was how they used their gifts once they were given the opportunity. John Maxwell says, "Talent is never enough." As a matter of fact, he even has a book by that title. Talent opens the door, but effort, determination, and perseverance keep it open.

Proverbs 18:16 states, "Giving a gift can open doors; it gives access to important people!" This text is not talking about a bribe. I believe that Solomon is challenging his hearers to work with all diligence and manage their talent. Because stewarding well the abilities that God has given us brings us significant success.

Another verse that speaks in a similar manner when it comes to stewarding our talent is Proverbs 22:29. It states, "Do you see any truly competent workers? They will serve kings rather than working for ordinary people."

Recognize your gifting, develop strategies to utilize your gifting in your work, and do it with all diligence. Over time, you will be noticed, you will get promoted, and you will have the chance to do things that others in your line of work only dream about. Once the gift takes you there, steward it with great determination and perseverance. Remember, talent opens the door, but it isn't enough to keep it open.

Giving a gift can open doors; it gives access to important people!

PROVERBS 18:16

How They Keep Score

Jack Welch was the CEO of General Electric for many years. Welch was known for making things simple. He once said, "If you want to succeed in any organization, find out who keeps score, how they keep score, and score."

Welch knew that as a leader, one of his greatest challenges and opportunities was to liberate his people so that they might perform for the company and be rewarded by the company. He gave opportunity, but he also didn't allow his subordinates to hijack the vision or take the rest of the team down. In this regard, he was tough with those who weren't pulling their weight. Consider this perspective when he talked about firing "jerks" in his company. He said, "Public hangings are teaching moments. Every company has to do it. . . . CEOs can talk and blab each day about culture, but the employees all know who the jerks are."

Proverbs 14:35 states, "A king rejoices in wise servants but is angry with those who disgrace him." American Christianity has largely avoided the conversation regarding authority and subordination as a means to honor God, but when you study the life of Jesus, you see it on almost every page.

As a man, you will most likely live your life both in and under authority. Scripture calls us to honor authority. When you do, life goes well for you. When you don't, there are consequences.

If you are under authority, remember that God has put people in places of authority, and he calls us to show them honor even if we don't like them. You see, God prepares you to lead by teaching you to follow. So deal wisely by honoring the king, and God will honor you.

If you are in authority, you are blessed when those under your authority honor your leadership. Bless them for doing so and give them the opportunity to score.

A king rejoices in wise servants but is angry with those who disgrace him.

PROVERBS 14:35

Always Right

Howard Cosell, the great commentator on *Monday Night Football*, was a man of strong opinion. Cosell was controversial, and he would rarely back down from others with his "take" on things, including his support of Muhammad Ali. Cosell was known to have said of his style, "Mommy, why does Daddy cuss the TV and call it Howard?"

Many on sports radio have taken this approach with their enthusiasm and opinion, but they lack the skill and wisdom of Cosell. This turns off the listeners because it is hard to continually listen to someone who thinks that he or she is always right.

Have you ever been around people who think they are always right? They love to tell you what you think. They love to put their two cents in, even when it doesn't concern them. When you try to contribute to the conversation, it is hard to get a word in edgewise.

Proverbs 12:15 says, "Fools think their own way is right, but the wise listen to others." Clearly there are two options for us to choose: the way of the fool, who isn't teachable, or the way of the wise, who is willing to stop and listen. If you choose the way of the fool, don't be surprised when your circle of community dwindles over time. It may take a little while for others to figure it out, but eventually they will fall away because no one delights in one-sided relationships.

A significant part of finding wisdom is simply being found listening. Delight in listening before airing your own opinion. You may just learn something about the other person, about life, and about yourself.

Fools think their own way is right, but the wise listen to others.

PROVERBS 12:15

Reset

It happens at some of the most inconvenient times. My wife hollers at me, "My hair dryer is out. Can you reset the breaker?" Invariably it is cold or raining, and I have to find a coat or umbrella and go out to the breaker box, where I find that everything is fine.

Then I think, *It's the GFCI outlet. It has tripped and needs to be reset.* This seems to happen about once a week, when the hair dryer and hair rollers are on at the same time. I go back inside to the GFCI outlet, hit reset, and all returns to bathroom bliss.

We, too, need a reset on a weekly basis. We need to power down all the noise that we allow into our lives that takes us away from God's purpose for us and focus on him. We need to hear the preaching of the Word of God. We need to be called up to praise him. We need to offer to him our resources for Kingdom use. We need to value his church and gathering with other believers.

Hebrews 10:23-25 states, "Let us hold tightly without wavering to the hope we affirm, for God can be trusted to keep his promise. Let us think of ways to motivate one another to acts of love and good works. And let us not neglect our meeting together, as some people do, but encourage one another, especially now that the day of his return is drawing near."

Hit reset on a weekly basis by going to and contributing to a local church. Over time, it will change your life for the good of your soul and the glory of God.

Let us not neglect our meeting together, as some people do, but encourage one another, especially now that the day of his return is drawing near.

HEBREWS 10:25

Seeing What Could Be

Ara Parseghian, two-time national champion head football coach for the Notre Dame Fighting Irish, once said, "A good coach will make his players see what they can be rather than what they are." In his eleven seasons at Notre Dame, Coach Parseghian never had a losing record. Immediately after taking over at Notre Dame, with the program coming off five straight losing seasons, the Fighting Irish nearly captured the 1964 National Championship in Parseghian's first year. That's leadership!

When Saul was king over Israel, the Philistines wreaked havoc on the Israelites. The Valley of Elah became the location for a great showdown between Israel and the Philistines. Goliath, the Philistines' champion, came forward and challenged anyone in Israel to a man-to-man battle, winner take all. For forty straight days, Goliath taunted Israel, until a young shepherd boy named David brought his brothers supplies at the front lines. When he heard the giant taunting the army of the Living God, the leader in David began to emerge. Quickly, he inquired about what would be done for the man who took the giant down.

I want you to see something really special in this story. Look at David's question in 1 Samuel 17:26: "What will a man get for killing this Philistine and ending his defiance of Israel?"

Notice Saul's evaluation of David: "Don't be ridiculous! . . . There's no way you can fight this Philistine and possibly win! You're only a boy, and he's been a man of war since his youth" (1 Samuel 17:33).

Do you see it? Saul said, "You're only a boy." David said, "What will a man get for killing this Philistine?"

Let's take a play out of Coach Parseghian's playbook and help our children grow in the faith of what God can do. Let's lead and inspire them toward greatness. To Saul, David was a boy. But I would argue that David was the only man on Israel's sideline that day.

Don't be ridiculous! . . . There's no way you can fight this Philistine and possibly win! You're only a boy, and he's been a man of war since his youth.
1 SAMUEL 17:33

Huge Small Things

When success comes your way, there is often an initial surprise in the accomplishment. Over time, the more successful you become, the easier it is to take the success for granted. When you begin to take success for granted, you will grow more and more discontent, and complacency can set in. When this happens, it can overcome you like a vicious animal on the prowl, and you find yourself in places doing things you would never have done before in a quest to find happiness and contentment once again.

This often happened to Israel. After they honored the Lord by keeping his covenant, he would bless them. In their blessings, they would forget the Lord, behave in such a way as to invoke the curses of the covenant (see Deuteronomy 28–32), and be disciplined by the Lord. Deuteronomy 32:15-16 gives us a description of this cycle:

> But Israel soon became fat and unruly;
>> the people grew heavy, plump, and stuffed!
> Then they abandoned the God who had made them;
>> they made light of the Rock of their salvation.
> They stirred up his jealousy by worshiping foreign gods;
>> they provoked his fury with detestable deeds.

When you take success and prosperity for granted, it leads you down paths that aren't pleasing to the Lord. One of the ways to guard against taking success for granted is to make a big deal out of small things. I challenge our church staff to never lose sight of the significance of the small victories, because those stories are powerful. Are they more commonplace than they once were? Yes. But they are still the victories we have been striving for from the beginning.

As you work, enjoy the huge accomplishment of the small things, as this makes the journey so much more meaningful. It also keeps you grounded in what really matters.

Then they abandoned the God who had made them; they made light of the Rock of their salvation. DEUTERONOMY 32:15

The Enemy's Playbook

Adversity is never neutral. It is used either as a catalyst to finish or as a weight to press you down.

I went through a significant professional challenge in which I dealt with adversity for more than nine months. I drew tremendous strength and counsel from the story told in the Old Testament book of Nehemiah.

Nehemiah is trying to rebuild the walls of Jerusalem when he is opposed by a group of adversaries. These men circulated rumors about him and repeatedly caused him significant challenges. Nehemiah 6:5-7 includes some of the rumors:

> The fifth time, Sanballat's servant came with an open letter in his hand, and this is what it said: "There is a rumor among the surrounding nations, and Geshem tells me it is true, that you and the Jews are planning to rebel and that is why you are building the wall. According to his reports, you plan to be their king. He also reports that you have appointed prophets in Jerusalem to proclaim about you, 'Look! There is a king in Judah!'
>
> "You can be very sure that this report will get back to the king, so I suggest that you come and talk it over with me."

The enemies of God have a simple playbook of lies, deceit, and fear. If you pay too much attention to the enemies' ways, they can derail you from what you were called to in the first place. So look at how Nehemiah responds to the adversity. He says, "They were just trying to intimidate us, imagining that they could discourage us and stop the work. So I continued the work with even greater determination" (Nehemiah 6:9).

Know the enemy's playbook, and let the adversity strengthen your resolve. Remember, the adversity will either press you down or cause you to rise up. Choose to rise up, and continue the work!

They were just trying to intimidate us, imagining that they could discourage us and stop the work. So I continued the work with even greater determination.

NEHEMIAH 6:9

Living Life through the Rearview Mirror

Have you ever been around someone who seems to be living life through the rearview mirror? This type of person seems to think that the only good times, the only best times, are the days gone by.

The great Tom Landry lived differently. He is known for the mind-set and attitude that declares today, and each day given to him, was a day full of opportunity. Landry said, "Today, you have 100 percent of your life left." What a great perspective! Though we don't understand all that we experience or why, we have a choice regarding how we will view our lives and the time God has given us.

Listen to the wisdom of Ecclesiastes 3:11: "God has made everything beautiful for its own time. He has planted eternity in the human heart, but even so, people cannot see the whole scope of God's work from beginning to end."

How do you view time? Each of us is given the same amount of time every day. What we do with our time, how we see time, and what we envision with the rest of our time will determine whether we live life looking at the rearview mirror or looking through the windshield. Knowing that you have 100 percent of your life left today, what will you do with it? What does your tomorrow look like? God is at work. Join him at making today, tomorrow, and the days to come something spectacular. He makes everything beautiful at just the right time!

God has made everything beautiful for its own time. He has planted eternity in the human heart, but even so, people cannot see the whole scope of God's work from beginning to end.　　　　　ECCLESIASTES 3:11

The Hard Work Hall of Fame

Houston's Christian radio station KSBJ hosted an event called "Born to Be Wild: A Man Journey" in February 2016. Heisman Trophy winner Charlie Ward and Super Bowl XLI champion head coach Tony Dungy were the featured guests, and Christian artist Brandon Heath led worship. Mark Merrill and Darrin Gray from All Pro Dad were a big part of the night. Because Darrin and I have established a heart connection, he invited my sons and me to join the behind-the-scenes action and attend the event.

At a VIP reception prior to the event, Coach Dungy was discussing his newly revealed acceptance into the Hall of Fame. He was excited that he was going to be inducted with one of his players, Marvin Harrison.

Dungy reflected on the uncommon work ethic of Harrison and Peyton Manning. If you have read any of Dungy's books, you know that the word *uncommon* means a lot to him. He first was captured by this word when his college head coach, Cal Stoll, told his players, "Success is uncommon, therefore not to be enjoyed by the common man. I'm looking for uncommon people." Given that Harrison, Dungy, and someday, Manning will all be inducted into the Hall of Fame, I would say that these men, through their hard work, truly are uncommon.

Notice how Scripture calls us to uncommon service to the Lord. Second Timothy 2:20-21 states, "In a wealthy home some utensils are made of gold and silver, and some are made of wood and clay. The expensive utensils are used for special occasions, and the cheap ones are for everyday use. If you keep yourself pure, you will be a special utensil for honorable use. Your life will be clean, and you will be ready for the Master to use you for every good work."

Today, set yourself apart for uncommon service to the Lord.

In a wealthy home some utensils are made of gold and silver, and some are made of wood and clay. The expensive utensils are used for special occasions, and the cheap ones are for everyday use. If you keep yourself pure, you will be a special utensil for honorable use. Your life will be clean, and you will be ready for the Master to use you for every good work. 2 TIMOTHY 2:20-21

What I Do vs. Who I Am

Former Baylor University quarterback Bryce Petty once said, "During my time at Baylor, I've learned that football is what I do; it's not who I am. When I began to truly understand what that meant, the sky was the limit for what I was capable of. It has freed me and given me peace to explore who I am spiritually, who God is, and what He's doing in my life."[55]

So much of our worth as men is tied to what we do. As a result, we can either derive a sense of well-being or loathe ourselves based on our performance on the competitive fields of life. But answering the question, "Who are you?" shouldn't be tied to what we do, because doing always flows from being.

Ephesians 1–3 speaks specifically of our identity. We were excluded, dead in our trespasses, foreigners and aliens to the covenants. Now we are in Christ, a union that always describes a life of benefits and an eternal glory. Notice what our identity looks like in Ephesians 1:13: "Now you Gentiles have also heard the truth, the Good News that God saves you. And when you believed in Christ, he identified you as his own by giving you the Holy Spirit, whom he promised long ago."

Five different times in the book, Paul reminds his readers of what they had been like before Christ and what they became after Christ. It isn't until Ephesians 4 that Paul begins to instruct them on what they need to do because of who they are.

Who are you? From what I see, if you are in Christ, you are identified as a child of God. Now let what you do flow from that understanding.

Now you Gentiles have also heard the truth, the Good News that God saves you. And when you believed in Christ, he identified you as his own by giving you the Holy Spirit, whom he promised long ago.　　　　EPHESIANS 1:13

---

55 "All In," *FCA Magazine* (November/December 2014): 9, http://www.fca.org/digitalmagazine /fcamagvol56issue6/.

Lombardi's Leadership Secret

In my interview with NFL Hall of Fame quarterback and Super Bowl champion Bart Starr, I asked him, "What was the secret to Vince Lombardi's leadership success?" Here is what Starr had to say about his former coach: "His own order of life and his leadership and so forth . . . he was truly one of those strong men, whose strength had grown initially and was there every day because of how he began his day and his devotion to God."

Isn't it fascinating that the secret wasn't his knowledge of the game, his knowledge of his players, or his ability to diagnose an offense and set his defense accordingly? According to Super Bowl I and II MVP Bart Starr, Coach Lombardi's leadership secret was that he began each day in time with God.

I have been around a number of successful people who have struggled to know how to have spiritual success. There is no need to complicate matters. Your reading *A Minute of Vision for Men* is a step toward spiritual growth. Reading a portion of Scripture and presenting your requests to the Lord in prayer are other great ways to spend time with God.

Psalm 119:15 states, "I will study your commandments and reflect on your ways." Nourishing your spirit for just a few minutes each morning is a great starting point for a life of adoration to the Lord. The more you grow in this area, the easier it will be to take the next steps.[56] Establishing a prayer and Bible study routine will ground you even further in the faith.

There is depth and power in a life of worship and devotion to God. As Vince Lombardi shows us, and as Bart Starr testifies, this devotion will impact every area of your life.

I will study your commandments and reflect on your ways.   PSALM 119:15

---

[56] A great next step would be taking time to go through the *One Year Bible*, published by Tyndale House Publishers. Their One Year line is a great way to digest Scripture over the course of 365 days.

The Poor Man Test

We were heading home from church one Sunday. My oldest, Brady, who was only two or three at the time, was bundled up in his car seat when we exited the freeway to head to the suburbs. We were on a tight budget, and we couldn't afford to live in town near our church.

A woman held up a sign asking for money. We had seen her on our way home from church more than once. As I took the left turn and passed right on through the light, Brady said to me, "Daddy, what does she want?"

I curtly responded, "Oh, Brady, she just wants some money. She needs some help."

With the faith and wisdom of a pure-hearted child, he said, "Well, Daddy, we've got to help her."

Immediately I turned the car around, stopped to see what I had in my pocket, and then proceeded to circle the freeway to come back around to the woman. When I rolled my window down and she approached, I asked her name, and I told Kathy that we wanted to bless her, and gave her some money.

While reflecting on that moment, I have wondered what it is about growing up that causes us to lose our innocent faith and cling to our money. Part of a maturing faith is putting your money on the line. It is the one area where God says, "Try me in this!" (see Malachi 3:10). For many people, money is the one area that they withhold from God. Jesus said, "Where your treasure is, there your heart will be also" (Matthew 6:21, ESV). In other words, look at where a man puts his money and you will see what has his heart.

One way to determine who or what has your heart is to look at your attitude regarding the poor. Proverbs 14:31 states, "Those who oppress the poor insult their Maker, but helping the poor honors him." Do you show contempt for the poor, or do you respect them and show them kindness? Is your treasure found in your wallet or in your obedience to God? What you do with the poor in your midst declares what you think about God.

Where your treasure is, there your heart will be also.   MATTHEW 6:21, ESV

The Use of Instant Replay

Baseball was the last of the major sports to adopt the use of instant replay. What was the delay? What kept them from being willing to go to the tape to make sure they had the right call? Hundreds of millions of dollars are invested for the players, owners, and fans to all have a great experience. Is it the pride of the umpire that kept Major League Baseball from reviewing their work in real time? You know what they say about instant replay: "The eye in the sky doesn't lie."

The pride of a man is a powerful thing. It can cause a nation to go to war, a man to leave his family, and a coach to ignore talent right under his nose because he doesn't want to be questioned.

Listen to the words of Solomon, king of Israel. Proverbs 24:32 states, "Then, as I looked and thought about it, I learned this lesson." I would advocate that we need to push the pride aside and use instant replay in our lives. We need to review our steps, our words, and our thoughts. We need to examine ourselves and allow others we trust to do the same, because it takes a humble man to review his ways. It takes an even greater humility to receive instruction.

When you rewind the tape, what do you see? Grace, kindness, and humility, or pride, arrogance, and strife?

Then, as I looked and thought about it, I learned this lesson.   PROVERBS 24:32

Will Power

Leon Jones was our church's maintenance man for over twenty-five years. He always had a smile on his face and nicknames for different kids at the church. One young boy named Will he called "Will Power." Without fail, when Leon would see Will, he would say, "Will Power," and Will would crack a smile and walk on.

It is interesting to watch kids grow and live up to the names that they have been given. Will is a very disciplined young man who is excited to learn and grow and absorb as much of life as he can.

Will isn't academically motivated as much as he is practically motivated. For example, Will already has his real estate license at the age of twenty-two because he wants to sell rural land and work his own land. He is also learning to become a welder. You see, Will is gifted with his hands, and he isn't afraid to work hard or try new things.

Will has already achieved a lot in his twenty-two years, and his life and nickname remind me of 2 Timothy 1:7, which states, "God has not given us a spirit of fear and timidity, but of power, love, and self-discipline."

Whatever your name or nickname, remember whose name you carry and seek to live up to his name. When you need willpower, ask the Lord, for he has given you a spirit of power, love, and self-discipline.

God has not given us a spirit of fear and timidity, but of power, love, and self-discipline.   2 TIMOTHY 1:7

The Impact of a Spiritual Father

Three-time Super Bowl champion coach Joe Gibbs speaks of a time when as an assistant football coach at the University of Arkansas, he found a spiritual father. This man, who managed a J. C. Penney department store and had very little athletic prowess, walked with God. His name was George Tharel.

George taught an adult Sunday school class at his church and had a tremendous impact on Gibbs. In my interview with Coach Gibbs, he said of his spiritual father, "George had a huge impact on me. . . . He took me under his wing. After I left Arkansas, we would talk every week, and I knew George was directed by the Lord, because he came from a completely different world and yet would say things to me where I knew that God had to have told him this."

What if the next Joe Gibbs is in your life and you are to be his George Tharel? Do you have a walk with God that would influence that young person to become as grounded and influential as Joe Gibbs? Can others seek counsel from you and know that you are clearly directed by the Lord?

Genesis 6:9 says of Noah, "This is the account of Noah and his family. Noah was a righteous man, the only blameless person living on earth at the time, and he walked in close fellowship with God." Walk with God and listen to his voice. There is no telling the impact you will have.

This is the account of Noah and his family. Noah was a righteous man, the only blameless person living on earth at the time, and he walked in close fellowship with God.

GENESIS 6:9

C'mon, Man

The guys on ESPN's *Monday Night Countdown* have made the phrase "C'mon, man!" a part of our everyday vernacular. This segment of the show is one of my favorites, because it features something absurd from the world of sports.

As I sat at my local car dealership getting a few last-minute tune-ups for my wife's truck, I had a "C'mon, man!" moment. Given that the car was still under warranty and the top of the lock had broken off, I asked the dealership to replace the broken part. After they performed the maintenance I needed on the SUV, the service adviser told me that the lock head wasn't covered under warranty. He said, "Because it's broken, we don't cover it under the warranty." I looked at him and said, "Isn't that exactly what the warranty covers?"

When you are told, "Three years, 36,000 miles, bumper to bumper," aren't the lock heads included? C'mon, man! What good is a warranty if what's warrantied isn't covered? I'm still shaking my head at this one.

Does your word have conditions on it? Do you leave people saying, "C'mon, man!" in their dealings with you? Unfortunately, we have lost the art of making our word our bond. We have lost the integrity of doing what we say, even when it costs us something. Proverbs 11:1 says, "The LORD detests the use of dishonest scales, but he delights in accurate weights." Don't sell your reputation by breaking your word. That is too high a price to pay!

The LORD detests the use of dishonest scales, but he delights in accurate weights. PROVERBS 11:1

The Importance of Saying Hello

Being the new person can be difficult. Tricia, a professional who had relocated to Houston from Canada, began coming to our church at the invitation of a member. Unbeknownst to me, she was assessing whether she would really consider our church as an option based on the warmth, or lack thereof, of our congregation. You see, she had faithfully attended a church nearby for nearly a year without anyone reaching out to her. She later told me about her first visit to our fellowship. She told the Lord that if someone came to her and spoke to her that morning, she would stay, confirming it as the Lord's leading.

At one of our dinners for new and prospective members, Tricia relayed how, during her first visit, I had come out of the worship center, heading to our guest reception, and walked right to her. Though she had moved out of the way of the traffic so that she could sit back and watch things develop, the Lord wanted to answer her prayer. She said, "And then you made a beeline to me and asked me, 'Are you new here?'" She said she had never been as thankful for a greeting as she had on that day, and she has been coming to our church ever since. She knew that this was where the Lord had led her.

Why can God's house be so cold relationally? What is our responsibility in receiving those who come to our churches seeking a place to worship with fellow believers? Romans 12:13 states, "When God's people are in need, be ready to help them. Always be eager to practice hospitality." One of the five promises that we make as a church leadership team is to provide warm fellowship to those who come in our doors. Our people have embraced and embodied it, and though we are not perfect, we believe a simple hello may be somebody's answer to prayer. Who needs your hello today?

When God's people are in need, be ready to help them. Always be eager to practice hospitality.   ROMANS 12:13

SEPTEMBER

A Different Way

Moneyball: The Art of Winning an Unfair Game is a book by Michael Lewis that details the journey of the Oakland A's and their general manager Billie Beane in their attempt to assemble a competitive team in a league that favors the rich-market franchises. Beane's approach was to set aside the subjective data—the so-called "collective wisdom" of baseball insiders that dominated the baseball world for nearly a hundred years—and assemble a team based only on their on-field performance—objective data called sabermetrics.

Beane's desire to take away the subjectivity and replace it with game-based objective data, such as slugging percentage and on-base percentage, was a revolutionary challenge to the old-school system. Beane looked at the game of baseball and asked, "What if . . . ?" Today, many front-office personnel have adopted the sabermetrics approach to assembling a baseball team because one general manager was willing to consider a different way.

What if we considered a different way when it comes to conflict with others? Have you considered another way when you are in a fight? Proverbs 25:21-22 states, "If your enemies are hungry, give them food to eat. If they are thirsty, give them water to drink. You will heap burning coals of shame on their heads, and the LORD will reward you."

The movie *Woodlawn* captures this different way, which in 1973 moved an entire city. Imagine what it can do in your life! The next time you are in conflict with another, ask the question, "What if . . . ?" and seek the different way of Proverbs 25.

If your enemies are hungry, give them food to eat. If they are thirsty, give them water to drink. You will heap burning coals of shame on their heads, and the LORD will reward you.   PROVERBS 25:21-22

Having a Deep Bench

The game that broke my heart in 1993 has been dubbed "The Comeback." Frank Reich, in for the injured starter Jim Kelly, was the hero, forever blessing head coach Marv Levy and the city of Buffalo. Reich led the Bills back from a 32-point deficit to win against my Houston Oilers with a final score of 41–38. Let's just say, it was a heartbreaking day for me and all of my friends as we looked on in disbelief.

This wasn't the first comeback engineered by Reich. As a matter of fact, as a backup quarterback for the University of Maryland Terrapins, he had led the Terps back from a 31–0 deficit to a 42–40 win over the University of Miami Hurricanes in 1984.

A football team's season is only as deep as their bench. Invariably, someone in a key position is going to go down and suffer an injury. Having depth on the bench with players ready to come in to give the team the spark they need is fundamental to winning in the long run.

Whether you lead an organization or feel like you are on the bench waiting for your chance to get in the game, remember these words: "Trustworthy messengers refresh like snow in summer. They revive the spirit of their employer" (Proverbs 25:13).

If you are the leader, keep in mind that there is nothing like having a bench full of faithful difference makers. If you are on the bench and hoping to get in to the game, prepare every day as if your number will be called.

Trustworthy messengers refresh like snow in summer. They revive the spirit of their employer.　　　　　　　　　　　　　　　　PROVERBS 25:13

Leading a Team

Legendary basketball coach Red Auerbach gave great counsel on leading a team. He once said, "Be and look prepared. Be a man of integrity. Never break your word. Don't have two sets of standards. Stand up for your players and show them you care on and off the court."

What great counsel for leaders! So many mistakes in leadership are made in violating the fundamentals of relationships. This counsel also has tremendous benefit for all of those who follow our leadership—whether it is our children, our employees, or the young athletes we coach in the local Little League.

Leaders of integrity come prepared, set a standard, and keep their word. Proverbs 11:3 states, "Honesty guides good people; dishonesty destroys treacherous people." Leaders of integrity want their followers to know that they aren't just important, but valuable, too. Pat Bowlen, the ailing owner of the Denver Broncos, has a reputation of being a man of integrity and standing up for his people. When his beloved Broncos once again won the coveted Lombardi Trophy in 2016, many of the same people in the organization who were there when they won it with John Elway as the quarterback were still there, with Elway as the general manager.

I am sure Bowlen wasn't perfect, but I'll bet you he also humbled himself when he was wrong. This is the only way to continually build love and affection over the long haul. So as you have opportunity to lead, keep these foundational principles in mind, and if you happen to make a mistake on one of them, don't be too proud to admit that you were wrong.

Honesty guides good people; dishonesty destroys treacherous people.
PROVERBS 11:3

Creating Moments

I've got to tip my hat to Tony and Heather Gray at Search Services in Houston. Tony and Heather are some of our closest friends, and I like them even more now because they included our family in an event they created for the release of the film *Star Wars: The Force Awakens*. But Tony and Heather didn't just invite us, they also invited all of their clients and their clients' families. They rented out a movie theater for a 4:45 p.m. showing on a Monday at the start of the Christmas holiday, just after the movie had come out.

At the theater, Tony got to address the crowd and introduce the people to a charity that his company supports before the movie rolled. More than three hundred people showed up at this moment to watch the next movie in the Star Wars episodes. When I saw Tony and Heather after the movie, I thanked them and said, "Man, I wish I had thought of this. This was great."

One of the things that good leaders do well is to create moments for others that encourage them, inspire them, communicate appreciation for them, and bless them. As you lead your family, are you creating moments that they will remember? What about your employees or clients? As you lead others, put them first, show them honor, and bestow blessings upon them. In Romans 12, I see two things that I want to leave with you today. Verses 6-8 state, "In his grace, God has given us different gifts for doing certain things well. . . . If your gift is to encourage others, be encouraging. If it is giving, give generously. If God has given you leadership ability, take the responsibility seriously. And if you have a gift for showing kindness to others, do it gladly."

Additionally, Romans 12:10 fits nicely with the first Scripture. It states, "Take delight in honoring each other." I want to challenge you today to lead zealously and honor those in your midst and make some really cool moments together.

In his grace, God has given us different gifts for doing certain things well. . . . If your gift is to encourage others, be encouraging. If it is giving, give generously. If God has given you leadership ability, take the responsibility seriously. And if you have a gift for showing kindness to others, do it gladly. **ROMANS 12:6-8**

The Wise Fool

The great players are known to find a way to expose their opponents' weaknesses. They study their opponents' technique to learn how to get into the heads of the people playing against them. Some players will bring up weaknesses from their opponents' personal lives to get under their skin as well.

If you were to spend a day or two with me, you would find that my weakness is struggling to listen effectively. One of the reasons why I don't listen well is because I speak too quickly. For instance, I will try to finish my wife's sentences without hearing her out or too quickly exert my opinion in a meeting. The older I get the more convicted I am of my need to speak less and listen more. Listening takes intentionality because of the distractions that are so prevalent in our lives today. Smartphones, the ever-present e-mail, and text messages create a dissonance with those we are in relationship with.

How can we be better listeners? First, listen with your eyes. Force yourself to maintain eye contact while in a one-on-one conversation. It takes effort and focus, but you will retain more of what was said if you lock in with your eyes. Second, listen with your heart by treating others how you want to be treated. As a result, don't hijack the conversation and make it about you. We all know people who seem to lie in wait for a chance to make the discussion about themselves. Third, listen with your mind. Do this by asking questions that pertain to the conversation at hand.

Scripture gives us wise advice for listening. Proverbs 18:13 states, "Spouting off before listening to the facts is both shameful and foolish." Proverbs 17:28 states, "Even fools are thought wise when they keep silent; with their mouths shut, they seem intelligent." Listen before you speak.

Spouting off before listening to the facts is both shameful and foolish.
PROVERBS 18:13

Third and Eight

All they needed was eight yards to keep the drive alive. The problem was that the tight end released into the flat and caught the ball at four yards, and the "Sam" linebacker cut him short at six.

Does this happen to your hometown team as often as it seems to happen to mine? For whatever reason, some offensive schemes leave the fans, the ownership, and the defensive side of the ball wondering about the competency and reliability of the offensive unit. When this happens, the entire team suffers.

You see, when your defense knows that the offense is going to go three and out, they lose heart. They then begin to ask, "Why am I working so hard if half of our game plan and half of our personnel are incompetent?"

To win consistently at any level requires an entire team effort. It demands excellence and absolute commitment to those you work with, those who employ you, or those who cheer you on from home. Not fulfilling your commitment creates an undertow of uncertainty that is hard to stop and repair. Look at the comparison Solomon makes in Proverbs 25:19: "Putting confidence in an unreliable person in times of trouble is like chewing with a broken tooth or walking on a lame foot."

If you are going to be successful, you have to learn to be faithful. You have to be reliable. So are you being faithful toward your employer, coworkers, and family? Make sure those around you can rely on you through your faithfulness.

Putting confidence in an unreliable person in times of trouble is like chewing with a broken tooth or walking on a lame foot.　　　**PROVERBS 25:19**

Third and Twenty-Two

I can never figure out why there isn't a play for third and twenty-two beyond the draw play. For many teams, the draw play is so predictable. Even the broadcasters know that on third and twenty-two, the offensive coordinator is going to call a running play. After it gets seven yards and the punt team comes on, they say, "Well, they just don't have a twenty-two-yard play in their playbook."

How do you react when your team calls a draw play on third and twenty-two? When my boys and I are watching our Texans and they run the draw on third and twenty-two, we jump out of our seats and scream at the TV, saying, "Throw the ball! Take a shot downfield! Throw deep!" Why accept defeat when you have world-class receivers and a grown man who can throw the ball seventy yards or more? I can't fathom it.

Let's consider our actions when our backs are against the wall. Why do we accept defeat so easily when the enemy has had his way with us? Why do we listen to his lies, believe we have lost, and throw in the towel?

I want to leave you with two Scripture passages to consider today. First, Ephesians 1:3 states, "All praise to God, the Father of our Lord Jesus Christ, who has blessed us with every spiritual blessing in the heavenly realms because we are united with Christ." Keep in mind, we have every blessing we need in Jesus Christ. There is a play in your playbook for third and twenty-two. Second, Romans 8:35-37 states, "Can anything ever separate us from Christ's love? Does it mean he no longer loves us if we have trouble or calamity, or are persecuted, or hungry, or destitute, or in danger, or threatened with death? . . . No, despite all these things, overwhelming victory is ours through Christ, who loved us." My friend, if it's third and twenty-two today, throw deep! He'll be right there with you.

All praise to God, the Father of our Lord Jesus Christ, who has blessed us with every spiritual blessing in the heavenly realms because we are united with Christ.

EPHESIANS 1:3

Where Did I Go Wrong?

Hall of Fame football coach Tom Landry said, "I have learned that something constructive comes from every defeat." Don't you wish you could get credit for such a wise statement? The wonderful thing about football is that every play is on film so that every movement can be reviewed, dissected, and analyzed. We don't have that luxury in our lives, but time in reflection can assist us in knowing where and why we were successful, as well as where and why we weren't.

When we lose, we need to allow defeat to shape us. You see, defeat has a way of causing us to reflect, take inventory, and bring about proper change. Defeat is fruitful because it causes us to ask, "Where did I go wrong?" This question leads to wisdom and knowledge because it exposes where and when we left the game plan to go our own way.

Hall of Fame coach Joe Gibbs's book *Game Plan for Life* is the fruit that has come from his defeat. In this book, Gibbs turns to eleven experts to examine the critical topics for which every man must have a plan.

Consider the words of Proverbs 4:5: "Get wisdom; develop good judgment. Don't forget my words or turn away from them." Have you left God's game plan for your life? He has wisdom and understanding available to you. As you read the Scripture and engage with the experts like those in Coach Gibbs's book, you will find the good judgment that you need so that there is fruit from the defeat and a win that is waiting in the wings.

Get wisdom; develop good judgment. Don't forget my words or turn away from them.   PROVERBS 4:5

Inspire Others to Greater Things

Jimmy Johnson, two-time-winning Super Bowl head coach of the Dallas Cowboys, once said, "Treat a person as he is, and he will remain as he is. Treat a person as if he were where he could be and should be, and he will become what he could and should be." Coach Johnson got it. He understood that it takes great insight, vision, and intentionality to move people.

In his book *InSideOut Coaching*, former Baltimore Colts defensive lineman Joe Ehrmann contrasts the leadership styles of transactional versus transformational coaches. He explains that transactional coaches move people with fear. The rare leader, the great leader, is transformational.

Ehrmann never had a transformational coach until he was playing lacrosse in the off-season at Syracuse University. An incredible athlete, Ehrmann wanted something more to do with his downtime. When he encountered the leadership style of his lacrosse coach, he knew that the leadership he had experienced up to this point centered on what the player could give the coach. When on the lacrosse team, he experienced what the coach could give to the player, which for Ehrmann was an entirely different outlook on life.

Jesus was a transformational leader. At his first encounter with Simon, the man we know as Peter, we see this exchange: "Then Andrew brought Simon to meet Jesus. Looking intently at Simon, Jesus said, 'Your name is Simon, son of John—but you will be called Cephas' (which means 'Peter')" (John 1:42). *Cephas*, in Aramaic, and *Peter*, in Greek, both mean "rock."

Transformational leaders see the possibility in others and invite them to that place. Transformational coaches raise the bar of expectation and instill belief that greater things are yet to come. If you truly want to lead well, consider the challenge, opportunity, and outcome of transformational leadership.

Then Andrew brought Simon to meet Jesus. Looking intently at Simon, Jesus said, "Your name is Simon, son of John—but you will be called Cephas" (which means "Peter").　　　　JOHN 1:42

Inspiring Generosity

It was 2008, and the Grapevine Faith Lions were playing the Gainesville State Tornadoes. Grapevine Faith, a private school, was well resourced. Gainesville State was made up of young men in a state-run juvenile facility.

Coach Chris Hogan of Grapevine Faith had a vision to create a pathway of generosity that flowed from one sideline to the other. He knew that the players of Gainesville State wouldn't have their parents in the stands, the cheerleaders cheering for them, or even a postgame snack.

What Hogan did that night taught everyone at the game a profound lesson. He challenged and inspired his fan base to become Gainesville State's fan base. He had his cheerleaders cheer on their sideline, as if they were the Gainesville State cheerleaders. He had his parents make a forty-yard sprint line with a banner that the Tornadoes of Gainesville State could run through. He even asked the parents to sit on the opposing sideline and cheer for Gainesville State and then made sure that every opposing player had a goodie bag after the game.

The results were incredible, and the Gainesville Tornadoes were given hope through a leader's generous heart. Psalm 112:4 states, "Light shines in the darkness for the godly. They are generous, compassionate, and righteous." Thanks, Coach Hogan, for a modern-day example of this verse. May we go and do likewise!

Light shines in the darkness for the godly. They are generous, compassionate, and righteous.

PSALM 112:4

Where Were You?

I was in line at Starbucks. I had just dropped off Brady, my then-nine-month-old baby, at his day care. On my way to work, I had stopped at Starbucks to get some fuel for my day, and the guy in front of me said, "Have you heard? Someone just flew a plane into the World Trade Center."

I remember where I was when President Reagan was shot. I remember where I was when the *Challenger* exploded, and I remember where I was when planes crashed into buildings on that September day.

By the time I made it to my office, many of my coworkers were huddled around a television to see what they could. Everything seemed to slow down, and it was all so surreal to realize that America was under siege.

After the third plane crashed, I left work to get Brady. Every instinct in me said, "I don't know what is happening, but I do know that I want my son to be with me if it happens to us here." So I got into my vehicle and picked up my son.

America has never been the same since. After two foreign wars, and additional terrorist assaults on Europe and our homeland, there is an anger and bitterness in our hearts that we don't often access. I believe that much of the anger of the 2016 presidential election was rooted in that moment in time when innocence for so many Americans was lost.

The "Where were you?" moments of life can really make a deep impact on you if you don't protect your heart. The 9/11 events of life, like your father walking out on you as a kid, or being betrayed by your spouse, leave deep wounds if you don't seek a way to have them healed.

It takes courage to pray the words of Jesus found in Luke 23: "Jesus said, 'Father, forgive them, for they don't know what they are doing'" (verse 34). May that be our prayer for those who have hurt us!

Jesus said, "Father, forgive them, for they don't know what they are doing."
LUKE 23:34

Becoming a Star

Hall of Fame coach John Wooden once said, "The main ingredient in stardom is the rest of the team." You know, one of the most significant things a leader can do is make much of his or her team.

If you are a fan of the NFL, you know names like Tamme, Amendola, and Welker, not because they were highly acclaimed coming out of college, but because as a late-round draft pick, a free agent, and a trade respectively, these players found themselves in a situation where the stars of their team made room for them. That's right, Tom Brady and Peyton Manning led effectively by seeking to make the most of every member surrounding them. Manning and Brady have done this year in and year out, and it has not only allowed these players to emerge, but it has also strengthened the entire offense, making them more diversified.

Hall of Fame leadership lets others emerge as significant contributors and stars while solidifying one's own place as a leader. Philippians 2:3-4 says, "Don't be selfish; don't try to impress others. Be humble, thinking of others as better than yourselves. Don't look out only for your own interests, but take an interest in others, too." Do those on your team see you making the most of their talents? Are you taking action that puts the ball in their hands? Take an interest in them and seek to put them in places where they can be successful, and watch your team begin to soar.

Don't be selfish; don't try to impress others. Be humble, thinking of others as better than yourselves. Don't look out only for your own interests, but take an interest in others, too.　　　PHILIPPIANS 2:3-4

Don't Let a Yellow Flag Define Your Season

From peewee football through the pros, yellow flags fly, and tempers flare when someone makes a mistake. Penalties cost an entire team, and it can make for some hard conversations in the moment and after a game. If a coach is not careful, he can fly off the handle and leave a young man feeling like one big mistake. Dads, we have the capacity to do the same thing, don't we?

The truth of the matter is that we all make mistakes and we all get penalized. Show me a man who thinks he is always right, and I will show you what a fool looks like.

You have probably heard the phrase "God doesn't make mistakes." Maybe it's a special paraphrase of Psalm 139:13-14, which states, "You made all the delicate, inner parts of my body and knit me together in my mother's womb. Thank you for making me so wonderfully complex! Your workmanship is marvelous—how well I know it."

Remember, God doesn't make mistakes. Instead, he redeems them. That is the good news of the gospel and one we must model when those on our team or in our home disappoint us. May we learn the important lessons from the mistakes we make, but let us not allow those mistakes to define the quality of our lives! There is nothing like the grace of God. Remember, in the life of the believer, his grace should abound.

You made all the delicate, inner parts of my body and knit me together in my mother's womb. Thank you for making me so wonderfully complex! Your workmanship is marvelous—how well I know it. PSALM 139:13-14

Leadership over the Long Haul

Since Tennessee Titans owner Bud Adams died in 2011, the controlling interest of the team has changed hands at least twice. In that time, they have had three coaching changes and one of the worst records in football. After receiving a first-round pick in the NFL draft in 2015 and selecting Marcus Mariota, the Titans were first in line for the draft with just a few weeks left in the 2015 season.

With instability in ownership comes instability in the front office, as the general manager and coaching changes have left the fans in Nashville longing for direction. Organizations that don't establish leadership and retain that leadership over the long haul tend to cycle through losing seasons over and over again. Finding, retaining, and empowering a leader to set a course and stay with it is vital to winning in every area of life.

In what areas do you need to ensure leadership over the long haul? How might things look if there was stable leadership in place? Proverbs 28:2 states, "When there is moral rot within a nation, its government topples easily. But wise and knowledgeable leaders bring stability." Remember, with solid leadership comes stability. Without it, the losses will keep piling up.

When there is moral rot within a nation, its government topples easily.
But wise and knowledgeable leaders bring stability.　　　PROVERBS 28:2

What Every Coach Hates

Coaches are interesting characters, aren't they? Each has his or her own idiosyncrasies. Each has his or her own language and personality. Some are fired up all the time—inspirational and continuously motivating their athletes. Others are calm, quiet, and seemingly unmoved by success or failure.

Vince Lombardi once said, "The quality of a man's life is in direct proportion to his commitment to excellence."

Excellence can be challenged by taking shortcuts. We do this in our thought life, our relationships, our work life, and in our treatment of others. Do you know what every coach hates? Shortcuts. Shortcuts undercut excellence, which undermines the entire effort of the team.

What shortcuts are you taking? Proverbs 8:13 speaks of four shortcuts that undermine excellence in our lives: "All who fear the LORD will hate evil. Therefore, I hate pride and arrogance, corruption and perverse speech."

As wisdom is personified, she proclaims what she hates—pride, arrogance, corruption (translated as "evil behavior" in the New International Version), and perverse speech. These are shortcuts that undercut excellence and God's work in our lives.

Why do we find ourselves taking these shortcuts? I think it's because it is easier to live for yourself and get puffed up with pride, living a life that declares you don't need God. Arrogantly promoting yourself to the front of the line so that others are pushed back is easier than going to the end of the line and waiting your turn.

Taking shortcuts in your work so that you will be more profitable is easier than paying the price to deliver the work with integrity. Corruption is always easier than integrity. Speaking curses comes so much easier than lifting up someone else with a blessing. Perverse speech flows right off the tongue.

Each of these shortcuts leads away from the life of wisdom that has great value. Take the longer, purer path, and enjoy the fruit that is borne through the excellence of your integrity.

All who fear the LORD will hate evil. Therefore, I hate pride and arrogance, corruption and perverse speech.   PROVERBS 8:13

Insurmountable

While doing the Insanity Max:30 Sweat Intervals workout, I found myself facedown in a plank position, being instructed to hop one leg out as if I were skiing downhill, while bending one knee in tight to the chest and extending it out toward the other leg. That move is called "ski abs/power knee." Just explaining the move is a challenge. These kinds of moves create a lot of soreness in my body. The pace and intensity is, as they call the program, "Insane." Doing that move made me want to quit. But when I stick with the workout, it changes my life.

Another thing that changed my life was spending time with Nick Vujicic when I had the privilege of interviewing him for my radio show. Nick leads a ministry called Life without Limbs.[57] Although Nick was born without arms or legs, he has traveled over three million miles and visited fifty-seven different countries ministering to people and sharing the love of Jesus Christ. The few hours I had with him will never be forgotten. Nick has overcome so much to, as he says, live a "life without limits."

What limits seem insurmountable to you? What is causing you to want to quit? From what Nick shared with me in our interview together, he would encourage you to look at John 9:3 and realize that whatever you are facing can bring glory to God.

John 9:3 states, "'It was not because of his sins or his parents' sins,' Jesus answered. 'This happened so the power of God could be seen in him.'" This is what God has done in Nick's life. He has displayed his power through Nick, and God can display his power through your life as well.

"It was not because of his sins or his parents' sins," Jesus answered. "This happened so the power of God could be seen in him."　　　　JOHN 9:3

---

[57] I want to invite you to take a few minutes today and visit www.lifewithoutlimbs.org. You will never be the same, and you will forever be inspired.

Every Part of Our Lives

Former Baylor quarterback Bryce Petty grew in his faith while at Baylor University. In a devotional for the Fellowship of Christian Athletes publication, *FCA Magazine*, Petty recalls that his friend Chris Wommack was the one who helped him learn how to integrate his faith into the sport he loves. Chris helped him learn to go "all in" for Christ. Petty says, "Chris dared me to take that a step further—or several steps further—and literally pray before each snap."[58]

Petty says, "If you've ever seen how fast our no-huddle offense operates at Baylor, that probably sounds completely nuts. But I really think it illustrates how God works in our lives. He wants every part of us." Petty then shares that sometimes his prayers were simply, "All right, God, here we go."[59]

Is your faith integrated into every part of your life? Allowing the Lord to have access and inform your work is a big struggle for guys. But remember, you are not defined by what you do but by who you are. Allowing the Lord to work in your life to develop and shape you will only bear fruit in what you do. Before you make decisions at work that will affect many, before you make that next sales call, before you operate on your patient, ask for the Lord's help and allow him to be involved in what you do.

First Thessalonians 5:17-18 states, "Never stop praying . . . for this is God's will for you who belong to Christ Jesus." Sometimes, like Petty, it's a quick, simple prayer.

Never stop praying . . . for this is God's will for you who belong to Christ Jesus.
1 THESSALONIANS 5:17-18

---

[58] Bryce Petty, "Bringing It Home Devotional: All In," *FCA Magazine* (November/December 2014): 14, http://www.fca.org/digitalmagazine/fcamagvol56issue6/.
[59] Ibid.

When the Storms Roll In, Have a Game Plan

In mid-December 2010, the Metrodome in Minneapolis was severely damaged by seventeen inches of snow that caused the Teflon roof to collapse. The Vikings, who were set to play the New York Giants, had to move their game to a Monday night and relocate the game to Detroit. The Vikings organization had been working toward a new stadium plan for quite some time, but until this happened, things were stalled. The roof collapse was the catalyst for building a new stadium.

I was recently visiting with a man who was telling me about a rough storm that was leading to a collapse in his marriage. This storm was vast and beyond the scope of his control, and much of the struggle had to do with the difficulties with his wife's work.

Those difficulties spilled over into the marriage, and they caused a great distance between the man and his wife. I had to say to him, "Sir, this storm is beyond your control and ability to fix. Once you understand that, you can develop a game plan for how to help your spouse."

What is your game plan for storms that roll into your family's life that are beyond your ability to control? My game plan is to be a refuge and shelter for those I love. It involves unconditional love, grace if needed, and tender care, continuously.

My hope is that when the storms come, my family sees the Lord in me, and I believe that this is what he looks like. Psalm 103:8 states, "The LORD is compassionate and merciful, slow to get angry and filled with unfailing love."

Decide today that when the storms come, and they will, you will strive to embody these characteristics of God's character. The best way to do that is to simply ask him to love your crew through you.

The LORD is compassionate and merciful, slow to get angry and filled with unfailing love.
PSALM 103:8

Hard Work

Vince Lombardi, Hall of Fame coach of the Green Bay Packers, once said, "The difference between a successful person and others is not a lack of strength or a lack of knowledge, but rather a lack of will." Hall of Fame coach Chuck Noll, who coached the Pittsburgh Steelers from 1969 to 1991, said, "Champions are champions not because they do extraordinary things, but because they do the ordinary things better than anyone else."

When you stop and think about these quotes, it calls you to take care of your own efforts, lest you become one of the greatest barriers to your success. You see, successful people aren't just given success, they earn it. They pay the fundamental price to be successful, whether that's getting up early for a morning workout, working late to get the extra know-how for the pending project, or finding time to study just a little bit more for their exam. They do ordinary things better than everyone else, and thus, they get the reward.

To be successful, you have to have the right attitude and the right atmosphere that leads to taking the right actions. Proverbs 14:23 says, "Work brings profit, but mere talk leads to poverty!" As you work today, pay the price, go the extra mile, and give your best. Set aside momentary enjoyment for long-term fulfillment. When the profits come through knowledge or fitness, increased revenue or responsibilities, you will find a sense of pride for your accomplishment. Be excellent in your work, for even before the Fall and the sin that entered the world, God gave man the great responsibility to work.

Work brings profit, but mere talk leads to poverty! PROVERBS 14:23

Taking Time to Listen

In their book *The Jersey Effect*, Hunter Smith and Darrin Gray unpack the blessings and challenges that go along with being a professional athlete. Smith, a ten-year punter for the Indianapolis Colts, talks about not only the impact of head coach Tony Dungy on his life, but Coach Dungy's interest in all of his life.

You see, Smith is also the lead singer of the Hunter Smith Band. He says to Coach Dungy in a letter, republished in his book, "Coaches are screaming. Players are working. An NFL practice is happening, and the head coach is interested in my dinky music career. That meant a lot to me, and it still does. No other coach I've been around has ever been that interested in anything in my life outside of how I could help the team win more games."

Dungy was simply modeling the love and leadership of our Lord, who still listens to us and for us today. First John 5:13-15 declares, "I have written this to you who believe in the name of the Son of God, so that you may know you have eternal life. And we are confident that he hears us whenever we ask for anything that pleases him. And since we know he hears us when we make our requests, we also know that he will give us what we ask for."

It is profound to know that our Lord loves to listen to us and is available for every part of our lives as he leads us. As we lead others, may we, too, be found listening to them, learning about them, and longing for their best! Take the time to listen, and you will double your impact.

We are confident that he hears us whenever we ask for anything that pleases him.
1 JOHN 5:14

The Rainbow Wig and John 3:16

Do you remember those times as a kid when, while watching a football game, you would see a crowd shot and that guy in a rainbow wig holding a John 3:16 sign? What's that all about? Now when you turn on *College GameDay*, signs are everywhere. Everybody has a message, and everyone wants to get noticed.

Social media is the "rainbow wig and John 3:16" sign of our day. It gives everyone fingertip access to blurting out their message so that those in their circle of influence can know exactly what they are doing, where they are going, and what they are thinking. Add the selfie photo, and you've got a great chance of being noticed.

John 3:16 declares that you have been noticed already. It states, "This is how God loved the world: He gave his one and only Son, so that everyone who believes in him will not perish but have eternal life." The beauty of the message of the guy with the rainbow wig is that God noticed you out of a crowd and declared his love for you by giving his one and only Son to pay for your sin. It's the best deal going, and when you grasp that message, it will change your life.

Have you taken Christ as your Savior? If not, simply pray, "Lord, I admit that I am a sinner in need of a Savior. Please forgive me for my sins. I take Jesus as my Savior, believing he died for me and rose again. Lord, come into my life and save me, I pray. In Jesus' name, amen."

This is how God loved the world: He gave his one and only Son, so that everyone who believes in him will not perish but have eternal life.   JOHN 3:16

Humble Talent

In separate conversations with the parents of one of my players, I told them, "It is such a delight to coach your son. Never have I seen such talent with such genuine humility." This young man was a standout athlete on our football team. Although he was extremely fast, determined, and gifted, he was also nervous. This made itself known before every kickoff, as he would try to get his helmet off before the vomit came out of his mouth. After he would throw up, I would look at his father and say, "I love it. You can't teach that!"

What I appreciated most about this young man was his reaction to adversity and his response when he was successful. When adversity came, he didn't back down from it. Instead, he shifted to another gear and pushed harder. Some kids can do that and not change the outcome at all. Few, like this one, can change the whole game. When he did change the game, he didn't dance or talk trash. He simply gave the ball to the referee and came to the sidelines.

Proverbs 11:2 states, "Pride leads to disgrace, but with humility comes wisdom." This young man was admired by his coaches and teammates, but he didn't seek that glory at all. He just went out for the next play, and when the game was over, he would come up to me, win or lose, and say, "Thank you, coach!"

Pride leads to disgrace, but with humility comes wisdom. PROVERBS 11:2

The Wisdom Store

Have you ever stored something? Most likely you stored something for a rainy day or for a celebration. In making preparations for a party, you set special things aside just for that occasion.

Cam Newton is famous for being a great quarterback and having certain antics and celebrations on the field. It appears that he has them planned out and ready to go. One of his classy celebrations is to take the football with which he scored and give it to a child seated in the end zone. The plan he has stored up in his mind makes kids' experiences great at the games.

Did you know that God has something stored up, and he's ready to give it to you today? Proverbs 2:7 states, "He stores up sound wisdom for the upright" (ESV). Whether you are going through a rainy day, a challenging season, or a catastrophe, wisdom is available to you.

If you are getting ready to celebrate a milestone of significance in your life or you are hoping to do something special, God also has wisdom stored up for you. As I write this, my wife and I are counting down the days until we celebrate our twentieth wedding anniversary. We think it is wise to acknowledge this milestone in a significant way, so we have been preparing for and planning our trip away together.

Whatever is before you, the heavenly Father has a storehouse of wisdom ready to pour out to you. Seek him, ask of him, and receive from him today!

He stores up sound wisdom for the upright.　　　　　　PROVERBS 2:7, ESV

Which Is It?

Football is such an emotional game that periodically players' tempers explode on the sidelines. These fuming players go off on others and get in their faces. It is interesting to see that at times, those being confronted will just stand there and say nothing, looking past the maniac, onto the field of play. It reminds me of Proverbs 26:4, which says, "Don't answer the foolish arguments of fools, or you will become as foolish as they are."

Then there are other times when the fool must be confronted. This happened to the Cowboys in 2015 when Greg Hardy, the troubled pass rusher, exploded on the special teams unit and their coach after another blown play that caused the Cowboys to fall behind again.

Dez Bryant, an embattled player also known for his own struggles, couldn't take it anymore and confronted Hardy. The wild scene became fodder for the network analysts later that day and well into the following week.

You see, after a time or two of a fool's ranting, it is appropriate to stand up to him and put him in his place. That is why I think it is fascinating that the very next verse, Proverbs 26:5, tells us to confront the fool: "Be sure to answer the foolish arguments of fools, or they will become wise in their own estimation."

Which is it? There is a time to let it go and a time to confront. Discerning which it is requires great wisdom. Consider seeking wise counsel from an outside voice before confronting a fool. That person's lack of proximity to the situation may be exactly what you need.

Don't answer the foolish arguments of fools, or you will become as foolish as they are.   PROVERBS 26:4

You Carry a Name

Richard Sherman, All-Pro safety of the Seattle Seahawks, made sure that everyone knew his name with his obnoxious behavior after swatting away a potential game-tying pass from San Francisco 49er Colin Kaepernick to Michael Crabtree in the 2013 NFC Championship game. In my opinion, Sherman, in a variety of postgame interviews, went on to embarrass himself, his family, and his teammates by the way he acted.

Do you think of all the NFL players in a certain light because of one man's comments? Maybe you do. Maybe you don't. But Sherman's unsportsmanlike actions certainly didn't boost the NFL's reputation.

Are you creating problems for yourself, those you work for, and your family by your actions? You see, you carry a name, and what you do with that name really does matter.

I often tell my kids, "You carry three names: Jesus' name, my name, and your name. Let's protect all three of those names because that's all we have." The most important of those names is Jesus' name. If you are a follower of Jesus Christ, then you are his representative. You carry his name with you everywhere you go. Second Corinthians 5:11 states, "Because we understand our fearful responsibility to the Lord, we work hard to persuade others. God knows we are sincere, and I hope you know this, too."

So what impression are you making on others? Does it align with what you say you believe? Are you pulling people toward Christ or away from Christ? Be consistent. Be gracious. And if you follow Christ, seek to be like him.

Because we understand our fearful responsibility to the Lord, we work hard to persuade others. God knows we are sincere, and I hope you know this, too.
                                                    2 CORINTHIANS 5:11

Walk This Way

John Madden, Super Bowl–winning head coach and legendary football broadcaster, once said, "The road to Easy Street goes through the sewer." I've been in a few sewers, but they still haven't led me to Easy Street. Instead, I have often found myself on Adversity Street.

When adversity comes, how can you know which road to take?

When I am facing adversity, I pray. I pray often. Sometimes it is just saying, "Oh, Lord, I need you" because that simple prayer is all I know to pray.

Often I will add to my simple prayers. First, I ask the Lord for wisdom: "Oh, Lord, I need your wisdom. Show me your way, O Lord. Make your will clear to me, I pray." In those prayers, I'm following the advice of James 1:5-8, which states, "If you need wisdom, ask our generous God, and he will give it to you. He will not rebuke you for asking. But when you ask him, be sure that your faith is in God alone. Do not waver, for a person with divided loyalty is as unsettled as a wave of the sea that is blown and tossed by the wind. Such people should not expect to receive anything from the Lord. Their loyalty is divided between God and the world, and they are unstable in everything they do."

Second, I pray for strength to endure. I say, "Father, strengthen me according to your word." Psalm 119:28 states, "I weep with sorrow; encourage me by your word." The word *encourage* means "to make strong."

Third, I ask for deliverance and safety to preserve my name, because it is all I've got. Proverbs 18:10 states, "The name of the LORD is a strong fortress; the godly run to him and are safe."

There is no Easy Street. But when you find yourself on Adversity Street, you can know how to walk down that road.

The name of the LORD is a strong fortress; the godly run to him and are safe.
PROVERBS 18:10

Value-Based Decision Making

A value is a principle or quality that is intrinsically desirable. It is an ideal that should govern decision making in business, school, athletics, dating, and marriage. As I coached my son Brady's football teams, one of our values on the football field was to try to always be a good sport.

When Brady was on the Aggies in fourth grade, we were up on Coach Winston's Longhorns by a few touchdowns. The game was winding down, and Brady, who was playing quarterback, was under center. Our offense was on the two-yard line, and Brady wanted to punch it in with a QB sneak. You see, he had yet to score a touchdown as a football player. I would have loved to have given him that opportunity to get into the end zone, but I had to keep the bigger picture in mind. In the grand scheme of things, the win was already in hand. We had beaten the Longhorns.

My value is to strive to have a good name. I knew that if I had allowed him to punch the ball into the end zone, it would have cost me influence with all of the coaches and league officials. As a result, my value governed my decision making over my emotion. As you can imagine, this disappointed my son, but it also taught him a bigger lesson. Instead of scoring, we took a knee and went out victorious with our name not only intact but on the rise. It took Brady two more years before he scored his first touchdown, but I believe it was worth the wait.

Listen to the conviction that governed Joseph's decision making when Potiphar's wife tempted him to sleep with her: "Joseph refused. 'Look,' he told her. . . . 'No one here has more authority than I do. [My master] has held back nothing from me except you, because you are his wife. How could I do such a wicked thing? It would be a great sin against God'" (Genesis 39:8-9). When we know our values, the hard decisions become much easier.

Joseph refused. 'Look,' he told her. . . . 'No one here has more authority than I do. [My master] has held back nothing from me except you, because you are his wife. How could I do such a wicked thing? It would be a great sin against God.
GENESIS 39:8-9

Check, Check

How much do you trust what others see? In offensive football, ten guys have to trust one guy to see what they need to see in order to execute the play as a unit. Many times a quarterback will look out across the heads of his offensive linemen to the secondary of the defense and see either a problem or an opportunity.

Quarterbacks love man-to-man coverage because in one-on-one situations, they can simply communicate a word or a hand signal to their receiver and change the play. In week two of the 2015 season, Jets quarterback Ryan Fitzpatrick used a hand signal to communicate with wide receiver Brandon Marshall to check out of a play into a fade route. That play went for six points and was crucial in the Jets' win over the Colts on *Monday Night Football*.

Do you trust what others see? If so, do you allow them to redirect you so that you can score? A good friend won't hesitate to speak words of counsel to you. If you live long enough, you will find yourself in situations where the problem you are facing exceeds your experience. When this takes place, you must have advisers, friends, or trusted confidants who will share from their experience and give you the necessary principles to navigate the choppy waters. Will you trust what they see?

Proverbs 25:11 states, "Timely advice is lovely, like golden apples in a silver basket." Learn to trust what others see and allow them the freedom to speak into your life. When you do, you will find that it is a game changer!

Timely advice is lovely, like golden apples in a silver basket.   PROVERBS 25:11

Magnolia Market and Chick-fil-A

On a holiday trip with my family, I went to the new and improved Magnolia Market in Waco, Texas. It was overflowing with shoppers looking at all the possible decorations for their homes and hoping to have a sighting of Chip and Joanna from the HGTV show *Fixer Upper*. Chip and Joanna have a strong faith in Christ and seek to honor him through their business and family life.

I love Chick-fil-A chicken, and with three or four Chick-fil-A restaurants in our area, I sit in their drive-through lines more frequently than I care to admit. This restaurant chain, founded by Truett Cathy, has held fast to its conviction of being closed on Sunday so that its employees can enjoy a day of rest and go to church with their families if they so choose. Cathy, a longtime Christian, had an unmistakable faith throughout his professional life.

Walking through the packed market and sitting in the overflowing Chick-fil-A drive-through lines, I have been reminded of the blessing of God on those who are clearly devoted to him.

Psalm 40:5 states, "O LORD my God, you have performed many wonders for us. Your plans for us are too numerous to list. You have no equal. If I tried to recite all your wonderful deeds, I would never come to the end of them." The psalmist can hardly contain his joy at the work of God on his behalf. When you have experienced it, it is profound and lasting. Show me an organization committed to honoring the Lord, and I will show you various ways that they have been favored by the Lord. Frankly, it is unmistakable!

O LORD my God, you have performed many wonders for us. Your plans for us are too numerous to list. You have no equal. If I tried to recite all your wonderful deeds, I would never come to the end of them. PSALM 40:5

Peace in an Ever-Changing World

Security is more important than ever, so it seems. Entering stadiums has always come with some sort of line and quick bag check. But the policies of the professional sports leagues' security protocols have created greater restrictions on everyone and what they can bring to the ballpark. My most recent trip to NRG Stadium included a thirty-five-minute wait in line to go through the metal detectors. One of the ladies in line had to return her purse to her car because it was too big. Living at peace in a world that is filled with terror can be a challenge.

From what I can see, the world has always had terrorists—people bent on causing fear and psychological, emotional, and physical harm. Proverbs 26 references an archer who wounds at random, and I imagine had there been firearms in the Bible, the author would have called him a gunman. Terrorists' ideology is dark and demonic, and there is nothing peaceful about it. But I believe that we can live at peace by being prepared and prayed up.

Peace comes by being prepared. The people of Israel have to fight for peace nearly every day. They do so by being vigilant. They use wisdom, common sense, and technology to assist them in their quest for daily peace.

Peace also comes by being prayed up. In Proverbs 1:33, wisdom invites us to listen and enjoy peace: "All who listen to me will live in peace, untroubled by fear of harm." Be prepared and prayed up so you can enjoy peace today.

All who listen to me will live in peace, untroubled by fear of harm.

PROVERBS 1:33

OCTOBER

A House Divided

At the halfway point of the 2015 NFL season, Jason La Canfora, of CBS Sports, reported that Houston Texans head coach Bill O'Brien was interested in the University of Maryland Terrapins head coaching job. After going 9–7 in O'Brien's first season, the team stumbled out of the gate and consistently failed to live up to their potential during the first half of the 2015 campaign.

If losing wasn't bad enough, general manager Rick Smith overruled Coach O'Brien's desire to immediately cut backup quarterback Ryan Mallett after he missed a team charter flight to Miami. Though Mallett was released a few days later, the damage was done. Immediately, the press began to speculate who would be let go first, Smith or O'Brien. You see, even the press knows that when there are factions within an organization, it cannot be successful and thrive.

Mark 3:24-25 states, "A kingdom divided by civil war will collapse. Similarly, a family splintered by feuding will fall apart." Are you feuding in your home, work, or ministry? If it continues, it won't be long until there is a huge shift that takes place. If we work to live in unity, we will accomplish more together over the long haul than we will apart in the moment. I want to challenge you to be a part of the solution and not a part of the problem. Remember the Lord's words that say, "Blessed are the peacemakers" (Matthew 5:9, ESV). Work to stay unified, because a house divided makes for a long, losing season.

Blessed are the peacemakers.   MATTHEW 5:9, ESV

The Case for Perseverance

On *Thursday Night Football* late in the 2015 season, the undrafted free agent Case Keenum had the third-highest quarterback rating for a single game in all of pro football history, as he led the St. Louis Rams past the Tampa Bay Buccaneers. Competing against rookie quarterback Jameis Winston, the number-one overall pick in the 2015 draft, Keenum out-shined Winston with his crisp, accurate passes, going 14 of 17 for 234 yards and two touchdown passes.

Keenum's journey to this place is a picture of resolve, commitment, endurance, and perseverance. He only had one offer to play Division 1 college football, and that was from Coach Art Briles at the University of Houston. When he graduated from college, Keenum was the most prolific passer in college football history, holding the record for the most touchdowns, yards, and total offense. Yet Keenum went undrafted to the pros. Signed to the practice squad by the Houston Texans, Keenum played whatever position the Texans needed on that squad to make a name for himself. In Houston, he went up and down on the depth chart, was cut, and was then picked up by the Rams.

After being cut by the Rams, he was re-signed by the Texans in the 2014 season. After that season, he was picked up again by the Rams. In 2015, after Nick Foles struggled for weeks on end, Keenum was named the starter and had the stellar performance noted above.

If only our faith could be as consistent as Keenum's commitment to football! The writer of Hebrews notes some great hall of faith examples for us in chapter 11 and then opens chapter 12 with a challenge: "Since we are surrounded by such a huge crowd of witnesses to the life of faith, let us strip off every weight that slows us down, especially the sin that so easily trips us up. And let us run with endurance the race God has set before us" (verse 1). Let's keep running with endurance.

Let us run with endurance the race God has set before us.　　　HEBREWS 12:1

Expectant Faith

There we were, sitting in the deer blind, waiting and waiting. It was my son Brady's fifteenth birthday weekend, and a generous friend in our church had invited us to his ranch in South Texas to hunt deer. It was the evening hunt, and having gotten up early that morning after a late arrival the night before, all we could think of was sleep. I even dozed off for a few minutes.

The sun was setting, and we thought it would be a fruitless day. We were having father-and-son time, but what we really wanted was to see an eight- or ten-point buck come out in front of us. As our thoughts wandered, there he was. It wasn't a deer or a hog, but a beautiful Texas bobcat.

Brady took aim, and as I was getting my binoculars up to see it up close, Brady pulled the trigger. My binoculars weren't in focus, so I had no idea if he hit it or not. When we got out of the blind and went to see if we got anything, we found the beautiful cat knocked down in his tracks.

Life, like hunting, takes patience and faith. At times, all we can do is position ourselves in the right place and wait. As we walk with the Lord, we trust him for the opportunities and the results. Psalm 37:1-11 is a special text for me when I find myself in a season of waiting. Psalm 37:5 speaks of God doing his part after we have positioned ourselves the best we know how. It states, "Commit your way to the LORD; trust in him, and he will act" (ESV). Live with such expectant faith that you are ready to take aim when the Lord prepares the way.

Commit your way to the LORD; trust in him, and he will act.

PSALM 37:5, ESV

Filled and Overflowing

When the Houston Astros won the 2015 wild card play-off game to head to the American League Division Series, they celebrated with a champagne shower in the visitors' locker room of the New York Yankees. This young team was ahead of schedule in reaching the play-offs, and their youthful zeal for the game showed as they fearlessly threw each pitch or swung for the fences.

The Astros were a first- or second-place team all year, and their hard work, love for the game, and love for one another paid tremendous dividends that overflowed in celebration as they sought to win in October. In the previous months, their character was shaped as they began to tail off at the end of the season. They fought to overcome this adversity and gained a wild card berth. They persevered and earned a spot in the final eight teams of the Major League Baseball season. It was exciting for the people of Houston to see, as it had been a long time since the Astros had been a contender.

Sports is a great mirror for life, but it isn't life. It can nevertheless teach us many things and encourage us to reflect on what really matters. Philippians 1:10-11 states, "I want you to understand what really matters, so that you may live pure and blameless lives until the day of Christ's return. May you always be filled with the fruit of your salvation—the righteous character produced in your life by Jesus Christ—for this will bring much glory and praise to God." What really matters is that we set ourselves apart for Christ and demonstrate his character. This will bring praise and glory to God.

I want you to understand what really matters, so that you may live pure and blameless lives until the day of Christ's return. May you always be filled with the fruit of your salvation—the righteous character produced in your life by Jesus Christ—for this will bring much glory and praise to God.

PHILIPPIANS 1:10-11

Is That Good Enough?

The question above was posed about the 2015 Texas Aggies on ESPN's *College GameDay*. In the 2014 campaign, the Aggies were blown out by the Alabama Crimson Tide, 59–0. As the Aggies prepared to face their SEC rival at Kyle Field, the commentators discussed if the changes made on the defensive strategy and personnel would be good enough for the Aggies to defeat the 2015 Crimson Tide. Commentators can always speculate and compare the previous year's squad against the current year's, but until it plays out, it is all only speculation.

Many people have the same question about their faith. They approach faith and God and the afterlife with the uncertainty of being good enough. They wonder, in their quiet moments when no one else is with them, *When this life is over, have I performed well enough?*

The beauty of the Christian Good News is that it begins with bad news. It declares that you are not ever going to be good enough. Romans 3:23 states, "Everyone has sinned; we all fall short of God's glorious standard." The bad news is clear: your efforts to please God are not enough.

But the gospel doesn't stop there. It is good news. If you keep reading, you see that Romans 3:24-25 states, "Yet God, in his grace, freely makes us right in his sight. He did this through Christ Jesus when he freed us from the penalty for our sins. For God presented Jesus as the sacrifice for sin." You are not saved by your good works, but by putting your faith and trust in the work that Jesus did for you on the cross. Be justified by putting your faith in him.

Yet God, in his grace, freely makes us right in his sight. He did this through Christ Jesus when he freed us from the penalty for our sins. For God presented Jesus as the sacrifice for sin. **ROMANS 3:24-25**

Take Time to Play

"Daddy, can you launch me?" This is a question I often get from my little girl, Carson. It is a question I used to get from her older brother Cooper, but he has outgrown my need to launch him.

When my daughter is asking me to launch her, she is asking me to pull her back on the swing as high as I can, count down, "5, 4, 3, 2, 1, 0!" and then she screams, "Launch!" Sometimes I make her give me a kiss between zero and launch. Then I release the swing and get out of the way. She laughs, exudes joy, and can't wait for me to do it again.

Sometimes I have made the mistake of saying no to her. She asks me, "Daddy, can you launch me?" and I reply, "Not now—I'm busy." There are times that I must say no, but when I can, I need to lead with the word *yes*.

Proverbs 3:27 says, "Do not withhold good from those who deserve it when it's in your power to help them." Leading with a yes when it comes to my time saturates my children with my love. It declares to them that they are a top priority in my life and that I love to give them what I have. So the next time you are prone to say, "No, not now—I'm busy," ask yourself, "Can I say yes here?" Take time to play, because like Brady and Cooper, pretty soon Carson won't be asking me to launch her anymore.

Do not withhold good from those who deserve it when it's in your power to help them.

PROVERBS 3:27

That Same Seven or Eight

If you are like me, you go on a diet, drop that first seven or eight pounds, and then get busy, frustrated, or just thrown off course by life, and stop your pursuit. I have probably lost fifty pounds over the past year. The problem is that it is that same seven or eight pounds that I'm losing, regaining, then losing again.

What keeps me from finishing? What is it in my character that causes me to settle for less than what is ideal for my health? What keeps me from breaking through to that next level of health, well-being, and appearance?

Proverbs 14:8 says, "The wisdom of the prudent is to give thought to their ways" (NIV). Have you considered your ways? What obstacles do you keep coming up against in your professional, relational, financial, or physical pursuits?

Whether it is the same seven or eight pounds for you, or some other barrier that you keep coming up against, I want to encourage you to give thought to your ways. If you see a pattern that has developed, put together a plan to overcome it. One of the best ways to do this is to engage an expert in the area where you need help. Seeking out a leader in your life—a trainer, a counselor, a financial adviser—can help you move past what's standing in your way and navigate the changes that are necessary. Don't let pride, excuses, or a lack of self-examination keep you from being the man God has called you to be.

The wisdom of the prudent is to give thought to their ways.

PROVERBS 14:8, NIV

A Judgment Call

During week four of *Monday Night Football* in the NFL's 2015 campaign, Detroit Lions receiver Calvin Johnson was about to score the game-winning touchdown on a quick pass from Matthew Stafford. Just before the goal line, Johnson was hit by Kam Chancellor, resulting in the ball being fumbled into the end zone.

As it was about to bounce out of the back of the end zone, Seattle Seahawks linebacker K. J. Wright illegally batted the ball out of the back of the end zone right in front of the referee. It was a wild play that had a number of possible outcomes. Unfortunately for the Lions, Wright wasn't penalized.

On the Tuesday morning sports talk shows, the hosts agreed that the referee's call was a judgment call, but if this action had been penalized, as it should have been, the Lions would have had first and goal at the half-yard line. The pundits declared that the referee's poor judgment cost the Lions another opportunity. The ironic thing about the play is that K. J. Wright's poor judgment could have cost his team the game.

Poor judgment is expensive. Our decision making is paramount if we are going to lead ourselves and others well. When it comes to adultery, look at the simple yet profound words of Proverbs 6. Verse 32 states, "The man who commits adultery is an utter fool, for he destroys himself."

From what I can see, no one ever sets out to destroy themselves. But if you allow your judgment to be clouded so that you behave like an utter fool, it will result in certain regret.

The man who commits adultery is an utter fool, for he destroys himself.

PROVERBS 6:32

OCTOBER 9
Leadership That's in Control

Does your leadership create confusion, chaos, or confidence?

Hall of Fame Dallas Cowboys coach Tom Landry once said, "Leadership is a matter of having people look at you and gain confidence, seeing how you react. If you're in control, they're in control." If you remember seeing Landry on the sidelines at Cowboys Stadium, he always wore his coat, tie, and fedora. His stoic presence never conveyed confusion or chaos. He was always in control.

Just as a team takes its cues from its leader, so does a family. So much of leading and following is caught through relationship. As a result, a leader's presence and ability to maintain order in his own life is mission critical. But when he loses control, all bets are off. That's why we need to let Proverbs 15:1 challenge us today. It states, "A gentle answer deflects anger, but harsh words make tempers flare."

How do you stay calm under intense pressure? What is the secret to leading when there is so much on the line? How can so many gain confidence from you? Tom Landry's secret was his relationship with the Lord Jesus Christ. Landry made no qualms about being a Christian, and his faith challenged him to live exceptionally. The best leaders I know have a relationship with the leader of leaders, Jesus Christ, that helps them stay cool under pressure. Many Christians pray Psalm 141:3 on a regular basis: "Take control of what I say, O Lord, and guard my lips." May you pray that today too.

A gentle answer deflects anger, but harsh words make tempers flare.

PROVERBS 15:1

The Best Tailgate Ever

If you ever get a chance to go to Oxford, Mississippi, on a Saturday in the fall, you will never be the same. The Grove, Ole Miss's legendary tailgate spot, is filled with thousands and thousands of Rebel fans dressed to the nines and excited for another chance to enter Vaught-Hemingway Stadium to see their Ole Miss Rebels engage in another epic SEC showdown.

The Grove is like no other tailgate I have ever been to. The anticipation of kickoff is in the air. You hear the chant of "Hotty-Totty" and then see the football team process through the "Walk of Champions" into the stadium. The food is rich and readily shared from fan to fan. The southern sweets are unparalleled.

Just like there is no place like the Grove, there is nothing as satisfying to your soul as wisdom. Proverbs 24:13-14 states, "My child, eat honey, for it is good, and the honeycomb is sweet to the taste. In the same way, wisdom is sweet to your soul. If you find it, you will have a bright future, and your hopes will not be cut short." The Scripture declares that God's wisdom is that by which the kings of the earth rule and reign. It says that God's wisdom is better than fine gold and choice silver. At one point in Solomon's teaching in Proverbs 4:7 he says, "Getting wisdom is the wisest thing you can do! And whatever else you do, develop good judgment." Take your own walk of champions by getting wisdom. When you do, you will never be the same!

Getting wisdom is the wisest thing you can do! And whatever else you do, develop good judgment.   PROVERBS 4:7

The Power of Words

In *The One Year Uncommon Life Daily Challenge*, Tony Dungy talks about how the locker room environment can be a breeding ground for "verbal bashings." He states that players, coaches, and staff often try to rationalize such remarks as joking. But Dungy knows that words have incredible power.[60]

With our words we have the ability to either build others up or tear them down. We often underestimate the significance of our words and how they truly affect others. When not used correctly, words can destroy, cause confusion, and create dissonance toward those whom we love the most. However, one encouraging and edifying word can bring joy and hope to those who need it most.

One of my sons had a coach who carelessly spoke words that actually made fun of him in front of others. The coach embarrassed my son with his careless remarks. He lost my son's interest that day.

That same son had a quarterback lesson with former NFL quarterback Sean Salisbury. Unbeknownst to Salisbury, my son had gone through a tough day the day before. Salisbury, who uses words to inspire his athletes effectively, spoke life into my son on an issue where his friends had made fun of him. It was a blessing that my son will never forget.

Proverbs 10:31-32 states, "The mouth of the godly person gives wise advice, but the tongue that deceives will be cut off. The lips of the godly speak helpful words, but the mouth of the wicked speaks perverse words." How do you use your words? Are you careful or careless? Do people come to you for advice, or do they try to avoid you because you have hurt them in the past? Let's be people who speak life into those closest to us. Watch your words, and use them as tools to build up those around you.

The mouth of the godly person gives wise advice, but the tongue that deceives will be cut off. The lips of the godly speak helpful words, but the mouth of the wicked speaks perverse words. **PROVERBS 10:31-32**

---

[60] Tony Dungy and Nathan Whitaker, *The One Year Uncommon Life Daily Challenge* (Carol Stream, IL: Tyndale, 2011), February 27.

The Price of Greatness Is Responsibility

In his book *Dad's Playbook: Wisdom for Fathers from the Greatest Coaches of All Time*, Tom Limbert says to fathers, "You have a tremendous impact on your family. Through your example, every day you show your children how to treat each other, how to handle adversity, and how to get things done. Make no mistake about it, it is a huge responsibility. But as the best coaches have shown us, the price of greatness is responsibility."[61]

Those words are heavy, aren't they? One of the reasons our nation is weakening is because men are giving up their responsibility to lead their families. This is the path of least resistance that follows the response of Adam in the Garden when at the fall of man, he passed the buck.

Look at how Adam tries to blame Eve for his actions. Genesis 3:9-12 states,

> Then the LORD God called to the man, "Where are you?" He replied, "I heard you walking in the garden, so I hid. I was afraid because I was naked." "Who told you that you were naked?" the LORD God asked. "Have you eaten from the tree whose fruit I commanded you not to eat?" The man replied, "It was the woman you gave me who gave me the fruit, and I ate it."

Guys, let's not pass the buck. I want to challenge you to take responsibility for your families. When you fail, admit it. When they fall, extend grace. Learn about them. Love them, and lead them to greatness.

The man replied, "It was the woman you gave me who gave me the fruit, and I ate it."

GENESIS 3:12

---

[61] Tom Limbert, *Dad's Playbook: Wisdom for Fathers from the Greatest Coaches of All Time* (San Francisco: Chronicle Books, 2012), 18.

Learning from Watching Film

One of the most revolutionary experiences for our peewee football league was the season we subscribed to Hudl, the online platform for watching practice and game film. As a coach, it cut my preparation in half because I was able to slow things down, view our successes and failures, and come to practice ready to make corrections and insert the game plan.

To grow in wisdom and insight, you don't need to subscribe to Hudl. No, you need to simply look around. Some of the greatest lessons you will learn come from watching the wise, older men in your midst. Find the one or two who exemplify who and what you want to be.

Chester Arnold was one of those men in our congregation. Chester was a deacon emeritus in our church. At ninety-five years of age, he went to be with the Lord. He had a servant's heart, he was joyful, and he was faithful to the end. His love, work, and devotion to the Lord and the church were immeasurable. When Chester was in his late seventies, we spent a week in Clarksdale, Mississippi, doing mission work in some of the more impoverished areas. Chester was such a short but strong man, and he outworked all of us. It was a joy to hear about Chester's service to our military, the way he met and married his wife, and the way he worked many years as an electrician.

Proverbs 16:31 states, "Gray hair is a crown of glory; it is gained by living a godly life." Take some time to get to know some of the elderly in your midst. These men can and will give you their wisdom if you watch and study their lives.

Gray hair is a crown of glory; it is gained by living a godly life.

PROVERBS 16:31

Put It in the Rearview Mirror

In his first golf tournament as a high schooler, a young freshman playing with upperclassmen hit a poor tee shot. This wasn't unexpected for the young golfer. But what made the young man's father proud was the maturity he saw developing in his son. Normally, it would take three or four more shots to overcome this one bad shot. But not this time.

Instead of being distracted by his past mistake, the young golfer got out his five iron and decided to go for it. With a tough lie, this young left-hander got over the ball and let it fly. The ball landed inches from the cup and resulted in a birdie for the hole.

How well do you put your mistakes in the rearview mirror? In Philippians 3:13-15, the apostle Paul says, "No, dear brothers and sisters, I have not achieved it, but I focus on this one thing: Forgetting the past and looking forward to what lies ahead, I press on to reach the end of the race and receive the heavenly prize for which God, through Christ Jesus, is calling us. Let all who are spiritually mature agree on these things."

Having a forward focus requires us to learn quickly from our mistakes so that we don't repeat them. It also requires us to receive fresh grace for our mistakes so that we don't beat ourselves up over them. So let's learn from this young golfer and the great apostle how to put our past behind us through the grace of Jesus and strive for God's purposes today!

No, dear brothers and sisters, I have not achieved it, but I focus on this one thing: Forgetting the past and looking forward to what lies ahead, I press on to reach the end of the race and receive the heavenly prize for which God, through Christ Jesus, is calling us. PHILIPPIANS 3:13-14

You Reap What You Sow

When the Houston Astros reached the play-offs in 2005, they decimated their farm system to build a team that would make it to the World Series that year. Unfortunately, the Astros lost four straight games to the Chicago White Sox in the series and didn't bring home a championship. Soon after this World Series run, Astros owner Drayton McClane decided he wanted to sell the team.

As a result, the rebuilding process of the farm club really struggled until the new owner of the Astros, Jim Crane, got to work. With experienced front-office leadership, the team aggressively drafted, traded, and reestablished their foundation of quality pitchers and players to make a run over the long haul. Ten years after their World Series appearance, the Astros won the 2015 American League wild card game against the New York Yankees.

Proverbs 14:14 states, "Backsliders get what they deserve; good people receive their reward." Just as the Astros lived for short-term success by sacrificing their future, we, too, reap the impact of our nearsighted decisions.

You see, our decisions today affect our tomorrow because mortgaging the future for fulfillment today comes at a high price. Whatever way you take, you can rest assured you will reap what you sow.

Backsliders get what they deserve; good people receive their reward.
PROVERBS 14:14

The Blessing of the Church

Some of the most generous people I have met are people who also have a lot of stuff. What I have learned about their generosity is that they use the things they have both for their enjoyment and as a way to bless others. Even with their vast amounts of possessions, they often think of others first.

As a pastor, I have been blessed by the people in my church who have been generous to so many in our city. They constantly amaze me with the way they share their time and resources: fighting human trafficking, investing in refugee communities, teaching people English, and funding our medical clinic. Their zeal for serving and giving is both refreshing and inspiring.

But what is truly humbling is seeing them meet the needs of those in our own church body. The call of our Lord is to build one another up in love. One of the ways we can do that is by sharing what we have. Yes, we enjoy what we have and rightfully so. But being openhanded and blessing our brothers and sisters in Christ is a key way to encourage them.

Galatians 6:10 states, "Whenever we have the opportunity, we should do good to everyone—especially to those in the family of faith." One of the lessons I try to impart to my children is that it is often through relationships in the church that we receive blessings—not through the sports leagues or the school, but the church.

As I reflect on it again, it's worth putting it in print: thank you, church, for the love you have demonstrated by giving freely what God has given to you.

Whenever we have the opportunity, we should do good to everyone—especially to those in the family of faith.   GALATIANS 6:10

What Carson Learned from #59

I had the chance to take my six-year-old daughter, Carson, on a date. We saw the Houston Texans play the New England Patriots at NRG Stadium. Our seats weren't great, but that didn't matter. We had a grand time. We were given the tickets because the night before the game, I spoke in the Texans chapel service. Each of my sons had experienced this special treat before, and now it was my Carson's turn.

Though tickets to the game were a great treat, it was the second pair of tickets that really got Carson excited. Those tickets were for the postgame players' reception, where family members and friends wait for the players to come out. It's a fun gathering where food is served and people are enthusiastic if the team has performed well. It is also a special way to get behind the scenes to meet a few of the players, which Carson was really hoping to do.

Though it was past 11 p.m., Carson was wide awake. Unfortunately, one of the players she had hoped to meet she only saw from afar, because after the embarrassing loss, he was leaving with quite a scowl on his face. One player she did get to meet, though, was Whitney Mercilus, #59, one of the players I had spoken with after the chapel service the night before. In the game, Mercilus had sacked Tom Brady on national television. Even after the loss, he was in good spirits, was gracious with his time, and took pictures with Carson.

On our way home, Carson asked, "Daddy, why was Whitney so happy and the other player (who will remain unnamed) so mad? Didn't they both lose?" I thought it a profound observation on her part. I said, "Carson, Whitney doesn't get his joy from winning and losing football games. He gets his joy from Jesus."

Where do you get your joy? In your performance, or in the Lord? Remember Isaiah 29:19 today, which states, "The meek shall obtain fresh joy in the LORD, and the poor among mankind shall exult in the Holy One of Israel" (ESV).

The meek shall obtain fresh joy in the LORD, and the poor among mankind shall exult in the Holy One of Israel. ISAIAH 29:19, ESV

The Voice of Pain

Randall Cunningham, the great NFL MVP quarterback of the Eagles and Vikings, writes about pain in his book *Lay It Down: How Letting Go Brings Out Your Best*. Randall is an authority on the impact of pain not just because of the physical abuse his body took on the football field but because of the deep pain he experienced through the loss of his two-year-old son in a drowning accident.

Cunningham writes of the voice of pain, "Pain says, 'Don't get up. Just lie here awhile.' Pain's voice is loud, perhaps the loudest voice you'll hear in your life."[62]

Has pain knocked you down? I want to encourage you to pick up Randall's book. I believe that his authenticity in dealing with excruciating pain can give you hope that you, too, can stand up and run another play. I also want to encourage you to press into the Lord in your pain.

Isaiah 61:1-2 describes the ministry of Jesus and how he dealt with and will deal with pain. It states, "The Spirit of the Sovereign Lord is upon me, for the Lord has anointed me to bring good news to the poor. He has sent me to comfort the brokenhearted and to proclaim that captives will be released and prisoners will be freed. He has sent me to tell those who mourn that the time of the Lord's favor has come, and with it, the day of God's anger against their enemies."

Jesus is near to those who mourn and to the brokenhearted. He can bring you the comfort you need. Also, let me remind you that there will be a day when he even puts death to death. Every tear will be wiped away. There will be no more suffering. The time of the Lord's favor will come.

The Spirit of the Sovereign LORD is upon me, for the LORD has anointed me to bring good news to the poor. He has sent me to comfort the brokenhearted and to proclaim that captives will be released and prisoners will be freed.

ISAIAH 61:1

---

[62] Randall Cunningham and Tim Willard, *Lay It Down: How Letting Go Brings Out Your Best* (Brentwood, TN: Worthy Publishing, 2013), 4–5.

OCTOBER 19
Building Trust

Trust is assured reliance on the character, ability, strength, or truth of someone or something. Hall of Fame NFL star Deion Sanders once said, "You don't earn another player's trust in games; you earn another player's trust in practice."

You see, trust is usually something that is built over time. Sanders was explaining that the trust teammates built during practice allowed them to play confidently during the game.

What about you? How do you build trust in relationships over time? Here are five simple principles to help you build trust:

1. Be reliable by doing what you say you are going to do.
2. Be honest, and always tell the truth as you speak from your heart.
3. Be open to others' thoughts and opinions. Stay teachable.
4. Keep confidences, and don't pass along gossip.
5. Show your integrity by being loyal and objective. Don't play favorites.

Joseph is an example of being trustworthy. When tempted to break his master's trust and sleep with Potiphar's wife, Joseph remained strong. Genesis 39:8-9 states, "Joseph refused. 'Look,' he told her, 'my master trusts me with everything in his entire household. No one here has more authority than I do. He has held back nothing from me except you, because you are his wife. How could I do such a wicked thing? It would be a great sin against God.'"

Clearly, Joseph decided in advance to be a trustworthy young man. Let's be people in the workplace and in our homes who keep and build trust!

How could I do such a wicked thing? It would be a great sin against God.
GENESIS 39:9

Friday Morning Breakfasts

For many years, I have taken one or both of my sons to breakfast on Friday mornings. We have talked about their sports teams, the college teams, the pro teams, and life in general.

On this particular morning, we had two separate encounters with individuals who looked very different from us. From outward appearances, it is safe to say that our lives had very little in common. In both moments, I led the conversation with a gracious greeting and quick smile. One of the gentlemen, who was standing at a traffic light, was soliciting funds. His sign read, "25 cents." I gave him a five-dollar bill and with a smile, told him that he needed to ask for more.

On the way to our destination, I then asked the son who was with me that morning to think through our two encounters. I told him that I hoped he saw that I treated both of the men we encountered with respect. I said, "The Scripture calls us to treat others the way we want to be treated." I then said, "You will encounter all sorts of people in your life. Lead the conversations with respect and a smile, and you will have a lot of peace in your encounters with others."

Looking back through the years, these moments of sharing chicken biscuits before school have led to some really great conversations where I have gotten to teach my sons. My prayer for them and for my daughter is what I see in Proverbs 23:23, which states, "Get the truth and never sell it; also get wisdom, discipline, and good judgment."

I want to be the dad that the next verse speaks of when I see wisdom flowing through the life of my children. "The father of godly children has cause for joy. What a pleasure to have children who are wise" (verse 24). The more I read the Scriptures, the more I am convinced that as a father, I have to lead my children to this place. Doing so with a chicken biscuit and a little honey is the tastiest way to go!

Get the truth and never sell it; also get wisdom, discipline, and good judgment.
PROVERBS 23:23

The Fantasy of Speculation

Fantasy football has turned into a huge industry. From weeklong leagues to season-long rosters, the hopes and dreams of so many football fans rise and fall on the health and performance of their fantasy players. Entire television and radio shows are based on fantasy football analysts reviewing past performance and providing future speculation. The gaming industry has invested heavily into the fantasy sports industry, and the government is trying to discern how to regulate it. Millions of dollars are traded every week based on speculation.

How cool would it be if you knew exactly who to pick because of their performance and ability to stay healthy? Some of this was depicted by Marty McFly, Doc, and Biff in the movie *Back to the Future Part II*. When Marty and Doc visit October 21, 2015, Marty purchases a sports almanac. Biff steals it, returns to 1955, and gives it to his younger self, who bets on games based on this knowledge. When they return to 1985, the conclusion for Biff is clear—he was very successful.

I think the words *fantasy* and *speculation* describe the movie's story line very well. But did you know that there is no need for speculation when we ask God for knowledge and wisdom? The next time you need knowledge, insight, and understanding, consider Proverbs 2:6: "The LORD grants wisdom! From his mouth come knowledge and understanding." I speculate that when you do, you, too, will be successful.

The LORD grants wisdom! From his mouth come knowledge and understanding.
PROVERBS 2:6

Play All Sixty Minutes

Former Tampa Bay Buccaneers head coach Greg Schiano was criticized when in his first season with the team, he had his defensive players go all out on a play when the opposing team's quarterback was taking a knee in the victory formation. When asked about it, Schiano defended his team's actions, indicating he was trying to change a culture and he wanted his players playing all sixty minutes. He wanted them to see the game to the end.

You know, if we learn to look to the end of a matter, we might save ourselves a lot of pain. For instance, when we enter into an adulterous relationship, we aren't looking to the end; we are only looking at what is right before us. We are so captivated by it that it actually blinds us.

As a result, we can't see the pain we will cause our wives, the devastation we will bring to our children, and the tragedy that will come when our ways get exposed. If we would see to the end, we would envision these moments and the pain the affair would create, and we would steer far away from that mistake.

Proverbs 5:3-4 warns us against the adulterous woman. It states, "The lips of an immoral woman are as sweet as honey, and her mouth is smoother than oil. But in the end she is as bitter as poison, as dangerous as a double-edged sword." Solomon was showing his sons the end of adultery with words like *poison* and *double-edged sword*. My friend, do you need to change the culture of your heart? Learn to see things to the end by heeding the Word of the Lord.

The lips of an immoral woman are as sweet as honey, and her mouth is smoother than oil. But in the end she is as bitter as poison, as dangerous as a double-edged sword. PROVERBS 5:3-4

Give It Four Minutes

I have a love-hate relationship with jogging. I love its benefits, but I hate every step—that is, in the first four minutes. In the first four minutes, my mind isn't focused, I am looking for the right music to listen to, and the stress that I put on my muscles creates pain that I don't terribly enjoy. It is amazing how tempted I am to stop before I have even begun. But I have come to realize that if I will give four minutes, I can go for forty or more.

There is something about going through uncomfortable moments for a short time that, if we keep going, enables us to go for quite a long time. When we choose to keep going, even when it is uncomfortable, our bodies, spirits, and minds adjust to the adversity and access stored energy to move us through. When it comes to fitness, embracing this adversity over and over again will lead to greater health, if we will just keep going. When it comes to trials in our lives, it is in the adversity that we are made stronger.

No matter what area of life you are dealing with, don't be afraid when you get uncomfortable. Second Timothy 1:7 states, "God has not given us a spirit of fear and timidity, but of power, love, and self-discipline." Keep going, and you will see that after those first four minutes, your strength will come, you will adjust, and you'll be just fine.

God has not given us a spirit of fear and timidity, but of power, love, and self-discipline. 2 TIMOTHY 1:7

The Power of a Team

In my interview with Hall of Fame quarterback Bart Starr, he made a comment on the power of a team. He said that *team* means "Together, everyone accomplishes more."

As much as we want to accomplish something, when it comes to working with others, we sometimes fail to see the benefit. As I coach my fourteen- and fifteen-year-old boys' basketball team, I continually challenge my players to trust each other. I have two boys who love to have the ball and try to score. Yet they consistently miss seeing the value of their teammates. They don't distribute the ball with trust, instead waiting until the last second to get a pass off. Sometimes the ball arrives too late because of their struggle to trust one of their teammates.

Contrast that with the fairly famous video clip of Tim Tebow saying to Demaryius Thomas something like, "Bro, I believe in you. You are going to catch the game-winning touchdown." On the first play from scrimmage of overtime when the Denver Broncos defeated the Pittsburgh Steelers, Tebow hit Thomas on a slant that went for eighty yards. It was the shortest overtime in the history of the NFL, lasting only eleven seconds.

We have a choice—to go it alone or to build up a team. Ecclesiastes 4:8 speaks to being alone. It comes just before Solomon declares, "Two are better off than one." Look at the harsh reality of depending only on yourself. Ecclesiastes 4:8 states, "This is the case of a man who is all alone, without a child or a brother, yet who works hard to gain as much wealth as he can. But then he asks himself, 'Who am I working for? Why am I giving up so much pleasure now?' It is all so meaningless and depressing."

When you realize that your fundamental role is helping others in your life, you will reap the benefits of that attitude. Remember, as Bart Starr says, "Together, everyone accomplishes more."

This is the case of a man who is all alone, without a child or a brother, yet who works hard to gain as much wealth as he can. But then he asks himself, "Who am I working for? Why am I giving up so much pleasure now?" It is all so meaningless and depressing. ECCLESIASTES 4:8

Keep It Moving

Momentum is an interesting thing. It is amazing how one drive, one shot, or one pitch can shift the entire momentum and mental outlook of a team. Getting momentum is almost euphoric. It gives a whole new perspective on a set of problems. The 2015 World Series champion Kansas City Royals captured the American League Division Series' momentum against the Houston Astros when they were able to stop Houston late in game four.

The Astros nearly had the game, up 6–2 in the eighth. But the Royals were able to get out of that jam and then punish the Astros to win game four. Kansas City, though down, never lost the expectant faith they'd had all season. They won game five and recaptured the momentum going into the World Series, where with this confidence, they defeated the New York Mets to clinch the 111th World Series title.

Do you have an expectant faith? Do you expect God to hear your prayer? Do you expect God to provide for your needs? Do you encourage those around you that God will move? Let me challenge your faith today. Hebrews 11:1 states, "Faith is the confidence that what we hope for will actually happen; it gives us assurance about things we cannot see." Today is an opportunity to recapture the momentum of your life by engaging an expectant faith. Whatever seems impossible to overcome, give it to your heavenly Father! Live with an expectant faith, because nothing is impossible with God.

Faith is the confidence that what we hope for will actually happen; it gives us assurance about things we cannot see. **HEBREWS 11:1**

Sitting in the Deer Stand

Do you hunt much? There is something special that happens when fall rolls around. We head to our sporting goods store, purchase our new hunting licenses, and prepare for opening day. One of the greatest gifts that a young man can receive is the gift of learning to hunt. We live in an increasingly urbanized society with weekends booked with sports and church commitments. After our battles on the athletic fields, we head home and jump right onto our tablets or phones and then turn on the television and watch college and pro football.

Time in the deer stand lets you get away from all the distractions of our modern world. It allows you to absorb all the sounds and smells of nature, and if you are fortunate, take aim at an eight- or ten-point buck. In those moments, you can experience the awe and wonder of God's creation like never before. It is good to be reminded of the simplicity and beauty of his creation, and it is also good to teach it to your children.

Ecclesiastes 12:1 states, "Remember also your Creator in the days of your youth." Some of the greatest moments I have had with my children came as we got out into nature, whether that be the Rocky Mountains in Colorado, the beaches of the Florida panhandle, or the vast acreage of South Texas. Exploring together, catching fish from the beach while playing in the surf, and hunting with my sons has created some amazing memories. As they say at REI, "Get outside." It will do you good.

Remember also your Creator in the days of your youth.　　ECCLESIASTES 12:1

Monday-Morning Quarterback Blues

Monday-morning quarterbacks are a dime a dozen. "They should have gone for it on fourth down." "He shouldn't have thrown it there." It is easy to be sitting on the sidelines of life, criticizing people who are actually in the game.

You may have a Monday-morning quarterback in your midst. It could be the team member who contributes little but talks a lot. It could be a family member who is constantly nagging you. Or maybe you are your own Monday morning quarterback, criticizing your own life.

As a pastor, I must confess that Mondays can be tough. You see, I naturally replay the film of the previous day in my mind and wonder how I really did. "Was anyone blessed? Did I truly minister to anyone? I could have said that better." I also reflect, not on the encouraging words from those in my church, but on the words of the people who don't hesitate to tell me what I could have done better.

When discouragement and despair come to you first thing in the morning, attack it. One of the best ways to shift the momentum of your day is to get a workout in, then seek inspiration by reading Scripture. Next, do something on your to-do list that is hard. Run, pray, and tackle a difficult task. Don't run from the despair, but hit it straight on. When you do, you will agree with the words of Psalm 118:24, which states, "This is the day the LORD has made. We will rejoice and be glad in it."

This is the day the LORD has made. We will rejoice and be glad in it.

PSALM 118:24

Winning in spite of Peyton Manning

Did you ever think you would see the headline above? If anyone has ever known how to win, it is Peyton Manning. In the 2015 season, the Broncos were sitting at 6–0 when *Sports Illustrated* declared that the Broncos were winning in spite of their Hall of Fame–bound quarterback.

Every team has moments when they are winning as a unit, even when key elements are struggling. Players have their ups and downs performing on the athletic field, and no one player will ever win the game for their team over the long haul on his or her own. This proved to be the case the entire 2015 season that led to the Broncos winning Super Bowl 50.

After Manning sat out for seven weeks because of injury, he was left sidelined for Brock Osweiler, who had performed well. When Osweiler struggled in the final week of the season, Manning returned to the game and never looked back. He led the team through the play-offs to the Super Bowl championship. But in that Super Bowl, the story was Wade Philips's defense that recorded seven sacks on the Carolina Panthers quarterback, Cam Newton.

Ecclesiastes 4:9-10 states, "Two people are better off than one, for they can help each other succeed. If one person falls, the other can reach out and help. But someone who falls alone is in real trouble." Just like the Broncos did all season, when your teammate is down, lift him or her up, because two together truly are better than one.

Two people are better off than one, for they can help each other succeed.
If one person falls, the other can reach out and help. But someone who
falls alone is in real trouble.   ECCLESIASTES 4:9-10

The Lord's Prayer and Football

Faith and football seem to go hand in hand. There is something about the battlefield of football that drives the highest profile coaches and players to huddle before a game and recite the Lord's Prayer. If you've ever been in the locker room or on the field with sixty-plus men bowing their knees and reciting this famous prayer in unison, you will never forget it. But what are they really praying?

David Jeremiah, in his book on the Lord's Prayer, declares that this prayer can be outlined with five words that start with the letter *P*:

Praise: "Our Father in heaven, hallowed be Your name."
Priorities: "Your kingdom come. Your will be done on earth as it is in heaven."
Provision: "Give us this day our daily bread."
Personal Relationships: "And forgive us our debts, as we forgive our debtors."
Protection: "And do not lead us into temptation, but deliver us from the evil one."

The prayer ends with a promise: "For Yours is the kingdom and the power and the glory forever. Amen."[63]

One of the truths that has ministered to me the most through the years is the last part of Matthew 6:8. Keep in mind that this verse comes right before we are taught this prayer by the Lord. Matthew 6:8 states, "Your Father knows exactly what you need even before you ask him!"

Keep that in mind when you pray. It should stir you to praise. It should challenge your priorities and give you confidence in God's provision. It should allow you to enjoy pardon in your personal relationships. It gives confidence in his protection and great meaning to his promises.

Your Father knows exactly what you need even before you ask him!

MATTHEW 6:8

---

63 Adapted from David Jeremiah, *Prayer: The Great Adventure* (Sisters, OR: Multnomah, 1997).

There's a Reason He Got Cut

When Houston Texans quarterback Ryan Mallet missed a training camp practice in August 2015 after Brian Hoyer was named the starter, it was reported that he overslept. During the regular season, after being knocked out for one play, he attempted to return, but he was refused the opportunity and was benched. Just before halftime, with one second still on the clock, Mallett left the field, going to the locker room and leaving his team behind. His actions spoke volumes.

A few weeks later, Mallett missed the team charter flight to Miami. He had to book and catch his own flight to join the team. The word from the media was that Coach O'Brien wanted to cut him even before the game. General Manager Rick Smith refused to terminate Mallett, because that would have left the Texans with only one quarterback for that game. As injury prone as the Texans have been at the quarterback position, Smith's wisdom prevailed, enabling Mallett to make one more game paycheck with the Texans. After the Texans suffered their worst defeat in team history, Mallett was cut and T. J. Yates was re-signed.

It was an unfortunate end to his time with the Texans, but as Proverbs 29:1 states, "Whoever stubbornly refuses to accept criticism will suddenly be destroyed beyond recovery." You don't have to be in the NFL to know that if you are habitually late and undependable, the organization that you are working for will move on from you. If you struggle with this, get your act together; otherwise, others will be saying of you, "There's a reason he got cut."

Whoever stubbornly refuses to accept criticism will suddenly be destroyed beyond recovery.   PROVERBS 29:1

A Person of Influence

People today are desperate for leadership. So often we limit our scope of influence and do not realize that we have the opportunity to make a difference in the lives of everyone with whom we come in contact. Everyone is a leader, because someone is always looking up to you no matter who you are. We will use our influence either positively or negatively.

As a young head coach at Florida State, Bobby Bowden came face-to-face with tragedy when one of his players was killed. Feeling the burden of this loss, Bowden took the time to talk to his players about eternity. A young graduate assistant, Mark Richt, was in the back of the locker room when Bowden explained the gospel. It was at that moment, when Bowden was imparting a life-giving message to his team, that Richt was influenced to give his life to Christ.

We need to broaden our vision and realize the influence that we carry to our extended family, friends, and coworkers—even the people we just pass throughout our day.

In Matthew 5:14-16, Jesus says, "You are the light of the world—like a city on a hilltop that cannot be hidden. No one lights a lamp and then puts it under a basket. Instead, a lamp is placed on a stand, where it gives light to everyone in the house. In the same way, let your good deeds shine out for all to see, so that everyone will praise your heavenly Father."

There are so many people you encounter each and every day, and you need to be mindful of them, seek to serve them, and be a blessing to them. This is the way to cultivate your influence.

You are the light of the world—like a city on a hilltop that cannot be hidden.   MATTHEW 5:14

NOVEMBER

Anything Goes

Some sports organizations can never get on the winning track. They have moments in the spotlight, but they don't have the leadership to make continued play-off runs, year in and year out. What their owners must realize is that everything rises and falls on the leadership that they put in place.

When Nehemiah arrived on the scene in Jerusalem, he found the city of his fathers with the walls torn down. The people of Jerusalem were oppressed and ruled by another nation. Nehemiah, a Jew, went with the favor and permission of Cyrus, the king of the Medo-Persian Empire, to rebuild the walls of this city and become its new governor.

Nehemiah found the people oppressed, not only by the outside nation that was ruling them, but also by their wealthier kinsmen. These upper-class Israelites were exacting usury on their brothers in a time of crisis, a practice forbidden in the law of Moses.

Listen to their cries from Nehemiah 5:4-5: "We have had to borrow money on our fields and vineyards to pay our taxes. We belong to the same family as those who are wealthy, and our children are just like theirs. Yet we must sell our children into slavery just to get enough money to live. We have already sold some of our daughters, and we are helpless to do anything about it, for our fields and vineyards are already mortgaged to others."

The point of the matter is clear. When things are a mess, the oppressed are even more oppressed. And when God's purposes are being reestablished in a place, sin must be confronted, and systems must change. It takes a leader to make this happen. Without leadership, you will find yourself in a land where anything goes.

We have had to borrow money on our fields and vineyards to pay our taxes. We belong to the same family as those who are wealthy, and our children are just like theirs. Yet we must sell our children into slavery just to get enough money to live. We have already sold some of our daughters, and we are helpless to do anything about it, for our fields and vineyards are already mortgaged to others. **NEHEMIAH 5:4-5**

NOVEMBER 2
The Last Sixty

When you think of the number sixty, what comes to mind? Does the name Chuck Bednarik ring a bell? Bednarik was one of the last players in the NFL who played both ways, playing center on offense and linebacker on defense. He was best known for a legendary hit on Frank Gifford.

Today's minute of vision marks the day when we are officially sixty days away from the end of the year. Let's think back to the first of the year. How did you start? I would expect that many of us started this year with a great zeal to make improvements—losing weight, changing careers, going back to church, or checking things off our bucket lists. What kind of progress have you made on your goals? Are you further along than you thought you would be? Did you already accomplish the goals that you set for yourself?

In your final sixty days of this year, how will you live to finish stronger than you started? What if you lived these final sixty days like you did the first sixty of this year? What kind of momentum would you have going into next year? What changes that you make now would you take to the next level next year? Listen, it isn't going to be easy. As a matter of fact, it may require you to play both ways, hit it harder than you have ever hit it before, and place yourself into an accountability relationship so you will finish what you started.

Ecclesiastes 3:1 states, "For everything there is a season, and a time for every matter under heaven" (ESV). Make the most of this final season of the year, and finish what you started.

For everything there is a season, and a time for every matter under heaven.
ECCLESIASTES 3:1, ESV

Brothers of Adversity

In any family, just like on any team, there is going to be conflict. The older my sons get, the more conflict they seem to have. I am constantly on them about being kind to each other and building each other up instead of tearing each other down. As a matter of fact, as the Christmas holidays were coming to a close one year, I commented to my wife that I was ready for the kids to go back to school.

We're not the only family who deals with conflict. A buddy of mine took one of my sons on an extended hunting trip with his sons, and when he returned, he said, "I sure hope your son isn't truthful with you about how my sons behaved toward each other." I looked at him and said, "Sounds like they are fighting for pack dominance."

Brothers fight, don't they? Sometimes it's a bit extreme, and if there isn't a moderator, they can end up really hating each other. But when there is good leadership in the home, the wrestling for dominance can actually be something that prepares them for the world that lies before them. You and I both know that it is a fight out there, and the last thing we want to do is send our sons into the fight unprepared.

Proverbs 17:17 states, "A friend is always loyal, and a brother is born to help in time of need." Sometimes that help is preparation for what lies ahead. If you have a brother, give him a call, reflect on your conflict, and thank him for helping you get ready for the life you are living today. He played a bigger part than you realize.

A friend is always loyal, and a brother is born to help in time of need.

PROVERBS 17:17

Can We Go Back?

Thirty-five degrees is really cold for sitting outside, even when you are bundled up from head to toe. It's even colder when you know you aren't the one getting to shoot the first deer, since it's your big brother's birthday hunt. It isn't a formula for quiet patience in the deer stand. At eleven years of age, this was a challenge for Cooper. After about forty minutes, he asked, "Can I go back?" Of course we said, "No!"

Going back is a reference to longing for comfort. When we get to difficult places in our lives, we often long to go back to the way things used to be. When we think like this, we oversimplify how good yesterday was because today seems pretty harsh. Discomfort leads to discontent, and all we can think about is what we left to arrive here.

This happened to the children of Israel after they cried out for deliverance from the Egyptians. The Lord had heard their cry and sent them a team of deliverers, Moses and Aaron. As these men led the Israelites out of Egypt, the people saw God do the miraculous. But I am struck by how quickly they forgot the way that God delivered them and what they were delivered from when the day in front of them seemed so difficult. The Israelites asked, "'Why is the LORD taking us to this country only to have us die in battle? Our wives and our little ones will be carried off as plunder! Wouldn't it be better for us to return to Egypt?' Then they plotted among themselves, 'Let's choose a new leader and go back to Egypt!'" (Numbers 14:3-4).

When I get to this point in the story, I want to throw it to the guys at ESPN's *Monday Night Countdown* for a quick "C'mon, man!" How quickly we forget all the Lord has done for us yesterday when what is before us today seems so difficult! When you ask the question, "Can we go back?" quickly tell yourself, "No," and keep moving forward, trusting the Lord.

"Why is the LORD taking us to this country only to have us die in battle? Our wives and our little ones will be carried off as plunder! Wouldn't it be better for us to return to Egypt?" Then they plotted among themselves, "Let's choose a new leader and go back to Egypt!" NUMBERS 14:3-4

The Power of Habits

Have you ever heard a quarterback talk about not remembering the second half of a football game? In its former days, the NFL didn't have the concussion protocols in place that it does today. As a result, teams would often run their players back out to the field for more of the same.

As concussion awareness has heightened, former players have begun talking about those moments when they just went out and performed, although everything was a blur. Quarterbacks have gone so far as to say that they have no memories of the rest of the game, but they just went out and did what they had been doing for years.

The many repetitions of three-, five-, and seven-step drops kicked in and took over when it was time to throw a pass. Their habitual practices served them as their subconscious minds did what their conscious minds were unable to.

It is amazing how deep our daily practices go into our lives. Some have speculated that up to 40 percent of our daily activities are performed out of habit. If this is the case, we ought to consider our ways to know that they are serving us well. Proverbs 4:26 states, "Mark out a straight path for your feet; stay on the safe path."

What are some of the habits that you have that you know aren't profitable? Are there practices that you engage in today that five years ago weren't tolerated? Consider the areas of alcohol, social media, and sexually explicit material. Have any of these taken hold so that you consistently find yourself regretting your conduct? Let your patterns serve you well by making a straight path for your feet.

Mark out a straight path for your feet; stay on the safe path.   PROVERBS 4:26

There's Got to Be More Than This

In a November 6, 2005, interview with *60 Minutes*, Patriots quarterback Tom Brady said, "Man, I'm making more money now than I thought I could ever make playing football. Why do I have three Super Bowl rings and still think there is something greater out there for me? . . . It's got to be more than this." Has your soul ever exposed itself in a similar way? Have you wondered if there is anything more to life? If accomplishments are the goal and prize, then you will end up with a great résumé but still feel empty. What is the key ingredient that is missing? What should the broader goal of your accomplishments be? We are to live for God's glory. When we live with our purpose in mind instead of living with his purpose as our aim, we come up short and lack lasting fulfillment.

Jesus spoke of the full and abundant life that is available to his followers. In John 10:10, Jesus said, "My purpose is to give them a rich and satisfying life." Other translations call it the abundant life. Don't confuse it with having lots of stuff. Instead, think of it as life with purpose, definition, and clarity for why you do what you do.

This abundant life begins at the Cross, where you discover your true value to God. It develops when you realize that God's purpose for your life is to glorify him in all you do. And it extends into eternity, where all things are made new. Begin to enjoy the abundant life by coming to God and allowing your purpose to be informed by his.

My purpose is to give them a rich and satisfying life.　　　　JOHN 10:10

Humility Comes before Honor

In the middle of the 2015 NFL season, Houston Texans head coach Bill O'Brien challenged his players to put the first half of the season behind them. Preparing to face the undefeated Cincinnati Bengals on *Monday Night Football* with a 3–5 record, O'Brien reportedly humbled himself when he challenged his players to move on from their first-half mistakes and bad plays.

O'Brien led the way in doing this by admitting to his team that he made a mistake in the first game of the year benching his quarterback, Brian Hoyer, for Ryan Mallett in the third quarter. That one decision seemed to take the team off course, and it wasn't until they were halfway through the season that O'Brien could look up and right the ship. I believe that when the leader admitted his mistake, it enabled the others on the coaching staff and in the locker room to feel like they, too, could get a fresh start.

O'Brien's admission to his team is a powerful example of humility that we would do well to learn from. Scripture gives us a choice between haughtiness and humility. Here are the results of each: "Haughtiness goes before destruction; humility precedes honor" (Proverbs 18:12).

Taking the bye week to look deeply into his team and his own decision making, O'Brien chose to use the key of humility to try to unlock the potential of his team. As a result, the Texans made a run and finished 9–7 for a second straight season under O'Brien, and they secured a wild card berth into the play-offs.

As you lead today, embrace humility. Don't be afraid to step back, take inventory, identify your mistakes, and admit them. When you do, you free others up to do the same.

Haughtiness goes before destruction; humility precedes honor.　　PROVERBS 18:12

Sometimes It Just Flows

When the Carolina Panthers defeated the Arizona Cardinals 49–15 to win the 2015 NFC Championship game and return to the Super Bowl, I thought, *Sometimes it just flows.* The Panthers crushed their opponents throughout the play-offs and found themselves going to the fiftieth Super Bowl having only lost one game all season.

When looking at both the offensive and defensive sides of the football, the Panthers demonstrated that they had the strongest team in the sport. But the Panthers didn't get there just by luck or happenstance. Their intentional plans for each phase of the game, their disciplined efforts to fix what ailed them, and their development as coaches and players paid huge dividends on the field. I often tell my children that preparation is the work. What happens when you get on the field flows out of that preparation.

Young David, the eventual king of Israel, had a zeal for battle. He knew how to win on the battlefield because he had prepared so diligently when caring for his father's sheep. First Samuel 17:36-37 records David's conversation with King Saul. David defended his desire and ability to go to battle with Goliath by stating:

> I have done this to both lions and bears, and I'll do it to this pagan Philistine, too, for he has defied the armies of the living God! The Lord who rescued me from the claws of the lion and the bear will rescue me from this Philistine!

I hope that you can have confidence today for the battles that you face because you have prepared yourself. Remember, preparation is the work, and after you have prepared, when you take the field, sometimes it just flows.

I have done this to both lions and bears, and I'll do it to this pagan Philistine, too, for he has defied the armies of the living God! The Lord who rescued me from the claws of the lion and the bear will rescue me from this Philistine! 1 SAMUEL 17:36-37

Taking Responsibility

One of the things that I don't particularly enjoy in my job as a pastor is listening to a husband and wife who aren't willing to get along. On one occasion, I was listening to a man complain about his wife, and he was struggling to know what to do. I told him to take up leadership by being responsible for setting the tone in his household. I told him to take a hard look at himself and change what he could control, which was himself.

The great Bear Bryant said, "Find your own picture, your own self in anything that goes bad. It's awfully easy to mouth off at your staff or chew out players, but if it's bad, and you're the head coach, you're responsible. If we have an intercepted pass, I threw it. If we get a punt blocked, I caused it. A bad practice, a bad game, it's up to the head coach to assume his responsibility."

Relationships are difficult when there is pride present. Pride is a divisive force. When Julee and I have struggled, it is because neither of us was willing to give an inch. We valued our pride and being right over being right with one another.

First Peter 3:8 states, "Sympathize with each other. Love each other as brothers and sisters. Be tenderhearted, and keep a humble attitude." Guys, I want to challenge you to take responsibility, as the leader, for the atmosphere in your homes. If things aren't going as you hoped, look in the mirror. Make course adjustments in yourself first and see how things begin to change. You get to set the tone, and your humble service will honor God, who in turn will honor you.

Sympathize with each other. Love each other as brothers and sisters. Be tenderhearted, and keep a humble attitude.　　　　　　　　　1 PETER 3:8

Early and Often

Hunters know that if they are going to get a good harvest during the various hunting seasons, they have to get out early. One of my buddies, who is a learned hunter, tells me that it is in the first and last thirty minutes of daylight when you will have the most opportunities. Getting out early before the sun is up is key.

One of the ways that hunters check to see if game is coming through to the feeders is by checking game trails and looking for tracks around the feeders. How often deer or hogs come to a certain spot can now be ascertained by hanging cameras in nearby trees. When motion is detected, the cameras capture the activity. Knowing how often deer or hogs come through to a particular feeding location over and against another will yield the greatest results.

Getting up early and often to read the Bible and pray also yields the best results. In his book *The Circle Maker*, Mark Batterson states, "Ultimately, the transcript of your prayers becomes the script of your life."[64] I can say that every bit of *A Minute of Vision for Men* was born in prayer, when I would get up early and go to the Lord often.

Jesus led with the early-and-often prayer strategy. Mark 1:35 states, "Before daybreak the next morning, Jesus got up and went out to an isolated place to pray." If you get up early and go often, you, too, will see the amazing harvest, season after season.

Before daybreak the next morning, Jesus got up and went out to an isolated place to pray.

MARK 1:35

---

64 Mark Batterson, *The Circle Maker: Praying Circles around Your Biggest Dreams and Greatest Fears* (Grand Rapids, MI: Zondervan, 2011), 14.

The Values of Champions

Coach Tony Dungy was a master motivator. He knew that he needed to stay a few steps ahead of his players. When asked what it takes to win as a team, Coach Dungy replied, "Hard work and togetherness. They go hand in hand. You need the hard work because it's such a tough atmosphere to win week in and week out. You need togetherness because you don't always win, and you gotta hang tough together."

You know these two ingredients are what make teams great champions. When individuals on a team fail to work hard, they fail to prepare for their potential. When there is division in the ranks of a team, it diverts the team's attention from what matters most.

If you are leading a team, not only do you have to embody these values, but you also have to expect them of others. Raise the culture of your team by teaching these values. Bring them to the forefront, and ask your team to respond accordingly.

I am sure you have heard the old adage "Don't expect what you don't inspect." Look for these values, and when you don't find them in play, challenge your teammates, and if you have to, make a change.

Proverbs 10:17 states, "People who accept discipline are on the pathway to life, but those who ignore correction will go astray." When you see your team members accepting discipline, celebrate it and let the rest of the team know what you see.

People who accept discipline are on the pathway to life, but those who ignore correction will go astray. PROVERBS 10:17

I Have to Apologize

At the 2015 Miss Universe Pageant, the host, Steve Harvey, concluded the evening with a huge blunder. He mistakenly crowned Miss Colombia as Miss Universe when the honor actually went to Miss Philippines. I don't know if there has ever been such a blunder like that in a pageant before. The most awkward moment was when the crown was removed from Miss Colombia's head and placed on that of Miss Philippines.

What I truly appreciate about Harvey's mistake is that he was humble, honest, and very remorseful. He apologized and took full responsibility for what had happened. Harvey owned his mistake.

As awkward and hurtful as that moment was, Harvey teaches us all that saying, "I'm sorry," and "Please forgive me," is so important. When I watched Harvey's response to his error, I thought, *Now here is a man who has apologized before. Here is a man comfortable with humility.* Though a huge star, Steve Harvey didn't hesitate to take full responsibility for the error and do so publicly.

You can tell a lot about a person who is willing to apologize in public. Proverbs 28:13 states, "People who conceal their sins will not prosper, but if they confess and turn from them, they will receive mercy." If there is something that you need to take responsibility for, go ahead and just do it. Find the grace that will put that mistake in the past and move forward in freedom.

People who conceal their sins will not prosper, but if they confess and turn from them, they will receive mercy. PROVERBS 28:13

A Wake-Up Call

On November 13, 2015, radical Islamic terrorists unleashed an attack on the city of Paris that killed more than 130 people. From attacking a theater where a heavy metal band was performing, to setting off three explosions outside a soccer stadium, to rolling up to an intersection bordered by two outdoor cafés and opening fire on those simply enjoying a cup of coffee, these Islamic State pawns executed an orchestrated plan to further their agenda of jihad. This same city had experienced an attack on the newspaper *Charlie Hebdo* just eleven months before, and the French government had been watching some five thousand suspected Islamic extremists living within France.

Our world has changed drastically since 9/11, and the questions we must ask individually and collectively are, Are we learning anything from these moments that should inform our way? Is our government doing all it can to protect us? What are our responsibilities as citizens to protect ourselves and watch over our neighbors?

Proverbs 1:32-33 states, "Simpletons turn away from me—to death. Fools are destroyed by their own complacency. But all who listen to me will live in peace, untroubled by fear of harm." Don't be lulled to sleep. Complacency destroys careers, families, communities, and nations. Stay alert and vigilant, because the enemy is real and he seeks to kill, steal, and destroy. Protect your family, your neighbors, and your community by turning to the wisdom of God to guard and guide your way!

Simpletons turn away from me—to death. Fools are destroyed by their own complacency. But all who listen to me will live in peace, untroubled by fear of harm.
PROVERBS 1:32-33

An Ox to the Slaughter

My oldest son, Brady, loves watching the Outdoor Channel. We live in the heart of the fourth largest city in the United States, and our street empties onto the inner loop freeway feeder. Our neighborhood is a far cry from the country. But Brady loves camouflage. He has a camouflage Bible, phone case, and hoodie. He wears boots whenever he has an opportunity to, and he can't wait for his next chance to get out of the city. He dreams of opportunities to hunt deer, hog, quail, and dove. During Brady's fifteenth birthday weekend, we went to a friend's ranch in south Texas and hunted his ten thousand acres. Brady killed a bobcat and a coyote. What a treat that was!

Just as a hunter lays a trap for his prey, the adulteress lays a trap for a man. You see, the Bible describes the adulteress as one lying in wait for those who lack judgment. With seductive words, the adulteress pleads for men to drink deep of love. The problem, though, is that love isn't present, only ruin.

Proverbs 7:22-23 states, "He followed her at once, like an ox going to the slaughter. He was like a stag caught in a trap, awaiting the arrow that would pierce its heart. He was like a bird flying into a snare, little knowing it would cost him his life."

My friend, don't ruin your life. Deny the adulteress, and flee her presence.

He followed her at once, like an ox going to the slaughter. He was like a stag caught in a trap, awaiting the arrow that would pierce its heart. He was like a bird flying into a snare, little knowing it would cost him his life.

PROVERBS 7:22-23

Blessed Yet Complaining

A church sign once read, "America: God's spoiled child." Is America spoiled? Though we are the most prosperous nation on the face of the earth, it seems we struggle with contentment. Instead of being thankful to the Almighty for abundant provision, we find ourselves complaining. We hardly celebrate the Thanksgiving holiday anymore. Instead, Thanksgiving Day has been reduced to Black Friday Eve.

A lack of gratitude leads to a bad attitude. For whatever reason, we find it therapeutic to complain. In a podcast about discontentment, Dr. Kevin Elko said, "We justify and camouflage our complaining as venting if that word puts a positive spin on it." But instead of finding a stress relief, it only allows us to see the deficiencies of a situation all the more.

First Thessalonians 5:18 states, "Be thankful in all circumstances, for this is God's will for you who belong to Christ Jesus." Let's stop for a few minutes today and count all of our blessings—from the food on our tables to the clothes on our backs. Let's allow an attitude of gratitude to permeate our hearts and our minds. An old hymn declares, "Count your blessings, name them one by one. Count your blessings, see what God has done." When we stop and take inventory of what we have, not only does it help us see all that God has given to us, but it also keeps us from seeing all of the deficiencies of a situation.

What do you have to be grateful for today?

Be thankful in all circumstances, for this is God's will for you who belong to Christ Jesus.   1 THESSALONIANS 5:18

Taking Longer to Recover

During the 2015 NFL season, Denver Broncos quarterback Peyton Manning surpassed the all-time passing yards champion, Brett Favre. However, Manning completed five of twenty passes for thirty-five yards and threw four interceptions in one game, so he was benched by Broncos head coach Gary Kubiak in that same game. This caused many to wonder if the end was near for Manning's career. After the game, it was reported that Manning had injured ribs and a tear in the plantar fascia in his foot. One commentator, a former NFL star, said, "I knew it was time to retire when it took my body until Saturday to recover from the previous Sunday." Indeed, at the end of the season, Manning retired from the game of football.

One of the ways you progress to the next place in your life is through a season of frustration. In the moment, frustration can be very challenging. When it occurs over and over again, week in and week out, it can be God's way of getting you to pick your head up and see what he may be doing to redirect your life. Frustration can be a great catalyst for progress if you will be thoughtful about it.

Remember these words from Proverbs if you sense the frustration you are experiencing is so that you will consider new paths: "Good planning and hard work lead to prosperity, but hasty shortcuts lead to poverty" (21:5). If you sense you are coming to the close of one season and embarking on a new one, take your time to be thoughtful, wise, and discerning. Make sure you take a path that honors God.

Good planning and hard work lead to prosperity, but hasty shortcuts lead to poverty.   PROVERBS 21:5

Norman vs. Beckham Jr.

Tom Pedulla's headline that appeared in the *New York Times* on the Monday after the premiere of *Star Wars: The Force Awakens* read, "Josh Norman's Defense Uncovers Odell Beckham Jr.'s Dark Side." In the tale of two halves, the Carolina Panthers pulled out a 38–35 victory over the Giants to go 14–0 with just two games left to play in the 2015 season, but that wasn't the big story of the game.

An emerging star for his sensational one-handed catches and freakish statistics, Odell Beckham Jr. was anything but classy during this epic battle at MetLife Stadium. Josh Norman covered Beckham like a blanket, and their blows during the game would have landed them both in the county lockup if they hadn't been on a field overseen by referees. The blow that led to Beckham's one-game suspension came about when Beckham speared Norman in the head with his own head, coming across a pile of tacklers with Norman in his sights. After the game, it came out that Norman himself had participated in some very controversial antics that got under Beckham's skin.

There are a number of Scriptures that come to mind when I see this type of performance played out on the field. But the Scripture that resonates the most is Proverbs 12:16: "A fool is quick-tempered, but a wise person stays calm when insulted." Don't show your annoyance at once. Grow in wisdom so that you will have it to show restraint!

A fool is quick-tempered, but a wise person stays calm when insulted.

PROVERBS 12:16

Lead by Example

Don Shula, two-time Super Bowl–winning head coach of the Miami Dolphins, said, "I don't know any other way to lead but by example." Our lives, like it or not, are examples of what is flowing through our hearts. Now that I have typed that, it kind of scares me to consider what example I have set over the last week or so. But leadership unfolds not just in speeches, strategies, and surveys. Leadership emerges from the example that the leader sets.

This begs us to ask ourselves, what example am I setting for others? What do my children, employees, friends, and clients see through me? When I am squeezed and things don't go my way, what picture am I giving to others? When there is abundance and I've had a banner year, will those in my midst see an attitude of gratitude? Will they hear me express thanks to God for his abundant provision?

Colossians 3 gives us a picture of how we might live as examples for our Lord. Just as we get dressed each morning, we must clothe ourselves with these qualities every day. Colossians 3:12-15 states,

> Since God chose you to be the holy people he loves, you must clothe yourselves with tenderhearted mercy, kindness, humility, gentleness, and patience. Make allowance for each other's faults, and forgive anyone who offends you. Remember, the Lord forgave you, so you must forgive others. Above all, clothe yourselves with love, which binds us all together in perfect harmony. And let the peace that comes from Christ rule in your hearts. For as members of one body you are called to live in peace. And always be thankful.

The only way that we will accomplish this is through the help of the Holy Spirit. So get dressed each day by asking the Holy Spirit to help you put on these qualities. Give him an all-access pass to your heart, and live this example out before those in your life.

Since God chose you to be the holy people he loves, you must clothe yourselves with tenderhearted mercy, kindness, humility, gentleness, and patience.

COLOSSIANS 3:12

Sensitivity to the Spirit

Have you noticed how sensitive people are today? With the popularity of Facebook, Twitter, and Instagram and the ability to sound off whenever we want about whatever we want to whomever will listen, we have become a highly sensitive society. It's easy to spew venomous rhetoric at those we disagree with, and as a result, we've lost a certain grace and etiquette.

Unfortunately, some of the most un-Christian rhetoric comes from those who post Bible verse memes on social media. It's easy to go on a rant because of an article someone posted or an opinion someone expressed, not worrying about who might see it or care what damage it will do.

What if our sensitivity shifted? What if, instead of being so sensitive about people's opinions and behaviors, we were sensitive to what God says regarding our emotions, our speech, and the way we engage others? One of my frequent prayers is that I would not crowd the Lord out but that I would listen for his voice.

First Samuel 3:8-10 shows us a beautiful way to listen for the voice of the Lord:

> So the LORD called a third time, and once more Samuel got up and went to Eli. "Here I am. Did you call me?"
>
> Then Eli realized it was the LORD who was calling the boy. So he said to Samuel, "Go and lie down again, and if someone calls again, say, 'Speak, LORD, your servant is listening.'" So Samuel went back to bed.
>
> And the LORD came and called as before, "Samuel! Samuel!"
>
> And Samuel replied, "Speak, your servant is listening."

May we, too, say, "Speak, your servant is listening."

Speak, LORD, your servant is listening.   1 SAMUEL 3:9

Being a Man by Being Thankful

Heisman Trophy winner Tim Brown writes in his book *The Making of a Man*, "I've met many people who are extremely successful in their careers. Some of them . . . are pretty quick to tell you about all they've done. It's "I, I, I." . . . They have a difficult time acknowledging the people who helped them along the way. More important, they fail to give God the credit for opening the doors to opportunity and giving them the skill to succeed."[65]

Have you stopped to take a look back at all the people who helped you get where you are today—parents, teachers, coaches, and friends? Each of us has someone who put in a good word on our behalf, made a phone call for us, or put his or her own name on the line, believing in our potential. Some even sacrificed their own positions for our well-being. Jonathan did this for David.

Take a look at 1 Samuel 18:3-4, which states, "Jonathan made a solemn pact with David, because he loved him as he loved himself. Jonathan sealed the pact by taking off his robe and giving it to David, together with his tunic, sword, bow, and belt." Jonathan gave up the throne for the sake of his friend, David.

Who has put their name on you? It is a humbling thing when another advocates for you. Call, text, or write to tell that person thanks. You'll be glad you did.

Jonathan made a solemn pact with David, because he loved him as he loved himself. Jonathan sealed the pact by taking off his robe and giving it to David, together with his tunic, sword, bow, and belt.   1 SAMUEL 18:3-4

---

[65] Tim Brown with James Lund, *The Making of a Man: How Men and Boys Honor God and Live with Integrity* (Nashville: W Publishing, 2014), 9–10.

The Investment Strategy of Kindness

Given the new play-off structure in college football, the Big 12, made up of ten major colleges, wonders each year how not having a championship game affects the possibilities of their teams getting into the play-off bracket. The 2014 Baylor Bears missed out on the brand-new college football play-off because of the lack of a championship game in the Big 12. The conference's leadership has indicated that they will not change the structure of how they crown a champion. If they continue to miss the play-off bracket, I would assume they may decide a change will be necessary. But to this point, it is fascinating to me when parties become so immovable because they think the way they do things is right.

Are you immovable? Here is another way to ask it: Are you right, or are you right? If you are struggling in a relationship, ask yourself, do I always have to win every argument? Do I always have to be right? You see, you can be right on the issues and all alone, or you can be right relationally and working toward the long haul.

If you have to win every debate, then pride is a major problem in your life. If you are not careful, you might just end up all alone. Look at the words of Proverbs 11:17, which states, "Your kindness will reward you, but your cruelty will destroy you." If you invest in relationships through kindness, you will have a great return for your life.

Your kindness will reward you, but your cruelty will destroy you.

PROVERBS 11:17

Saying Thanks

What are you thankful for today? I am thankful for John Pickul. John is in his seventies, but you wouldn't know it. No, John is much younger than his age.

Why is he so young? First, John has a joyful spirit and loves to get as much out of life as possible. Second, John is cool. You see, John drives the bus for our middle school students for their "Middle School Madness" youth ministry outings. Not only does John drive the bus, but he also dresses in all black and plays laser tag with the kids. We were tossing around things that we were thankful for in our staff meeting, and this awesome report about John Pickul stood out to me.

What stands out to you for which you are thankful? When you stop and take inventory of the things you can be grateful for, your ability to be content goes way up. Additionally, your desire to complain goes way down. You see, thanksgiving is an antidote to dissatisfaction, discouragement, and despair.

Are you thankful? If so, does it show? I think John is thankful for his health; for his wife, Iola; for his family; for the Houston Livestock Show and Rodeo; and for his ability to enjoy so much of this life. When you are around a guy like John, you can't help but be thankful as well.

Psalm 100:4-5 states, "Enter his gates with thanksgiving; go into his courts with praise. Give thanks to him and praise his name. For the LORD is good. His unfailing love continues forever, and his faithfulness continues to each generation." For what are you thankful? Let the Lord know through a prayer of thanksgiving.

Enter his gates with thanksgiving; go into his courts with praise. Give thanks to him and praise his name. For the LORD is good. His unfailing love continues forever, and his faithfulness continues to each generation.

PSALM 100:4-5

From QB to Professor

Dr. David Klingler is an associate professor of Bible exposition at Dallas Theological Seminary. David has become a good friend of mine over the years, and I admire him for letting God use him to do the very thing he loves most: teaching the Bible.

A former Heisman Trophy candidate and first-round draft pick of the Cincinnati Bengals, Klingler remembers being challenged by his friend and pastor Voddie Baucham Jr. to do more with his life than play football and train horses. Baucham challenged him to go to seminary and be used by God to teach the Bible to others.

Over time and through a series of events, David embraced that challenge. The more he studied, the more he grew to love the Word of God. He earned a master's in theology and then a doctorate in Old Testament studies. Now not only is he raising two fine young men, but he is also living a life that has exponential impact.

Isn't it amazing how challenges spoken into our lives at just the right time can plant seeds that come to fruition years later? Romans 8:28 says, "We know that God causes everything to work together for the good of those who love God and are called according to his purpose for them." Let's commit to live out our calling and watch how God can take seeds planted and turn them into fruitful purpose.

We know that God causes everything to work together for the good of those who love God and are called according to his purpose for them. **ROMANS 8:28**

Say Please and Thank You

We are often like that young son who looked at his dad one day and said, "Hey, Dad, I can say *please* and *thank you* in Spanish." His father, unimpressed with what his son had learned at school, responded, "How come you never say it in English?"

If you had been one of the ten lepers who were healed in Luke 17, do you think you would have returned to Jesus to say thank you? I have always wondered if I would be one of the nine who left, or if I would have been the one who came back to express his thanks.

You see, I am still amazed by this story, because this day marked a radical shift in the lives of these men. No longer would they be deemed "unclean" and be avoided by all of society. Now they were free of those labels and the awful illness that suppressed their lives. Yet still, only one of them returned to give thanks.

How often do you stop and thank God for his provision, his protection, and the lack of persecution in your life? The reality is that we could never thank God enough for all that he has done for us. I am certain that there is so much more that we don't see for which we should be thankful. Yet we have trouble being truly thankful for the blessings we can see and know we have been given.

Luke 17:17 shows us the glory that should be given to the Father. It states, "Jesus asked, 'Didn't I heal ten men? Where are the other nine? Has no one returned to give glory to God except this foreigner?' And Jesus said to the man, 'Stand up and go. Your faith has healed you.'"

Take the time to give glory to God today for all that he has done for you. What ten things do you know that he has given you from his hand? Write them down, and then thank him for each by name.

Jesus asked, "Didn't I heal ten men? Where are the other nine? Has no one returned to give glory to God except this foreigner?" And Jesus said to the man, "Stand up and go. Your faith has healed you."   LUKE 17:17

Getting Stuck in the Mud

On a Saturday after Thanksgiving, my sons, my brother-in-law, and I got into a duck blind just before sunup. The ducks began to fly overhead, and we were able to bag a few. Shortly thereafter, though, the action stopped. After sitting in the cold for an hour, it was time to go in. As we were heading back, one more duck began to circle the pond. No longer in the blind, I thought, *This duck's not that stupid, is he?* Although my brother-in-law told me it was probably best to just head in, I shot the duck out of the air, wounding it. Something in me just couldn't leave that duck landing right in front of me without taking aim.

The duck started to swim away, beginning an adventure to try to kill it and get it out of the pond. My brother-in-law and I split up, deciding to take different paths to the duck. At the far edge of the pond, I took one step, and I immediately knew I was in trouble. After two more steps, I began to sink, now stuck up to my hips in mud.

Have you ever succumbed to temptation? I knew it was probably best just to go in, but shooting the duck out of the air seemed like great fun. The ramifications of that decision led to great struggle and derailed me for quite some time. Temptation is all around us. That is why Jesus teaches us to always be on the alert. He says in Matthew 26:41, "Keep watch and pray, so that you will not give in to temptation. For the spirit is willing, but the body is weak!" Don't give in.

Keep watch and pray, so that you will not give in to temptation. For the spirit is willing, but the body is weak!   MATTHEW 26:41

People and Stuff

The holidays have become about people and stuff. In recent years, "Black Friday" news reports have shown hundreds of people lined up in front of stores for great discounts on electronics and video games. Some people even camp out two or three days in advance to be the first in line. When the doors are opened, the people rush in to get their hands on a limited supply of that must-have item. Needless to say, some people get out of sorts with others in their pursuit, and conflict ensues.

When we read about Jesus' birth, though, we see the antithesis of what holiday shopping has become. There weren't crowds of people present at his birth, and there wasn't anything very appealing about the stuff surrounding him in that stable, either.

But the irony of the birth of Jesus is that it was about both people and stuff. Jesus came to redeem people from sin and death, and we can worship him, as the Magi did, by bringing him a tribute from our things as a sacrifice of praise. Matthew 2:11 states, "They entered the house and saw the child with his mother, Mary, and they bowed down and worshiped him. Then they opened their treasure chests and gave him gifts of gold, frankincense, and myrrh."

I want to challenge you to make this holiday season different. Don't just make it about people and stuff. Make it about Jesus, and bring to him both your heart and a gift of tribute from that which he has given to you!

They entered the house and saw the child with his mother, Mary, and they bowed down and worshiped him. Then they opened their treasure chests and gave him gifts of gold, frankincense, and myrrh.　　MATTHEW 2:11

Leave with Class

My two older brothers are Aggies. As we got together for dinner heading into the 2015 Christmas holiday and the college football bowl season, I asked, "What's the deal with your Aggie quarterbacks?" You see, in the same week, two of their quarterbacks, Kyle Allen and Kyler Murray, both the number-one-ranked quarterbacks of their respective classes coming out of high school, left Texas A&M looking to play somewhere else.

Not only was this a blow to the program, but it seemed their timing couldn't have been any worse, leaving two weeks before the Aggies would play in the Music City Bowl. From the outside looking in, it seemed that something just wasn't right at Kyle Field. With that said, my oldest brother, Keith, responded, "Even if they were treated poorly, there's a better way to leave than two weeks before the bowl."

Leaving well seems to be a lost art because we don't think about our reputations over the long haul. Each of us is going to leave our employment at one point or another. Listen to Proverbs 22:1, which states, "Choose a good reputation over great riches; being held in high esteem is better than silver or gold."

When we leave a job, we will say more about our character in that moment than we did during the entire time of our service there. When we follow Christ as Savior and are on his team, his name on the front of the jersey matters so much more than our name on the back.

Choose a good reputation over great riches; being held in high esteem is better than silver or gold.

PROVERBS 22:1

Roethlisberger, Vick, and Jones

The Pittsburgh Steelers weren't yet halfway through the 2015 NFL campaign when they had already gone to their third-string quarterback, Landry Jones. Jones, a star at the University of Oklahoma, said after a come-from-behind victory over the Arizona Cardinals, "I just can't believe I got in the game."

Here is a guy who has been the best player on the field wherever he has gone throughout his entire amateur football career. But when he turned pro, he found himself waiting behind Ben Roethlisberger and Michael Vick for an opportunity to live out his childhood dream.

Waiting is hard for athletes, but it is even harder for young wives who can't conceive. Yes, waiting is hard for a backup point guard or catcher, as they are eager to get in the game and show what they can do. But waiting is even harder on a young father who is watching his son battling cancer.

Throughout my pastoral ministry, I have had to walk with people through some very difficult trials and challenges. Occasionally, there is a great victory that emerges through these trials. I am not sure what you may be waiting for God to move on. As I have had to wait, and as I have walked with others in their seasons of waiting, I will confess to you this harsh reality: waiting is hard, and you don't always get what you want.

But there are also times when the victory is so sweet, words can't really express the beauty of what has taken place. You see, there is nothing like that moment when you, like Landry Jones, get to take the field and get the victory you have been longing for. May the words of Proverbs 13:12 bless you today: "Hope deferred makes the heart sick, but a dream fulfilled is a tree of life."

Hope deferred makes the heart sick, but a dream fulfilled is a tree of life.
PROVERBS 13:12

Say "Cheese"

Have you ever let your circumstances steal your joy? I know I have. I have learned that if your joy is based on your circumstances, you are destined to be disappointed. This was reinforced to me while Christmas shopping at the mall, where I saw a little boy getting his first picture with Santa Claus. He was a tiny thing, probably fourteen to sixteen months of age.

He was dressed in his dark blue corduroys, a plaid shirt, and little leather shoes. His mom had picked out just the right outfit for that first picture with Santa. There was only one problem. When his mother sat him alone next to the fat man in red pajamas with the long, white beard, the boy didn't like it. As a matter of fact, it scared him so much that there was no way he was going to smile. Instead, the look on his face was utter terror.

The photographers were trying to make him smile. Santa's little helper was making funny faces, and Mom was trying to get him to say, "Cheese." But nothing seemed to help.

There is so much in your life that will steal your joy right out of you if you let it. But remember, if you belong to the Lord Jesus Christ, this world is not your home. Romans 14:17 states, "The Kingdom of God is not a matter of what we eat or drink, but of living a life of goodness and peace and joy in the Holy Spirit."

Place your hope in Christ, the one who is unchanging, so that you will have joy even when your circumstances change.

The Kingdom of God is not a matter of what we eat or drink, but of living a life of goodness and peace and joy in the Holy Spirit.   ROMANS 14:17

The Life That Is Truly Life

In one installment of the comic strip *Cathy*, the main character is stuck in a Christmas-shopping traffic jam while she is trying to do her normal shopping. The cartoonist does a great job showing the reader Cathy's frustration. When Cathy gets to the point of exasperation, no longer able to move, she screams out, "If stores really understood the holiday spirit, they'd open an express lane for the greedy."

We live in an increasingly materialistic society. The scandals of Wall Street and the housing bubble collapse were because of the deadly sin of greed. Many people were deeply affected by the consequences of the decisions of those who were greedy.

Yet what we have failed to realize is that our quest to possess will ultimately possess us unless we intentionally combat it with an antidote. Do you know the antidote to greed? Scripture says the antidote to greed is generosity. As a matter of fact, the apostle Paul gives Timothy instructions on what to teach the wealthy in his congregation so that they won't be captured by greed. Here are his words in 1 Timothy 6:17-19:

> Teach those who are rich in this world not to be proud and not to trust in their money, which is so unreliable. Their trust should be in God, who richly gives us all we need for our enjoyment. Tell them to use their money to do good. They should be rich in good works and generous to those in need, always being ready to share with others. By doing this they will be storing up their treasure as a good foundation for the future so that they may experience true life.

The last phrase of verse 19 is translated in *The Message* as the "life that is truly Life."

Decide today to be generous. Be rich in good deeds and live for a purpose that is greater than yourself.

Teach those who are rich in this world not to be proud and not to trust in their money, which is so unreliable. Their trust should be in God, who richly gives us all we need for our enjoyment.   1 TIMOTHY 6:17

DECEMBER

Keeping It Merry

John Grisham's *Skipping Christmas* portrays a couple who decide that they would rather forgo the Christmas holiday than spend the thousands of dollars associated with Christmas because of the pressures of the culture. The book is a great read with many fun twists and turns, and it exposes one of the challenges of Christmas: keeping the holiday merry.

During the month of December, the demands on our time go up, as the expectations of others have us going from the malls to buy gifts, to holiday parties to make small talk, and to our kids' schools to see their Christmas programs. As Christmas Eve approaches, the pressure of buttoning things up at work, wrapping the gifts, packing the car, and getting the kids nicely dressed for Christmas Eve services mounts, making the Christmas holiday feel anything but merry. The rat race of Christmas can make "skipping Christmas" very tempting.

How can we keep Christmas merry? I believe it all involves directing our hearts toward Christ at the beginning of each day. Consider getting up a few minutes early and spending time with your first cup of coffee reading the Christmas story in Matthew 1–2 or Luke 1–2. Consider grabbing that morning cup and reading John 1:1-14. As John declares in verse 14, "The Word became human and made his home among us. He was full of unfailing love and faithfulness. And we have seen his glory, the glory of the Father's one and only Son." Let's begin our days with our hearts focusing on the true meaning of Christmas, and protect our joy.

The Word became human and made his home among us. He was full of unfailing love and faithfulness. And we have seen his glory, the glory of the Father's one and only Son.　　　　　　　　　　JOHN 1:14

DECEMBER 2
A Blue Christmas

In *A Charlie Brown Christmas*, Charlie Brown just can't get into the Christmas spirit. His little friend Linus observes, "Charlie Brown, you're the only person I know who can take a wonderful season like Christmas and turn it into a problem."

For many people, the Christmas holidays are a time of difficulty instead of joy. Maybe this is the first Christmas you will experience without someone you loved deeply. Or maybe you are struggling in a key relationship or having difficulty making ends meet.

Did you know that you can still have joy in the midst of your struggle? When you understand the heart of Christmas, the joy that is beyond your circumstances will carry you. During this season, when you feel alone, lost, or forgotten, turn to Isaiah 26:3: "You will keep in perfect peace all who trust in you, all whose thoughts are fixed on you!" Fix your mind, your emotions, and your will on the one who will give you peace during this holiday season.

The earth has dealt with difficulty since the very beginning when man chose a path of sin that led to death. But even in that moment, we see God's promise of redemption: "I will cause hostility between you and the woman, and between your offspring and her offspring. He will strike your head, and you will strike his heel" (Genesis 3:15).

Hundreds of years after that first promise was given, the Son of God was born, so that our God would restore that which was broken in the Garden long, long ago. He will make all things new. May the Lord grant you a merry Christmas!

I will cause hostility between you and the woman, and between your offspring and her offspring. He will strike your head, and you will strike his heel.
GENESIS 3:15

A Christmas Fanatic

One of my favorite *Peanuts* cartoons has Lucy coming to Charlie Brown and saying, "Merry Christmas, Charlie Brown. Since it's this time of the season, I think we ought to bury past differences and try to be kind."

In the next frame, Charlie Brown says, "Why does it just have to be 'this time of the season'? Why can't it be all year long?"

Then Lucy looks at him and exclaims, "What are you, some kind of fanatic?"

As Christmas draws near, I want to encourage you to seek to reconcile relationships within your family. There is nothing like celebrating Christmas with your family relationships intact.

Ephesians 4:31-32 states, "Get rid of all bitterness, rage, anger, harsh words, and slander, as well as all types of evil behavior. Instead, be kind to each other, tenderhearted, forgiving one another, just as God through Christ has forgiven you." To reconcile a relationship, you have to choose to humble yourself and forgive the one who has offended you, even before you see each other. Humility means going first. When this grace is reciprocated, it is powerful. Past mistakes are forgiven and forgotten, and those who were separated are reunited. But let's not just do it for a family gathering during the holiday. Let's work toward right relationships all year long.

Get rid of all bitterness, rage, anger, harsh words, and slander, as well as all types of evil behavior. Instead, be kind to each other, tenderhearted, forgiving one another, just as God through Christ has forgiven you. EPHESIANS 4:31-32

A Note in His Locker

When Robert Griffin III cleaned out his locker at the end of the 2015 season, he left a message for the sports world to see. Referencing Dr. Kent M. Keith's "Paradoxical Commandments," which chronicles nine different responses to make when you are hurt or offended by others, the note was a mature way for Griffin to leave the Washington Redskins after a tough season.

Griffin's journey in the NFL is a fascinating one. Once called a rock star by teammate Santana Moss, seemingly owning the nation's capitol, Griffin went through tremendous highs in his rookie season, only to be matched by equally difficult lows in his remaining time playing in Washington. During his final season with the Redskins, Griffin was essentially inactive for most of the season. It certainly isn't the script RG3 would have written for himself.

When things don't go your way, how do you respond? My first thoughts are often the most ugly, and if kept unchecked, they can cause great damage to my reputation or to others in my life. Jesus often taught principles that seemed so paradoxical to human nature. The hardest principle to employ might be the one found in Luke 6:28-29: "Bless those who curse you. Pray for those who hurt you. If someone slaps you on one cheek, offer the other cheek also. If someone demands your coat, offer your shirt also."

The way of Jesus is different, but that is because his Kingdom is not of this world. Dr. Keith's final comments in the "Paradoxical Commandments" put all of these matters into perspective when he says, "In the final analysis, it's between you and God; it was never between you and them anyway." Live with this end in mind when others come against you.

Bless those who curse you. Pray for those who hurt you. If someone slaps you on one cheek, offer the other cheek also. If someone demands your coat, offer your shirt also. LUKE 6:28-29

A Great Leader

On December 5, 2013, the world lost a great man in South African president Nelson Mandela. The Nobel Peace Prize winner was known as the man who ended the dark days of apartheid in South Africa. Archbishop Desmond Tutu said of him, "He awed everyone as a spectacular embodiment of . . . forgiveness, and he saved our land from the bloodbath that most had predicted would be our lot."

Mandela had a way of turning hearts, and he had a great impact in both the quantity of lives that he touched and the degree with which he did it. This came because he followed a man much greater than himself, Jesus of Nazareth. You see, as great as Nelson Mandela was, his accomplishments pale in comparison to the greatness of Jesus. Mandela was able to save many people in South Africa because of his efforts to turn the tide, but Jesus has and will save people from every nation, tribe, and tongue from eternal condemnation.

When the angel appeared to Mary in Luke 1:31-32, he said to her, "You will conceive and give birth to a son, and you will name him Jesus. He will be very great and will be called the Son of the Most High." I love that the angel says, "He will be very great." What a wonderful statement. Can you imagine being Mary, hearing about her son being very great?

Have you put your trust in Jesus? He is great and greatly to be praised!

You will conceive and give birth to a son, and you will name him Jesus.
He will be very great and will be called the Son of the Most High.

LUKE 1:31-32

A Christmas Surprise

Have you ever struggled to buy a gift for your wife? I remember, as a young married man, making my wife cry one Christmas. I didn't realize just how bad I was at buying gifts until that moment. My experience reminds me of the man and woman who were still mad at each other from the previous Christmas. She was mad at him for the gift he got her. He was mad at her for being mad at him. When he got up the courage to ask her what she might want for Christmas, she said in her sarcastic tone, "Just surprise me." So that year, at three in the morning, he leaned over and yelled, "BOO!"

Guys, let's be honest. If you're like me, you struggle buying the right gift for your significant other. What I have learned through the years is that good gift giving includes considering what, when, and how. That's what to give, when to give it, and how to give it with a memorable, special delivery. Master what, when, and how, and you will go a long way toward putting a smile on your wife's face.

This, by the way, is how God gave his Son. Galatians 4:4-5 states, "When the right time came, God sent his Son, born of a woman, subject to the law. God sent him to buy freedom for us who were slaves to the law, so that he could adopt us as his very own children." Jesus is the perfect gift, who came at just the right time in a memorable delivery.

When the right time came, God sent his Son, born of a woman, subject to the law. God sent him to buy freedom for us who were slaves to the law, so that he could adopt us as his very own children. **GALATIANS 4:4-5**

What God Wants for Christmas

Have you ever wondered what God wants for Christmas? It may surprise you.

A missionary who worked among some of the most impoverished people in Africa had just finished preaching the morning message. As it was time to take up the offering, the missionary was moved by what he saw. You see, he had already wondered what those in attendance could possibly put in the offering baskets.

When the baskets were passed, some put in seemingly valuable things they had scavenged from the trash heap. Those who were fortunate to work placed a few coins into the basket.

One woman, who clearly was destitute, looked at the plate as it was coming by. As she sat there and held it, the others in the church service looked at her, wondering what she would do. It was as if time had stopped. Suddenly, she stood up and stepped into the basket, offering herself to the Lord.

I believe that this woman got it exactly right. You see, she gave all she had, and that is all God wanted. This story reminds me of Romans 12:1-2, which states, "Dear brothers and sisters, I plead with you to give your bodies to God because of all he has done for you. Let them be a living and holy sacrifice—the kind he will find acceptable. This is truly the way to worship him. Don't copy the behavior and customs of this world, but let God transform you into a new person by changing the way you think. Then you will learn to know God's will for you, which is good and pleasing and perfect."

The best Christmas present that you can give God is yourself.

Dear brothers and sisters, I plead with you to give your bodies to God because of all he has done for you. Let them be a living and holy sacrifice—the kind he will find acceptable. This is truly the way to worship him. Don't copy the behavior and customs of this world, but let God transform you into a new person by changing the way you think. Then you will learn to know God's will for you, which is good and pleasing and perfect. ROMANS 12:1-2

The Peace of Christmas, PART 1

As a kid, I used to love shaking snow globes. I recently saw a snow globe with a reindeer driving a red station wagon with a Christmas tree on top. The expression on the face of that reindeer was one of all-out exertion. While preparing for Christmas celebrations, I often feel like that reindeer flying ninety miles per hour down the snow globe roads of life with all sorts of pressure swirling around. Living this way can leave me longing for peace.

One of the reasons we fail to find peace not only during the holidays but during the rest of the year is because we have a wrong definition of peace. You see, when the snow globe of life swirls beyond our control, we feel panicked, stressed, or anxious. We look to the world's definition of peace—an absence of conflict and freedom from any strife or dissension—and get discouraged when that peace doesn't come. If this is our understanding of peace, there will always be a collision with the reality of the world and the peace that we want.

The peace of the Scripture is called shalom, which means to be secure, whole, and complete. This peace focuses more on character than circumstances.

Isaiah 9:6-7 shows us that the peace we all need is anchored in the incarnation of Christ and the inauguration of his Kingdom: "For a child is born to us, a son is given to us. The government will rest on his shoulders. And he will be called: Wonderful Counselor, Mighty God, Everlasting Father, Prince of Peace. His government and its peace will never end. He will rule with fairness and justice from the throne of his ancestor David for all eternity. The passionate commitment of the LORD of Heaven's Armies will make this happen!"

Do you want this peace that Jesus brings? Romans 5:1 states, "Since we have been justified by faith, we have peace with God through our Lord Jesus Christ" (ESV). Peace with God comes when we put our faith in Christ. Do you have this peace?

Since we have been justified by faith, we have peace with God through our Lord Jesus Christ.　　　　　　　　　ROMANS 5:1, ESV

The Peace of Christmas, PART 2

If you think about it, most sports teams get good news only in the off-season. Their good news comes to them based on circumstances like trades, the signing of free agents, and draft picks. Throughout the season, most of their news is bad—injured players, conflict in the front office, disgruntled fans, and ending the season with a loss. If sports teams felt peace only when they received good news in the off-season, they'd be in a lot of trouble the rest of the year. Instead, most teams continue to focus on the end goal, no matter what their present circumstances.

The peace of the Bible helps us focus on the end goal no matter what our present circumstances may be. You see, the peace of Christ is always available and ever increasing. Isaiah 9:7 states, "His government and its peace will never end."

When we as believers know that God's grace and peace are not bound, we ought to always be experiencing his peace flowing through our lives. But the problem is that we don't often know that we can have it in ample supply.

So how do we access his peace? The answer is easy. Simply ask for it. That is what we see in Philippians 4:6-7. It states, "Don't worry about anything; instead, pray about everything. Tell God what you need, and thank him for all he has done. Then you will experience God's peace, which exceeds anything we can understand. His peace will guard your hearts and minds as you live in Christ Jesus."

Do you need peace? Just do what this Scripture says and ask. When you experience his unmistakable peace, you can keep moving forward no matter what the season.

Don't worry about anything; instead, pray about everything. Tell God what you need, and thank him for all he has done. Then you will experience God's peace, which exceeds anything we can understand. His peace will guard your hearts and minds as you live in Christ Jesus. PHILIPPIANS 4:6-7

The Peace of Christmas, PART 3

The great theologian C. S. Lewis writes in his classic *Mere Christianity*, "If you read history you will find that the Christians who did most for the present world were just those who thought most of the next."[66] As we have been studying Isaiah 9:6-7, we have seen that peace is found in a relationship with the Prince of Peace and that it is ever increasing and always available. Today we will discover that it will fully be realized in the culmination of his Kingdom.

Isaiah 9:7 states, "He will rule with fairness and justice from the throne of his ancestor David for all eternity. The passionate commitment of the LORD of Heaven's Armies will make this happen!"

Notice the first sentence of this verse. The word *eternity* reminds us that God rules and reigns now and will rule and reign forevermore. The everlasting peace he gives leads to overflowing hope in our lives. Romans 15:13 states, "I pray that God, the source of hope, will fill you completely with joy and peace because you trust in him. Then you will overflow with confident hope through the power of the Holy Spirit."

Believe, be filled, and overflow with hope, because the peace of Christmas is everlasting. May the peace of Christ be yours in abundance!

I pray that God, the source of hope, will fill you completely with joy and peace because you trust in him. Then you will overflow with confident hope through the power of the Holy Spirit.   ROMANS 15:13

---

[66] C. S. Lewis, *Mere Christianity* (New York: HarperCollins, 2001), 134.

Christmas Shopping

Knute Rockne, legendary head football coach of the University of Notre Dame, once said, "Football is a game played with arms, legs, and shoulders, but mostly from the neck up." Coach Rockne was referring to how football is a physical game but the advantage goes to those who use their minds by developing and executing a game plan. No quality coach goes into a game without a good plan and preparation.

My wife always has a game plan when she goes shopping. I am amazed at her ability to navigate the mall. It's as if she has a sixth sense for scoping sales, beating the crowd, and finding a parking spot. As you go out Christmas shopping, you might want to prepare with a game plan.

Scripture is God's game plan for our lives. It helps us understand what is in bounds and what is out of bounds. It helps us navigate relationships, gives wisdom for finances, and directs us as parents. The Bible gives us a picture of victory for our lives by inviting us to a personal relationship with God's Son. Scripture enables us to renew our minds so that we can know where to set our feet and how to have vision for our lives.

Scripture also tells us about the depth of impact it has on our lives. Hebrews 4:12 states, "The word of God is alive and powerful. It is sharper than the sharpest two-edged sword, cutting between soul and spirit, between joint and marrow. It exposes our innermost thoughts and desires." God's Word helps us from the neck up and through every part of our lives so that we can know how to honor him.

The word of God is alive and powerful. It is sharper than the sharpest two-edged sword, cutting between soul and spirit, between joint and marrow. It exposes our innermost thoughts and desires. HEBREWS 4:12

Dear Santa

In his book *Children's Letters to Santa Claus*, Bill Adler shares some of the funniest letters from the hearts of little boys and girls. Here is one of them:

> *Dear Santa,*
> *"In my house there are three boys. Richard is two. Jeffrey is four. Norman is seven. Richard is good sometimes. Jeffrey is good sometimes. Norman is good all the time. (Signed) Norman."* [67]

Don't you love how Norman compared his behavior to his brothers'? We often do the same thing before God, as we compare ourselves to our peers. When we do this, we feel pretty good about ourselves.

Jesus tells a story of this dynamic in Luke 18:10-12: "Two men went to the Temple to pray. One was a Pharisee, and the other was a despised tax collector. The Pharisee stood by himself and prayed this prayer: 'I thank you, God, that I am not a sinner like other people—cheaters, sinners, adulterers. I'm certainly not like that tax collector! I fast twice a week, and I give you a tenth of my income.'"

In the letter above, Norman represents the religion of "Do" that pervades so much of the religious thinking of this world. Do enough good, and you may just earn God's approval! But the problem with this is that the standard keeps changing according to the actions of our neighbors.

The gospel of Jesus Christ is different. The gospel of Jesus Christ declares what was "Done" on our behalf to satisfy the just standard of God's law. My friends, the number one distinction of the gospel of Jesus Christ is that what you cannot do in meeting the just standard of God, Jesus did for you two thousand years ago on a cross.

Is your faith one where you "Do," in order to get ahead spiritually? Or have you fully trusted what God has "Done" for you in Jesus Christ?

It is only by God's grace that you have been saved!　　　　EPHESIANS 2:5

---

[67] Bill Adler, *Children's Letters to Santa Claus* (New York: Birch Lane, 1993).

Intentional Gift Giving

During the Christmas season, many Christians all over the world follow the Advent calendar to guide their Christmas celebrations. Advent is described as a season of "waiting and anticipation" that involves the four Sundays leading up to Christmas. Each Sunday has a separate theme: hope, peace, joy, and love. In many traditions, an Advent wreath with different colored candles, which are lit each Sunday, symbolizes this progression through the Christmas season. It all culminates in a Christmas Eve lighting of the Christ candle in the center of the wreath, declaring that Christ has come.

In our home, during the days of Advent, my wife, Julee, sets out on her Christmas shopping. She is the best gift giver in the family, finding exactly what she wants to give, at the best price, with coupons and free shipping if she orders it online. She is a shark when it comes to finding the best deal. She is a blessing when it comes to giving great gifts. She loves to give to each person in our family things that they will enjoy and that they want.

When I look at my wife's gift giving, I am reminded of the intentionality with which God gave his Son to us. When you examine the promises of the Old Testament and the arrival of the baby Jesus, you see this beautiful thread through Scripture, of God at work behind the scenes to bring forth the Messiah! Seven hundred years before Jesus' arrival, Isaiah the prophet proclaimed in Isaiah 7:14, "The Lord himself will give you the sign. Look! The virgin will conceive a child!"

This Advent season, as we remember how Israel had to wait in anticipation, let's also enjoy the gift that has been given just for us. Never forget the intentionality of God's love to you as you celebrate the birth of Christ this Christmas.

The Lord himself will give you the sign. Look! The virgin will conceive a child!
ISAIAH 7:14

Baby Jesus in a Car Seat

Watching young children celebrate Christmas is so much fun. Decorating with them can often be laborious, but seeing their reactions to the Christmas tree or the manger scene is worth the extra work. One pastor tells a story of a child helping his mommy and daddy unwrap the manger scene and put it in its prominent place in their home.

"Here's a sheep," he said with joy, as he pulled it out of the box. "And here's a cow," he continued. As he came to the shape of the baby in the manger, he thought it looked like his little brother when they would load the car and head out. The little boy exclaimed with great zeal, "And here's baby Jesus in his car seat!"

Like this little child, we may not fully understand all the details of God, but that doesn't mean we can't take delight in what we do know. Remember, the story of Christmas is the story of God with us. Isaiah 7:14 states, "The virgin will conceive a child! She will give birth to a son and will call him Immanuel (which means 'God is with us')."

Like this little boy who didn't understand it all but was eager to participate, all you need to truly partake in Christmas is childlike faith to delight in the gift of God's Son, Jesus. He has been the promised one from the very beginning.

She will give birth to a son and will call him Immanuel (which means "God is with us").
ISAIAH 7:14

Assisting the Valet

We called for the car about twenty minutes before checking out of our hotel. It was the Christmas holidays, and the valet said it would be thirty minutes because there were about twenty cars in front of us. When we got to the hotel lobby at the appointed time, we waited alongside the rest of the guests who were in line. After fifteen minutes, I went to the valet stand to simply see where our vehicle was in the mix.

Jordan, the valet manager, called to see when our Ford Expedition would be brought down. He started asking questions, hung up, and proceeded to work with other guests. At this point I knew what my gut already believed—something was wrong. After a few more minutes, I inquired about our truck again. He called, but they didn't have an answer for us.

Finally, I looked at Jordan and asked, "Well, is someone looking for my truck? If not, I will go and find it." Jordan, a young college student who realized my patience had worn thin, looked at me and said, "Let's go find it together."

It took us some time to get to the garage, locate the vehicle, and find the keys, but Jordan thanked me for staying patient. I told him, "Jordan, I am trying to learn to not fret over things outside my control."

Psalm 37:8 states, "Stop being angry! Turn from your rage! Do not lose your temper—it only leads to harm." There was no point in getting angry about the situation. Anger would have only ruined the day we had at Sea World after finally finding our truck.

Stop being angry! Turn from your rage! Do not lose your temper—it only leads to harm.   PSALM 37:8

We Are So Blessed

Each Christmas my brother Troy and his family make their way from Dallas to Houston for a family Christmas gathering the weekend before Christmas Day. This particular Christmas was our year to host the larger family get-together, and in addition to Troy and his crew, my brother Keith and his family, my sister Kim and her family, and my parents joined us. Not counting our dog, Bella, there were eighteen of us gathered for Christmas dinner. As usual, my wife, Julee, had things just perfect, and we had a wonderful time together.

At our family gatherings, there are the usual conversations that happen as we talk about sports, politics, and our kids. We each talk about our work and then maybe make mention of our hobbies. I would imagine it is very similar to your Christmas with family as well.

On the way out the door, my father embraced me and said, "Son, we are so blessed." I said, "Amen. We sure are." Then he went on to say, "Yes, but even just getting together without strife is a far cry from what I grew up with." It seems that my dad would go back and trade just about anything for peace with his family.

What if we began to think of prosperity in terms of peaceful relationships more than possessions? Proverbs 17:1 states, "Better a dry crust eaten in peace than a house filled with feasting—and conflict." We must do our part to promote peaceful relationships with those in our lives. May your family gatherings this Christmas be filled with Christ's peace!

Better a dry crust eaten in peace than a house filled with feasting—and conflict.   PROVERBS 17:1

Rich Tradition

When your six-year-old describes a run to Chick-fil-A for milkshakes before heading to view Christmas lights as a tradition, you know you have established something special. There are many rich traditions at Christmas, and so many of them are full of deep meaning. But the trap that we can fall into, if we aren't careful, is the trap of traditionalism.

Traditionalism proclaims that holidays or other moments are incomplete unless the tradition is observed. Traditionalism mandates things be done a certain way because that is always the way they have been done.

Tradition, on the other hand, emerges naturally, over time, as something valued and treasured because of the significance of its meaning. Tradition is to be celebrated, not because of the way it is done, but because of its meaning and what it represents.

Jesus battled traditionalism every day, especially on the Sabbath. He lived in a time when the ritual of the Sabbath came before the reason for the Sabbath. Regulation became the driving force, and it choked the life right out of the important day.

In Mark 2:27 Jesus says, "The Sabbath was made to meet the needs of people, and not people to meet the requirements of the Sabbath." Keep the life in your traditions by making sure the ritual doesn't take precedence over the reason.

The Sabbath was made to meet the needs of people, and not people to meet the requirements of the Sabbath.
                                                                    MARK 2:27

A Mature Man of Faith, PART 1

Christmas stories, plays, and sermons this month have us thinking about the star, stable, and shepherds. We hear about Mary, the baby Jesus, and the wise men. We're reminded that there was no room in the inn. We may hear a performance of Mary's Song from Luke 1 that proclaims, "My soul magnifies the Lord," and wonder what it must have been like to carry the Messiah.

Less often do we hear a message about Joseph, but Joseph is vital to the story too. You see, Joseph is a picture of a mature man of faith. Look at what Scripture says about Joseph when he found out Mary was with child. Matthew 1:18-20 states, "This is how Jesus the Messiah was born. His mother, Mary, was engaged to be married to Joseph. But before the marriage took place, while she was still a virgin, she became pregnant through the power of the Holy Spirit. Joseph, to whom she was engaged, was a righteous man and did not want to disgrace her publicly, so he decided to break the engagement quietly. As he considered this, an angel of the Lord appeared to him in a dream."

Do you see the character of Joseph on display? He was a just man who was unwilling to shame others, and he gave thought to his ways. We would be wise to develop our character so that when someone disappoints us, we respond in the same manner.

Joseph, to whom she was engaged, was a righteous man and did not want to disgrace her publicly, so he decided to break the engagement quietly.

MATTHEW 1:19

A Mature Man of Faith, PART 2

Yesterday we began to see a bit about Joseph and his depth of character. I have called him a mature man of faith because of his reaction when he was disappointed by his fiancée, Mary. Joseph had already paid the dowry for Mary—the high, high price he had given her father. He had entered into the covenant relationship, had drunk the cup of the covenant, and had gone to prepare a place for Mary, to come back and take her as his wife.

After Joseph heard of her being with child and responding with thoughtfulness, the angel appeared to Joseph and told him not to be afraid to take Mary as his wife. Matthew 1:20-21 tells us, "'Joseph, son of David,' the angel said, 'do not be afraid to take Mary as your wife. For the child within her was conceived by the Holy Spirit. And she will have a son, and you are to name him Jesus, for he will save his people from their sins.'"

What did Joseph do after his visit with the angel? Matthew 1:24-25 says, "When Joseph woke up, he did as the angel of the Lord commanded and took Mary as his wife. But he did not have sexual relations with her until her son was born. And Joseph named him Jesus." Was Joseph afraid? Yes. Was obeying God risky? Yes. Did it require a sacrifice? Absolutely. Yet Joseph obeyed.

Remember, a mature man of faith listens to God's instruction and obeys it. We would be wise to do the same.

"Joseph, son of David," the angel said, "do not be afraid to take Mary as your wife. For the child within her was conceived by the Holy Spirit. And she will have a son, and you are to name him Jesus, for he will save his people from their sins." MATTHEW 1:20-21

A Mature Man of Faith, PART 3

We may look at Joseph only as a guy who became the father of a baby that wasn't his offspring and raised him as his own. We may think, *What character! What obedience to God's plan! And what sacrifice!*

Although all those thoughts apply to Joseph, we miss the true purpose of his sacrifice. As a mature man of faith, Joseph's sacrifice meant that others would find joy. When mature men of faith give sacrificially, others can find joy.

Consider how many people in the years since Jesus' birth have come to know the joy of the Savior. Joseph, who was just an ordinary man, had an incredible part to play in the genealogy of Jesus. Joseph may have been ordinary, but his extraordinary obedience gave us an amazing example to follow.

Remember the words of Luke 2:10-11 today as the angels announced the birth of Jesus to the shepherds: "The angel reassured them. 'Don't be afraid!' he said. 'I bring you good news that will bring great joy to all people. The Savior—yes, the Messiah, the Lord—has been born today in Bethlehem, the city of David!'"

This announcement of joy is for you, too. Thankfully, the Father in heaven saw to it to give Jesus an earthly father of great faith so that we, too, might experience this joy.

The angel reassured them. "Don't be afraid!" he said. "I bring you good news that will bring great joy to all people. The Savior—yes, the Messiah, the Lord—has been born today in Bethlehem, the city of David!"

LUKE 2:10-11

The Gift of Intentional Time

Ann Landers shares the power of intentional time in her answer to a reader's question. In the story, Landers reports that a young attorney was reflecting on the moment when his life changed because of his father's gift of time.

The attorney told Landers that the greatest gift he had ever received was a gift he got one Christmas from his dad. It was a note saying, "Son, this year I will give you 365 hours, an hour every day after dinner. It's yours. We'll talk about whatever you want to talk about. We'll go wherever you want to go, play whatever you want to play. It will be your hour!"

That dad not only kept his promise to his son but renewed it every year.

Intentional time in the life of any relationship is powerful, as it declares one's love. In a parent-child relationship, it declares to the child his or her worth, their great significance. In a marriage, it can be the chance to connect after a busy day, week, or season. Intentional time blows wind into the sails of a relationship.

Genesis 29:18 shows us Jacob serving Laban for seven years for the privilege of marrying his younger daughter, Rachel. It states, "Since Jacob was in love with Rachel, he told her father, 'I'll work for you for seven years if you'll give me Rachel, your younger daughter, as my wife.'" There is nothing like making time for what we value the most. As busy as you are, I want to encourage you to give the gift of intentional time this Christmas season. If you do, it can change the course of your life and those in it.

Since Jacob was in love with Rachel, he told her father, "I'll work for you for seven years if you'll give me Rachel, your younger daughter, as my wife."

GENESIS 29:18

The Manger and the Gift of Diapers?

In a cartoon capturing the innocence of little ones, three small boys come to the manger scene bearing gifts. The first two are holding gold and frankincense, the gifts of the Bible story. But the third little boy is more practical. He comes with a box of disposable diapers! I bet that would have put a smile on Mary's face. This gift would have been one of practical love. Practical love is the kind of love that meets needs.

The gift of Jesus we celebrate at Christmas was given out of God's practical love for us. Galatians 4:4 states, "When the right time came, God sent his Son, born of a woman, subject to the law." God's practical love is a tangible love. It is incarnational love. It is the love of Christmas.

Is there a way you can lavish practical love on your family this Christmas? Practical love may involve sacrifice. Sacrifice was required when God made his love practical by giving his Son to die in our place. Sacrifice was required when the Son of God left heaven's glory to take on flesh. Consider Luke 2:6-7 and the vast exchange Jesus made for you and me—the throne of heaven for a feeding trough for livestock: "While they were there, the time came for the baby to be born, and she gave birth to her firstborn, a son. She wrapped him in cloths and placed him in a manger, because there was no guest room available for them" (NIV).

While they were there, the time came for the baby to be born, and she gave birth to her firstborn, a son. She wrapped him in cloths and placed him in a manger, because there was no guest room available for them.

LUKE 2:6-7, NIV

The Paradox of Christmas

The illustrations section of sermons.com has a humorous and potent story called "The Scene at Bethlehem," named for Titian's famous painting. You see, as the story goes, a father and his son were looking at Titian's painting of the birth of Christ. The inquisitive boy asked his father why the baby Jesus was placed in a pile of straw and an awful cradle like the one in the painting. Logically, the father answered that Mary and Joseph were poor and that they really couldn't afford anything more.

The son then responded with another question that brought a chuckle from the father: "If they were poor, why would they pay so much to have an expensive artist paint this picture?"

One of the things I love best about the Christmas story is that Jesus can identify with every man and woman. He can identify with the poor because he was born in a manger, in a stable, among livestock. At the same time, he was worshiped as the "King of the Jews" by the wise men, who brought him gold, frankincense, and myrrh.

The more you study Jesus' life, the more you will see that whatever you are going through, no matter how difficult, he can identify with your situation. Have you thought about the King of kings being betrayed, abandoned, and tried as a criminal? The prologue of John's Gospel captures this paradox beautifully. John 1:1-3 and 10-12 state,

> In the beginning the Word already existed. The Word was with God, and the Word was God. He existed in the beginning with God. God created everything through him, and nothing was created except through him. . . . He came into the very world he created, but the world didn't recognize him. He came to his own people, and even they rejected him. But to all who believed him and accepted him, he gave the right to become children of God.

What a paradox!

In the beginning the Word already existed. The Word was with God, and the Word was God.
JOHN 1:1

Christmas Brings Us Together

One of my favorite Christmas services at our church is the presentation of Handel's *Messiah*. With string players from the Houston Symphony and a one-hundred-voice choir, Handel's *Messiah* brings together new people, longtime church members, and many former church members who have moved away.

From the moment of his birth, Jesus began to bring people from far and wide to himself to worship. The shepherds came by the announcement of the angels. The magi came from the East because of the appearance of the star.

If all you do this Christmas is gather with family and friends and you fail to worship Jesus, you have missed the most important point of Christmas. His birth was the arrival of God, taking on flesh to redeem all of mankind from our sin problem. His ministry brought joy, life, and healing to so many in Israel. His teaching and miracles compelled his disciples to say, "Surely, this is the Messiah." His life that brought light to so many caused his enemies to seek to take it away. One of the most compelling points of the Good News of Christ is that his death and resurrection not only brought people to God, but it also brought about reconciliation among them.

Ephesians 2:14 declares, "Christ himself has brought peace to us. He united Jews and Gentiles into one people when, in his own body on the cross, he broke down the wall of hostility that separated us." In Ephesians 3 Paul calls this a mystery that was kept hidden. What a marvelous God we have! Truly Christmas brings us together!

Christ himself has brought peace to us. He united Jews and Gentiles into one people when, in his own body on the cross, he broke down the wall of hostility that separated us.
EPHESIANS 2:14

A Christmas Mess

Christmas morning is messy. Once the kids tear into the presents, the wrapping paper, packaging, and the toys themselves get strewn about the floor. On Christmas Day, my family stays put in our home, enjoying both a great breakfast and dinner prepared by my lovely wife. We snack throughout the day and enjoy the sweets of the season. On any other day of the year, Julee would be clamoring for the house to be picked up, but not on Christmas Day. On Christmas Day, it's okay to leave it messy, because we're celebrating Jesus' birthday, and the evidence of that is a beautiful sight.

When we look at the conditions in which Jesus entered the world, it's easy to conclude, as the Skit Guys have, that "he came to get messy." From the messy conditions of his birth to the geopolitical landscape into which he was born, Jesus' birth was the first Christmas mess, and it, too, was a beautiful sight.

You see, things were about to get cleaned up. To the tribes of the north in the region of Galilee of the Gentiles, a light was dawning. Joy was on its way. It may have gotten worse before it began to get better, but a Kingdom of everlasting and ever-increasing peace was inaugurated. That's why the angel could proclaim to those messy shepherds in Luke 2:10-11, "Don't be afraid! . . . I bring you good news that will bring great joy to all people. The Savior—yes, the Messiah, the Lord—has been born today in Bethlehem, the city of David!"

Was it a mess? Yes, but oh, what a beautiful sight! Merry Christmas!

Don't be afraid! . . . I bring you good news that will bring great joy to all people. The Savior—yes, the Messiah, the Lord—has been born today in Bethlehem, the city of David!
LUKE 2:10-11

Saying Good-bye

It was the day after Christmas. My oldest son, Brady, had just joined up with his buddy Parker and Parker's dad and brother to hunt deer at their family's ranch. He was going to be gone for four or five days. Brady was prepared in every way possible with clothing, money, ammunition, and weapons. But he was also prepared mentally with a chat from me about his personal and operational security.

To make sure that Brady is listening, I often take him to breakfast for our important conversations. On the day of his hunting trip, we grabbed a chicken biscuit and discussed the various ways something could go wrong. I told him, "Brady, there will be loaded guns in your hands and in the hands of your friends. You have to be vigilant about your safety and about theirs as well." He agreed and told me that he would take the greatest care. I then mentioned that it would be during the in-between times of the hunt when his guard was down that he and his friends would be most susceptible to getting hurt—whether it be on the four-wheeler or in an accident with a firearm.

Saying good-bye that morning wasn't hard, because I trusted my son and the Davidsons, but I also said good-bye knowing that something could go horribly wrong. Maybe it was the heightened awareness of the dangers of hunting that had my antenna up, knowing that if there were an accident, I might not ever see my son again.

But the reality of all our lives is that we are not guaranteed tomorrow. We say hello and good-bye every day, not knowing if we will see our loved ones again. Since this is the case, it is so important that we seek to live at peace with one another. Ephesians 4:32 states, "Be kind to each other, tenderhearted, forgiving one another, just as God through Christ has forgiven you." Value your relationships, knowing none of us is guaranteed tomorrow.

Be kind to each other, tenderhearted, forgiving one another, just as God through Christ has forgiven you.
EPHESIANS 4:32

Made for a Purpose

In his book *Quiet Strength*, Tony Dungy talks about his journey through the NFL. He relives one of the greatest years of his career, 1978, and calls it a miracle year. That year, Dungy was healthy, he led his team in interceptions, and the team won the Super Bowl. He says, "Despite all the good things that occurred that year, I can still look back and say that 1978 was the first season in my life in which sports weren't the most important thing to me. . . . God had me here for a reason, and it wasn't just to play ball."[68]

Have you stopped to think that maybe there is more to your life than what you do? How can the next year be a standout year for you?

It begins with discovering the love of God through a relationship with Christ. It continues by developing in your faith and your belief that God has a plan and purpose for you. Then you deploy your God-given influence for his purpose and glory. This is the progression of any man of great faith. After he has discovered Christ, he spends time developing in his faith. As he develops, he realizes that he has been gifted uniquely to serve Christ with his talents. He then deploys that talent to make an impact on the world around him.

Matthew 5:14 states, "You are the light of the world—like a city on a hilltop that cannot be hidden." This is the potent influence that you have as a follower of Christ. Cultivate it, and use it for God's purpose and glory.

You are the light of the world—like a city on a hilltop that cannot be hidden.

MATTHEW 5:14

---

[68] Tony Dungy and Nathan Whitaker, *Quiet Strength: The Principles, Practices, & Priorities of a Winning Life* (Carol Stream, IL: Tyndale, 2007), 51.

Change at the Top

The media calls it "Black Monday," the first Monday after the NFL season, when the firing of coaches begins. For weeks or even months leading up to this Monday, the pundits begin to ask the question, "Who is on the hot seat this season?" Speculation begins, and then that day arrives. If a coach who was on the proverbial "hot seat" survives, you can rest assured that he has made many changes to his coaching staff on offense, defense, and special teams.

When an owner makes a change at the top of the organization, it is because he or she feels that there is a culture shift that has to be made. Fully aware of the coach's abilities, the owner chooses this change because in this environment, with these players, he or she doesn't see a way forward.

Owners set the culture of the environment by establishing values, defining what a win looks like, and setting goals toward that win. Then the owner works to establish buy-in from the team's coaches. His or her expectation is that the coaches would work to get this buy-in from their players.

Oftentimes in life, leaders, like team owners, can only take their teams so far, and then a change is needed for both the team and the leader. Even Moses could only lead Israel so far before it was Joshua's turn. Deuteronomy 34:4 states, "The LORD said to Moses, 'This is the land I promised on oath to Abraham, Isaac, and Jacob when I said, "I will give it to your descendants." I have now allowed you to see it with your own eyes, but you will not enter the land.'"

As the leader, remember, you are only going to take your people so far. Then there will be a day when the next leader is selected. Make the most of your journey, but hold on to your role loosely.

The LORD said to Moses, "This is the land I promised on oath to Abraham, Isaac, and Jacob when I said, 'I will give it to your descendants.' I have now allowed you to see it with your own eyes, but you will not enter the land."

DEUTERONOMY 34:4

Grandma Drivers

A December 29, 2015, headline in *USA Today* read, "Older Model Drivers." Written by Terry Byrne and Janet Loehrke, the statistic underneath the headline said, "The fastest-growing demographic among a record-high 214.3 million licensed drivers in the U.S. is age 85 and older. Up 2.9%." When I read that, I couldn't help but chuckle a bit because it reminded me of Mrs. Billie Barlow.

I performed Mrs. Barlow's funeral earlier in December 2015 and had the privilege of honoring her for a life well lived. She was a woman who played by the rules, had a determined way about her, and wanted her independence as long as she could have it. She had that independence up until the morning she died. She was fully dressed and ready for her ride, Mrs. Marion King, to take her to the Senior Adult Christmas Party at the church. She was found on the floor, with her Bible open nearby.

Mrs. Barlow voluntarily gave up driving just a year before as her eyesight began to deteriorate. Prior to that, she volunteered at a school and at a reading center, teaching people to read, up until her early nineties. You see, Mrs. Barlow was an educator, and after she retired from the teaching profession, she continued to use her teaching gift in these ways and also to teach children's Sunday school at church. She loved to serve others in these wonderful ways and did so for many years.

Mrs. Barlow's life reminds me of Proverbs 16:31, which states, "Gray hair is a crown of glory; it is gained by living a godly life."

Who are the elderly in your midst? They each have a story, and it is one we can learn from if we will take time to listen.

Gray hair is a crown of glory; it is gained by living a godly life.

PROVERBS 16:31

Be Resolute

It's that time of year again—time to look back and reflect as we close out this year and time to look ahead and be resolute as we begin a new year. What were your resolutions at the beginning of this year? What will they be this next year? I am going to continue my pursuit of weight loss.

I realize that one of the reasons why I make resolutions each year is because I get frustrated with different parts of my life. Frustration isn't fun, but I believe that if harnessed correctly, frustration can be a great tool for change.

Are you frustrated? Make a resolution to change. You see, resolutions are a good tool for us. They help us refocus our priorities and catalyze us forward to progress.

You may be frustrated with your spiritual life but may not know where to begin. Or you may be frustrated with your work life. Perhaps you may be frustrated because of your past mistakes. Take a look at Ecclesiastes 7:3 with me. It states, "Sorrow is better than laughter, for sadness has a refining influence on us."

Do you want to get better? Look at your frustration and learn from it. Where did you change course? Where did you lose your way? Where did you err? Know that you aren't defeated if you keep moving forward. Let's make this next year our best yet!

Sorrow is better than laughter, for sadness has a refining influence on us.
ECCLESIASTES 7:3

Final Greetings

Joe Strauss, a staff writer for the *Baltimore Sun*, chronicled Cal Ripken Jr.'s last game in the major leagues. Ripken had a storied career, playing in twenty-one seasons and surpassing Lou Gehrig's consecutive-games-played streak. Ripken was known as the ironman of baseball, playing in 2,632 straight games. When it was time for him to play his last game, Ripken said, "One question I've repeatedly been asked these last few weeks is how do I want to be remembered. My answer has been simple: To be remembered at all is pretty special. I might also add that if I am remembered, I hope it's because by living my dream I was able to make a difference. Thank you."[69]

In many different translations of Scripture, each of the Pastoral Epistles close with an editor's heading that reads, "Final Greetings." In this section of the letter, the apostle Paul sends personal words to various people in that church who hold a special place in his heart.

In Acts 20:32, as Paul has called the elders of the church of Ephesus to meet with him before he heads to Jerusalem, he gives them a final greeting. It is a tough good-bye, but one where he knows he has given all he could to them for their benefit. Acts 20:32 states, "I entrust you to God and the message of his grace that is able to build you up and give you an inheritance with all those he has set apart for himself."

My hope is that after spending a minute a day with this book over the past year, you would discover that the Lord, through his Word, is able to give you an inheritance that does not fade. Stay in his Word, and grow in his grace. Here is a final blessing. Numbers 6:24-26 states, "May the LORD bless you and protect you. May the LORD smile on you and be gracious to you. May the LORD show you his favor and give you his peace."

May it be so!

I entrust you to God and the message of his grace that is able to build you up and give you an inheritance with all those he has set apart for himself.   ACTS 20:32

---

[69] Cal Ripken Jr., quoted by Joe Strauss, "Goodbye, No. 8," *Baltimore Sun*, October 7, 2001, http://www.baltimoresun.com/sports/bal-sp.ripken07oct07-story.html.

Acknowledgments

The task of writing a book and getting it to market has many layers, with many people involved. I want to begin by thanking the Lord for giving me this opportunity. It is by his grace, favor, and inspiration that I have anything of value to offer.

Thank you, Julee, my amazing wife and best friend. I love doing life with you and am so blessed by the home you have created for our family. Brady, Cooper, and Carson, thanks for your support in the time it took to finish the manuscript. I love being your daddy, and I love every day we have all under one roof.

John and Cherie Lindley, I'll never forget our lunch at Piatto. Your gift is still making an extraordinary impact. We won't fully know what it looks like until we see Jesus.

David Gow at Gow Media and SB Nation Radio, thank you! Your vision for these one-minute radio spots has gone beyond what either of us could have imagined. I wish I could have gotten a few more wins against you in our days of coaching in the SFL, but then I wouldn't have learned as much as I did after you handed me my tail!

To the team at SB Nation Radio—Craig Larson, Mike Pearson, John Granato, Sean Salisbury, Steve Bunin, David Philpott, and Mike Carrell—you guys are a real blessing. Thanks for making me feel right at home.

I want to thank Dan Hall, my coach, mentor, and friend. Thank you for speaking truth into my life even when I don't want to hear it. Wounds from a friend can be trusted. You really deliver what your brand, On Course Solutions, promises.

Paul Posoli, your book to Matthew changed so much for me. Thanks for sharing it with me. I would rather coach with you than against you any day!

Mark Sweeney, with Mark Sweeney and Associates, thank you for always being honest with me and for putting your name on this project. You see further because of the wisdom God has given you. I am humbled to have you represent me as my literary agent.

Dave Koch, Larry Meyers, and Chad Shoppa at Westar Media Group, thank you for the way you take ideas and turn them into reality! You have grown our influence, as you promised you would.

To the West U Baptist and Crosspoint Church family—so much of me and this work comes from my time with you. Thank you to the executive council and personnel committee for working with me to bring this to a broader audience.

Jeff McMurrough, Michael Sam Jr., Laura Hatfield, Liana Fairbanks, and Shannon Tanner—you all have been a great encouragement to me on this project. Thanks for your help.

Jennifer Dean, thank you, thank you, thank you! What a gift you have been through this entire project. Thanks for bringing your gifts to the Lord every single day.

To my new friends at Tyndale House Publishers: Jon Farrar, thank you for seeing the possibilities. Stephanie, Kara, Kristen, and Erin, thank you for the diligence on every page. You all are a joy to work with.